PENGUIN BOOKS

LANGUAGE PLAY

David Crystal was born in 1941 and spent the early years of his life in Holyhead, North Wales. He went to St Mary's College, Liverpool, and University College London, where he read English and obtained his Ph.D. in 1966. He became lecturer in linguistics at the University of Wales, Bangor, and from 1965 to 1985 was at the University of Reading, where he was Professor of Linguistic Science for several years. He is currently Honorary Professor of Linguistics at Bangor. His research interests are mainly in English language studies and he has been much involved with the clinical and remedial applications of linguistics in the study of language handicap.

David Crystal has published numerous articles and reviews, and his books include *Linguistics* (Penguin 1971, second edition 1985), *Child Language Learning and Linguistics*, *Introduction to Language Pathology*, *A Dictionary of Linguistics and Phonetics*, *Clinical Linguistics*, *Profiling Linguistic Disability*, *Who Cares About English Usage?* (Penguin 1984), *Listen To Your Child* (Penguin 1988), *Rediscover Grammar*, *The English Language* (Penguin 1988), *The Cambridge Encyclopedia of Language*, *Pilgrimage*, *The Cambridge Encyclopedia of the English Language*, *An Encyclopedic Dictionary of Language and Languages* (Penguin 1994) and *English as a Global Language*. He is also the editor of the Cambridge family of general encyclopedias.

David Crystal now lives in Holyhead, where he works as a writer, lecturer and consultant on language and linguistics, and a reference books editor. He is also a frequent radio broadcaster. In June 1995 he was awarded the OBE.

LANGUAGE PLAY

David Crystal

Illustrations by Ed McLachlan

PENGUIN BOOKS

PENGUIN BOOKS

Published by the Penguin Group
Penguin Books Ltd, 27 Wrights Lane, London w8 5tz, England
Penguin Putnam Inc., 375 Hudson Street, New York, New York 10014, USA
Penguin Books Australia Ltd, Ringwood, Victoria, Australia
Penguin Books Canada Ltd, 10 Alcorn Avenue, Toronto, Ontario, Canada m4v 3b2
Penguin Books (NZ) Ltd, Private Bag 102902, NSMC, Auckland, New Zealand

Penguin Books Ltd, Registered Offices: Harmondsworth, Middlesex, England

First published 1998
3 5 7 9 10 8 6 4

The Acknowledgements on pp. ix-x constitute an extension of this copyright page
The moral right of the author has been asserted

Set in 10/12.5 pt PostScript Adobe Minion
Typeset by Rowland Phototypesetting Limited, Bury St Edmunds, Suffolk
Printed in England by Clays Ltd, St Ives plc

CONTENTS

List of Games People Play   vii
Acknowledgements   ix

1 THE LUDIC VIEW   1

2 THE AMATEURS   9
INTRODUCTION   9
ENJOYING THE JOKE   12
DIALECT HUMOUR   18
FUNNY SOUNDS AND VOICES   24
NONCE WORDS AND MEANINGS   30
SOUNDS AND SPELLINGS   36
LIMERICK LAND   45
EVEN TOTAL NONSENSE   49

3 THE ENTHUSIASTS   54
INTRODUCTION   54
THE LANGUAGE ENTHUSIAST   54
MISSIONS IMPOSSIBLE   56
THE LUDIC TOWER OF BABEL   61
BUILDING HIGHER TOWERS   72
GEMATRIA, AND ITS LEGACY   80
GRID GAMES   83
AND FINALLY . . .   89

4 THE PROFESSIONALS   93
INTRODUCTION   93
THE ADVERTISERS   94
THE HEADLINE WRITERS   101

THE COMEDIANS 105
THE COLLECTORS 116
THE COMIC WRITERS 127
THE AUTHORS 137
THE ARTISTS 148
THE THEOLOGIANS 155

5 THE CHILDREN 159
INTRODUCTION 159
THE FIRST YEAR 159
GROWING UP 164
THE LANGUAGE OF THE
PLAYGROUND 173
TOWARDS EDUCATION 178
THE LOGICAL CONCLUSION 182

6 THE READERS 183
INTRODUCTION 183
THE LUDIC GAP 184
THE MISSING PLAY 188
FROM CREATIVITY TO
INTERVENTION 195
OTHER DOMAINS? 204
A NEW CLIMATE? 211

7 THE FUTURE 218
INTRODUCTION 218
WHY PLAY? 219
THE FINAL STEP 222

Notes 227
Index 238

THE GAMES
PEOPLE PLAY

1	PING-PONG PUNNING	2
2	BON MOTORISTS	6
3	DIALECT PLAY	20
4	MOUTHPLAY	26
5	NONCENESS	34
6	THE FIRST COMIC ALPHABET?	42
7	ACROSTIC POETRY	58
8	MARY HAD A LIPOGRAM	64
9	PLAYING AT QUESTIONS, STOPPARDLY	74
10	TRANSPOSITIONAL POETRY	78
11	THE FIRST CROSSWORD	86
12	TOM SWIFTIES	90
13	ADS AT PLAY	96
14	NEWSPLAY	102
15	GOONPLAY	114
16	RULES RULE, OK	118
17	ESSA ON THE MUEL	128
18	POETIC PLAY	140
19	CARTOONOGRAPHS	153
20	CHILD'S PLAY	168
21	BEGINNING AT THE BEGINNING	174
22	GRAMMATICAL PLAYTIME	206
23	DEAR READER	214

ACKNOWLEDGEMENTS

For permission to reprint copyright material, the editor and publishers gratefully acknowledge as follows:

for *Counting-Out Rhymes* edited by Roger D. Abrahams and Lois Rankin 1980, to University of Texas Press, 1980; for 'The Wonderful O' by James Thurber, 1957, to Helen Thurber and Rosemary A. Thurber, reprinted by arrangement with Rosemary A. Thurber and the Barbara Hogenson Agency; for 'Log of the Laggard Bros' by Keith Waterhouse to David Higham Associates; for Alan Coren's article 'August 1985', from *Punch*, to Liberty Publishing, 1996, reproduced by permission of Punch Ltd; for *Cohen's Cornucopia* by Mark Cohen, 1984, to Lutterworth Press; for 'Baa baa, black sheep' from *Father Koala's Nursery Rhymes* by Kel Richards, 1992, to Scholastic Australia, 1992; for *The Meaning of Liff* by Douglas Adams and John Lloyd, 1983, to Serious Productions, reprinted by permission of Pan Books; for *Ernest the Heroic Lion-Tamer* by Damon Burnard, 1993, to A. & C. Black, 1993; for *Wordplay*, 1992, to John Langdon; for *Move Over Mrs Markham* by Ray Cooney and John Chapman, 1972, to Warner/Chappell Plays; for *The Franglais Lieutenant's Woman* by Miles Kington, 1986, to Robson Books Ltd; for 'T'Babby Born in a Mistal' from *Ee By Gum Lord* by Arnold Kellett, 1996, to Smith Settle; from *The Name of the Rose* by Umberto Eco, 1984, to Secker & Warburg; for an extract from *The True Story of the 3 Little Pigs* by Jon Scieszka, 1989, to Viking Penguin, a division of Penguin Putnam Inc.; for an extract from *The Symbolic Species* by Terrence Deacon, 1997, to Viking Penguin, a division of Penguin Putnam Inc.; for an extract from, *Rates of Exchange* by Malcolm Bradbury, 1985, to Viking Penguin, a division of Penguin Putnam Inc.; for 'The Silent Bugler' from *The Lost Goon Shows*, by Spike Milligan, 1988, to Robson Books Ltd; for extracts from *The Goon Show Scripts*, to the Woburn Press, copyright © 1972, Spike Milligan; for *Get Thee to a Punnery* by Richard Lederer, 1988, to Wyrick & Company; for an extract from *Fox In Socks* by Dr Seuss, 1965, to International Creative Management, Inc.; for extracts from *Making the Alphabet Dance: Recreational Word Play* by Ross Eckler, 1995, to St Martin's Press Inc.; for *The Complete Monty Python Book*, to Random House UK Ltd on behalf of Monty Python; for extracts from *Rosencrantz and Guildenstern Are Dead* by Tom Stoppard to Faber & Faber; for extracts from *Dylan Thomas: The Collected Letters* edited by Paul Ferris, 1985, to David Higham Associates; for extracts from *Waiting for Godot* in *The Complete Dramatic Works* by Samuel Beckett, 1986, to Faber & Faber; for extracts from *The Birthday Party* by Harold Pinter, 1960, to Faber & Faber; for extracts from *The Radiant Way* by Margaret Drabble, 1987, to Weidenfeld & Nicholson.

Every effort has been made to contact or trace copyright holders. The publishers would be grateful to be notified of any additions that should be incorporated in the next edition of this volume.

1

THE LUDIC VIEW

Everyone plays with language or responds to language play. Some take mild pleasure from it; others are totally obsessed by it; but no one can avoid it. Indeed, as we enter the twenty-first century, there seems to be more of it about than at any previous period of linguistic history.

The aim of this book is to show that this is so, to investigate why it is so, and then to ask why the playful (or 'ludic') function of language is important for our appreciation of language as a whole. Ludic language has traditionally been a badly neglected subject of linguistic enquiry – at best treated as a topic of marginal interest, at worst never mentioned at all. Yet it should be at the heart of any thinking we do about linguistic issues.

We play with language when we manipulate it as a source of enjoyment, either for ourselves or for the benefit of others. I mean 'manipulate' literally: we take some linguistic feature – such as a word, a phrase, a sentence, a part of a word, a group of sounds, a series of letters – and make it do things it does not normally do. We are, in effect, bending and breaking the rules of the language. And if someone were to ask why we do it, the answer is simply: for fun.

But enjoyment and fun are not words which usually come to mind when we start to think about what language is and why it is used. We tend to adopt a more sober perspective. What is language for? The conventional answer talks about people 'communicating' with each other, in the sense that one person sends a meaning, a message, a thought, an idea, and another person receives it. The whole point of language, it is assumed, is to foster the transmission of knowledge, however this is defined – as concepts, facts, opinions, emotions, or

1 PING-PONG PUNNING

A domestic sitting-room. Evening. Janet and John are in the middle of a conversation with Peter and Jane. Janet is telling a story about what happened when their respective cats met in the street.

JANET: . . . And so there was a sort of confrontation between Crumble and Splash –

JANE: Catfrontation, you mean. (*Laughs.*)

JANET: Well, all right, catfrontation, if you insist – and they stood by the –

PETER: Near cat-astrophe, if you ask me. (*Groans all round.*)

JANET: I wasn't asking you, Peter!

PETER: Sorry, I didn't mean to be categorical. (*More groans all round.*)

JANE: This sounds like it's becoming a catalogue of disasters. (*Peals of laughter.*)

PETER: I don't think John approves of all this jocularity, when Janet's trying to tell us a perfectly serious story.

JANE: You know what John's being, though, don't you.

JANET: What?

JANE: A catalyst! (*More laughter all round.*)

PETER: I thought that was what happened to moggies when they'd drunk too much. (*Further groans.*)

any other kind of 'information'. Why use language? – for 'the expression of thought', says the *Oxford English Dictionary*; for 'expressing thought or feeling', says *Chambers*; for 'communicating ideas or feelings', says the *Longman Dictionary of the English Language*.

But if this is all there is to language, what are we to make of the *catfrontation* episode presented in the panel on p. 2? Read it now. Here we have a fragment of a conversation recorded between four people: Janet and John are husband and wife, as are Peter and Jane. (The human names are false, but not randomly chosen – as we shall see in

JANET: Oh, that's Christmas-cracker standard.

PETER: Of course, you know what Splash would get if he stayed outside for too long?

JANE: What?

SUSAN: Catarrh. (*More laughter all round.*)

JANET: Anyway, to get back to the point . . .

JOHN: Yes, get on with your catechism, Janet. (*Mock cheers.*)

Chapter 6.) The two couples are friends, and they live near to each other. They have got together for an evening, and the extract is taken from a point about 1.5 wine glasses into the occasion. It's easy to see what is happening. Jane's inspired piece of ingenious word formation, *catfrontation*, has sparked off a word-play mood. Peter and Jane try to outdo each other by finding words beginning with *cat-* which can be plausibly related in meaning to the conversational topic. Eventually John joins in, abandoning his mock-reluctance – and actually adds *catapult* to the list a few minutes further on.

Judged by any professional standards of comedy, the efforts of these four conversationalists range from the pathetic to the brilliant. But that is not the point. The real point is that all are having an excellent time. They do not mind that the conversation has been temporarily disrupted, and are happy to keep the main story in suspension. They applaud each other's cleverness, using groans and laughter, and nothing else seems to matter. The humour bounces back and forth between them, in an almost competitive spirit – which is why this kind of behaviour has sometimes been called 'ping-pong punning'.

It is difficult to see how ping-pong punning can possibly fit in with the view that the purpose of language is to communicate ideas. For what new knowledge is being transmitted between the participants, as they bounce jokes off each other? None. What have they learned, at the end of the sequence, that they did not know before? Nothing. There seems to be a tacit agreement that none of their language is to be taken at its face value, while the exchange is in progress – that no sentence is to be interpreted as containing any real information. The feline situation is not truly a catastrophic one. John is not really being a catalyst. Nor would Splash really develop catarrh. The rules governing literal discourse have been suspended, while everyone delights in verbally showing off.

This conversation gives us a hint of what the world of language play is like. It is not that it lacks rules: when we play language games – as any games – there must always be rules. Rather, the rules of ludic language are different from those which govern other uses of language. In particular, there are special ways of speaking, and often special facial expressions, to show that an utterance in a conversation is intended as a piece of wordplay. The part of the word which is the focus of the pun (*cat-* in this conversation) is usually pronounced in a more careful or prominent manner, and the speaker often looks quizzical or smug. Listeners are expected to make energetic use of just a small range of possible responses, such as the forced (or real) groan. And – very important – the participants must not make the same pun twice in a single sequence. We would never find an exchange like this:

JANE: *This sounds like it's becoming a cat-alogue of disasters.*
PETER: *I think Splash must have read about it in a cat-alogue.*

No one would consciously re-use someone else's pun, any more than they would listen to someone telling a joke, then tell the same joke all over again. (However, unlike jokes, instances of word-play *are* available for re-use *later* in the same conversation, as we shall see in Chapter 2.)

If the *catfrontation* exchange were an isolated instance, it would hardly deserve an extensive commentary. But pun-capping sequences of this kind are a very common feature of informal conversations, especially between people who know each other well. As James Boswell said, 'A good pun may be admitted among the small excellencies of lively conversation.' Men and women seem to use them equally. Nor do they seem to be restricted to particular ages, professions, or educational backgrounds. While the *catfrontation* conversationalists were evidently educated enough to be able to use such words as *catalyst*, ping-pong punning as a genre of word-play does not rely upon learnèd examples, and usually taps into words which most people know. For example, in another conversation, the sight of a chair with an arm missing elicited the quip *Don't worry, it's 'armless* – a pun that has probably been made (along with *'armful* and *out of 'arm's way*) thousands of times around the English-speaking world, by people from all educational backgrounds, as they encounter damaged armchairs or someone with an arm in plaster.[1]

Personality, of course, can't be ignored. To say that 'everyone engages in language play', as I did at the beginning of this chapter, is not to say that everyone engages in the *same kind* of language play. Some people are good at puns, and never miss a chance to drop one into a conversation; others never use them and cannot stand people who do. Jonathan Swift remarked: 'Punning is a talent which no man affects to despise, but he that is without it.' But, as we shall see, those who do not wish to be involved in ping-pong punning do not thereby cut themselves off from the world of language play. People who do not practise one form of language play always favour another. If it is not puns, then it might be puzzles. If not puzzles, then panel games.

2 BON MOTORISTS

'A pun,' as American writer Christopher Morley once said, 'is language on vacation' – an appropriate description, indeed, for the off-duty linguistic behaviour displayed by our *catfrontation* conversationalists. And nowhere is this description more lovingly explored than in a paperback by a fellow-American, writer and teacher Richard Lederer, *Get Thee to a Punnery* – a book dedicated to the proposition, unequivocally asserted at the beginning of his third chapter, that 'language is fun'.

From a fine collection of punny material, I single out these (genuine) examples of playful personalized car licence-plates. There are, he thinks, over 2 million Americans – 'bon motorists', as he calls them – who have their own vanity plates. These commonly identify the profession of the owner (left column), but they also often do no more than express an identity or sense of humour (right column). A more succinct form of everyday language play it would be difficult to find.

YRUILL	doctor	HIYAQT	flirt
YRUFAT	aerobics instructor	10SNE1	tennis buff
IOPER8	surgeon	XQQMOI	Miss Piggy fan
IC2020	eye doctor	HIOSVR	Lone Ranger fan
4CAST	weather forecaster	DOIOU2	habitual debtor
2THDR	dentist	EIEIO	farmer named McDonald[G2]

If not panel games, then poetry. Ludic language exists in hundreds of different genres and adds enjoyment to our daily lives in many routine ways. It is not just a matter of humour, or laughter: enjoyment encompasses much more.

Chapter 2 will develop this argument: I shall claim that it is part of the normal human condition to spend an appreciable amount of time actively playing with language within some of these genres, or responding with enjoyment to the way others play. Chapter 3 devotes

Car name-puns are less easy to arrange in Britain, where index-marks are traditionally arbitrary number-letter combinations. Most identity-conscious car-owners have to settle for their initials. But with judicious manipulation (such as allowing a 5 to read S, so that we can create such forms as 5EXY, MYA55) there are many playful possibilities, some of which have been known to fetch a tidy sum at auction.

A brief extract from Lederer's saga of Wang Xianfeng (a Chinese girl who was discovered in 1987 apparently having been brought up by pigs) shows how the *catfrontation* type of exchange can become the motivation for a whole story.

Wang Xianfeng was an enthusiastic little pig gal. She squealed with delight over the works of Francis Bacon and went whole hog and hog wild for cartoon characters like Porky Pig and Miss Piggy, movies like *Porky's*, novels like *Swine Flu Over the Cuckoo's Nest*, and plays like *Pygmalion* and *Hamlet*, which she loved to ham up . . .

In a wry gloss on this text, Lederer considers himself to be a 'terminal and interminable victim of witzelsucht' (literally 'wit-seeking'), evidently defined by *Stedman's Medical Dictionary* as 'a morbid tendency to pun while being inordinately entertained thereby'.

Can't fault that. Nor the aptness for this book of a quotation he ascribes to Alleen Pace and Don L. F. Nilsen: 'Language play is the new frontier of English'.

itself to the cases where the time involved in ludic behaviour becomes truly significant – possibly even excessive; and Chapter 4 reviews ways in which you can devote your whole life to it – and be paid for it at the same time. Chapter 5 asks where the need to play with language comes from. Was Samuel Beckett right to assert, in *Murphy*, 'In the beginning was the pun'? I look back over the course of child language acquisition, and suggest that, if we do have a 'language instinct', as some authors have maintained,[2] then it is indeed chiefly for language play. I shall go so far as to claim that it is a sign of communicative breakdown, or even pathology, when people avoid playing with language. Chapter 6 then presents the case for introducing children to the ludic dimension when they are learning to read and write, as well as later on, when they encounter the traditionally gloomy world of grammar.

By the final chapter, I hope to have demonstrated that we need to alter our definitions of language to give proper recognition to the importance of language play. For only in this way can we reach a satisfactory understanding of what is involved in linguistic creativity.

2

THE AMATEURS

Whatever else Janet, John, Peter and Jane do with language in their professional lives, when it comes to language play they are very definitely amateurs. Unlike the range of people whose activities are described in Chapter 4, they receive no payment for their ludic behaviour. They haven't had any formal training in order to engage in language play. Nor are there any official regulations governing what they do while they play with the language, or where and when they do it. No doubt they would think it absurd even to begin thinking about their behaviour in such terms.

Indeed, the whole point about conversational language play is that it is unregulated and anarchic. We let our hair down. Anything goes. We take risks – for it is always possible that a piece of word-play will fall flat, be misinterpreted, or go over the listener's head. With language play, moreover, everyone is equal – in the sense that, once we have achieved adult levels of fluency in a language, we have acquired all the tools and expertise we need in order to play with it success-fully. And as Chapter 5 shows, this ability grows gradually and unself-consciously through the immense amount of ludic practice which is part of the normal experience of childhood. None of this is to deny, as already mentioned, that some people are cleverer at language play than others; and with some types of language game, as we shall see in the next chapter, it is possible to train ourselves to achieve very high levels of skill. But, in principle, the same ludic licence is available to everyone.

Anything goes? Yes. Any aspect of linguistic structure is available to become the focus of language play. We can alter the pronunciation, the writing system, the grammar, the vocabulary, the patterns of

9

spoken or written discourse, or any combination of these. Within pronunciation, for example, we might play with the vowels, the consonants, the way syllables are made up, the way syllables combine into words, the pitch, loudness, speed, and rhythm of speech, or the range of vocal effects that are usually summed up as 'tone of voice'. To illustrate just one of these: consonants. British artist and illustrator Graham Rawle has had considerable success with his 'Lost Consonant' series, drawn in the *Weekend Guardian* since 1990, and now available in several collections in the form of postcards. Each card portrays an activity as described in a normal English sentence; but one of the words in the sentence has lost a consonant, yielding a different word and a bizarre situation, and this situation Rawle solemnly portrays in the associated picture. Typical sentences (from his collection No 5) are:

His solicitor had sent him a copy of the daft contract.
Doreen bought an earthenware bowl made by the local otter.
Clive was trying to revere his car round the corner.
Every evening he took a short troll round the garden.

Playing with consonants is just one of dozens of possible ways in which we can depart from the norms of pronunciation in order to achieve a special effect. In the case of grammar, there are thousands of possible deviations. In the case of vocabulary, there are tens of thousands.

In practice, of course, only a small number of these deviations turn up with any frequency. The critical point is that a piece of language play is effective only if we first recognize the rules of the language for what they are, and can sense when they are being broken. For example, it is possible to play with spelling in order to make a special effect. The aura of childhood surrounding *Winnie-the-Pooh* is partly conveyed by such spellings as *picknicks, piglit, missige, rabbits frends*, and *100 aker wood*.[1] The contrived spelling of a person's name may say something about the character, such as *Count Smorltork* in *The Pickwick Papers* or the tutor, *Thwackum*, in *A History of Tom Jones*. And Ogden Nash gives us:

> Better a parvenu
> Living luxuriously on Park Arvenu
> Than a Schuyler or a Van Rensselaer
> Living inexpensselaer.

These orthographic jokes work only because we know the standard spellings. There would be little point in trying to make a joke which relied on people recognizing a mis-spelling in a word such as *diarrhoea*, which most of us cannot spell at all. Similarly, if a story told to a group of listeners in the heart of England depended on their appreciating the difference between, say, a Dublin and a Cork accent, or between an American and a Canadian accent, it would be unlikely to succeed – for few English people are aware of these contrasts. The same issue arises in relation to jokes which rely on obscure vocabulary or unfamiliar dialect grammar. Robert Graves once remarked that any English poet has to 'master the rules of grammar before he attempts to bend or break them'. This is a good point, but it applies to more than grammar, to more than poetry, and to more than English: all features of ludic language, in all genres, and in all languages, require that the participants should be aware of the rules of the game before they begin to play.

Listening to informal everyday conversation, it is possible to discern a number of ways in which people follow this general principle – deviating happily from their normal linguistic behaviour, but only within very familiar linguistic territory. Generally, also, only one kind of deviation takes place at a time. If we are playing with sound effects, our grammar and vocabulary tend to stay stable. If we play with vocabulary or grammatical structure, we leave pronunciation alone. Such constraints are important, for without them the language can disintegrate to the point of unintelligibility, and the whole point of the game would be lost. As we shall see later, a sign of highly sophisticated language play, such as is found in poetry or in the fantastic lexical creations of James Joyce, is the way several linguistic levels can be successfully manipulated at the same time.

ENJOYING THE JOKE

I suggested at the end of Chapter 1 that language play involves far more than just humour: as we shall see later, it can be a part of some highly serious activities. Likewise, humour involves far more than just language play: comedy may arise directly out of the (non-verbal) situation as much as out of the language, as any good farce illustrates – and a mime artist can create humour without using any words at all.

But even within the world of verbal humour, by no means everything is the result of language play. Take these three old jokes:

'I say, I say, I say: Would you like to play with my new dog?'
'Does he bite?'
'I don't know. That's what I want to find out!'

MAN AT AUCTION: *I've bid a great deal of money for this parrot. Are you sure he talks?*
AUCTIONEER: *Of course I'm sure. He's the one who's been bidding against you!*

SMITH (on the golf course) *stops and bows his head when a funeral cortège passes by in the distance.*
BROWN (very impressed): *That was a very nice gesture, old man.*
SMITH: *Well, she was a good wife to me, after all.*

There is nothing unusual about the language used in these jokes. Whatever humour you might squeeze out of them comes from the absurd or unexpected nature of their situations, and not from their language, which is straightforward and colloquially standard. There is no bending or breaking of linguistic rules here.

By contrast, the following set of jokes do have a linguistic basis. They all involve a type of word-play, with a different aspect of linguistic structure being implicated in each case.

o Jokes which play with the way a word imitates sound:

> *'Doctor, doctor, I've just swallowed a sheep!'*
> *'How do you feel?'*
> *'Very baaad.'*

o Jokes which play with the vowels or consonants in the pronunciation system:

> *'I'd like a fur coat, please.'*
> *'Certainly, madam. What fur?'*
> *'To keep myself warm, of course.'*

o Jokes which play with the spelling or punctuation in the writing system:

> *'What did one sheep say to the other?'*
> *'I think ewe are bewetiful.'*

o Jokes which play with word boundaries:

> *BE ALERT. This country needs lerts.*

o Jokes which play with the grammatical structure of the sentence:

> *'Dad, what are all those holes in the new shed?'*
> *'They're knot-holes.'*
> *'What do you mean "They're not holes"? I can put my finger right through them.'*

o Jokes which play with the meaning of words:

> *'What do you get if you cross a sheep with a kangaroo?'*
> *' A woolly jumper.'*

o Jokes which play with the assumptions behind a dialogue:

> TEACHER: *Where are you from, Julie?*
> JULIE: *Wales, Miss.*
> TEACHER: *What part?*
> JULIE: *All of me, Miss.*

About two-thirds of the jokes in a typical collection rely on language play, and the vast majority of these involve puns of some kind.

It is a moot point, of course, whether these jokes count as humour. The published genre goes out of its way to stress that its jokes are not at all likely to make you laugh. On the contrary, the authors threaten to make you groan, retch, or vomit. They warn you to keep away. One collection, *1000 Jokes for Kids of All Ages* has a sequel, *Oh No! Not Another 1000 Jokes for Kids*. Another collection is called *The Most Awful Joke Book Ever*. A third is called *Sick as a Parrot*, and subtitled *The World's Worst Jokes.*[2] Its back-cover blurb reads:

> *This is really the best of the worst jokes you will find. Our author has made himself very sick collecting them.*
>
> *We guarantee that you will scream, bang your head and lose your friends if you repeat these jokes.*
>
> *Take care, you have been warned! This book is not for the squeamish.*

Any Martian observing a human child reading a joke book of this kind, or two children reading jokes aloud to each other, would have no idea what was going on. The definitions and characterizations of humour it would have learned about from contemporary accounts, such as Howard Jacobson's *Seriously Funny*, all emphasize the role of laughter.[3] Well, if humour is to be judged by the laughing it generates, then what we have here is not humour, for laughter is conspicuous by its absence. Rarely does even a flicker of a smile cross the children's faces. And all parents have experienced the awfulness of being asked to listen to a series of such jokes, read aloud in a deadpan tone by a child who waits confidently for an uproarious reaction.

Joke exchanges are carried on in deadly earnest, like a verbal duel –

mouth-to-mouth combat. Bang, bang: you're (linguistically) dead. Indeed, the gun analogy has not escaped the notice of literary commentators: as Charles Lamb put it, in *Popular Fallacies*, a pun 'is a pistol let off at the ear; not a feather to tickle the intellect'. Nor has the notion of a battle: many a Shakespearean critic has drawn attention to the 'pun-duelling' between pairs of lovers in the plays. Molly Mahood puts it well, in *Shakespeare's Wordplay*: 'Most of the witty wordplay in Shakespeare is either wanton or aggressive. The liveliest exchanges are between those pairs of lovers who fight their way to the altar, for their wordplay is doubly tendentious in being at once both hostile and seductive'.[4] And at least one character has no doubts about the wounds that can be inflicted. Boyet reflects ruefully, towards the end of *Love's Labour's Lost*:

> *The tongues of mocking wenches are as keen*
> *As is the razor's edge invisible . . .*
> > *Their conceits have wings*
> *Fleeter than arrows, bullets . . . (V.ii.256)*

Guns again. And certainly, as we see one suitor cut down another with a verbal blow, our response is more the cheer, the admiring intake of breath at the fast draw, than the belly-laugh. We thoroughly enjoy the linguistic fight.

It is the same with the children. Whether they laugh or not, there is no doubt that they are hugely enjoying themselves when they read joke books or swap jokes with each other. And enjoyment, rather than humour, is what language play is chiefly about.

Where do the jokes in joke books come from? Often, I imagine, from other joke books – for it is the easiest thing in the world to retell a joke so that it sounds original. This is what we do all the time, after all, when we repeat a joke we have heard: we replace names and other details, keeping only the essential plot and the punch line. It is a commonplace experience to be listening to an apparently new joke, then to realize from the punch-line that we have heard it before. No one has the time or patience to check through a pair of joke books to see just how many items are in common: it would be a difficult task, in any case, because the jokes are randomly distributed, and all kinds of minor differences get in the way. For instance, two of the above books contain the following:

DOCTOR: *Those pills I gave you to help you remember things – how are they working?*
PATIENT: *What pills?*

'Doctor, I'm getting very forgetful.'
'I see, Mr Bloggs. Now when did you first notice this trouble?'
'What trouble?'

And, despite the obvious differences, the next two are essentially the same:

A slow-thinking country lad was complaining to his friend about his illness.

'Oi can't keep nuttin' on moi stomach. The doctor gimme some pills – but they rolled orf in the night!'

'My doctor told me to take two of these pills on an empty stomach.'
'Did they do any good?'
'I don't know. They keep rolling off in the night.'

In such cases, it is impossible to prove whether one came from the other, or whether they originated in independent senses of humour. Copyright in jokes is an implausible notion, and several joke books actually state explicitly that the copyright is in the collection, or in the arrangement of the collection, and not in the individual jokes themselves.

Because the word-play in a joke is often very simple, it is likely that many jokes are spontaneously recreated thousands of times each year. It does not take much to see the phonetic correspondence between *spag* and *spook* to produce 'What does a ghost eat? Spookhetti'. As the old saying says:

> *A pun's the lowest form of wit,*
> *It does not tax the brain a bit;*
> *One merely takes a word that's plain*
> *And picks one out that sounds the same.*

Similarly, because jokes are often formulaic, it is easy to generate dozens of new exemplars in a single joke-swapping session. Easy targets are jokes which begin *Doctor, doctor . . .* or *Knock, knock . . .*, or the many jokes which work within a theme, such as elephant jokes and Irish jokes. Children at a certain age do this all the time, as we shall see in Chapter 5, and it doesn't take much to make adults join in too, as we have already seen in Chapter 1. The kind of spontaneous play we saw there, based on the word *cat*, could very easily become the basis of a new joke fashion. A thousand *cat* jokes for kids? Why not?

Sometimes it is the technique of the joke which is simple. 'What's the difference between . . .' jokes often rely on a simple transposition of initial sounds:

What's the difference between . . .
. . . a robber and a church bell?

One steals from the people and the other peals from the steeple.
. . . a kangaroo and a lumberjack?
One hops and chews and the other chops and hews.

There is a vast number of 'rhyming pairs' in English (such as *steal/peal, steeple/people, hop/chop, chew/hew*), and it is not difficult to find a combination which makes some sort of sense – though, it has to be admitted, some substitutions are extremely creative and ingenious, deserving our admiration. John Dryden's comment that the pun is 'the lowest and most grovelling kind of wit' is not always apt. Still, you might disagree with me after working your way through *1000 What's What Jokes For Kids.*[5]

Joke creation, in short, is not a specialist, professional matter. Though some can earn their living by it, the ability to see links of sound and meaning between words is part of the normal process of language learning, and anyone who has achieved a reasonable level of conversational fluency in a language has, by definition, acquired all the tools needed to begin joking in it. What level is that? The evidence of Chapter 5 suggests that it need only be equivalent to that of a child of about three or four. But few of us who have learned a foreign language have achieved even that level of linguistic competence. I spent seven years learning French in school, and have used the language often since, but I do not recall ever having sufficient intuition to be able to make a French joke, even though the techniques are exactly the same in English and French.

DIALECT HUMOUR

The difference between our limited ludic abilities in a foreign language and the powerful abilities we have in our mother tongue is especially clear when we consider dialect humour. Regional dialects and (especially in England) class dialects are a rich source of conversational language play, for everyone is aware of at least some dialect differences, even if they can imitate them only in a rough-and-ready way. It is enough that the dialect is vaguely recognizable from the attempt at an imitation. English people who begin a joke about the Scots by saying 'Hoots, mon, the noo', or about the Welsh by saying 'Look you, boyo', are labouring under a serious illusion if they think that the members of these two nations habitually talk like this. For the stereotype to be successful in the context of joke telling, it is sufficient if people think that they do. And no social group is exempt from stereotypes – as English people are sometimes surprised to find when they travel abroad and encounter a comedian who presents a biting satire of an upper-class English accent.

Quite often, indeed, there are stereotypes within the stereotypes: the English may laugh at the Irish, but the Irish from Dublin often make jokes at the expense of the Irish from Cork – and I have heard people from Cork joke about people from Kerry. (My research stops there: I never got as far as Kerry to establish who the people there joke about.) The same jokes go the rounds. 'Have you heard the one about the man from X?' All that is necessary is that the teller and listeners are not from X, and that X has a reputation for being away from the centre of civilization, with its people lazy, backward, or in some way dense. Such jokes have no trouble crossing dialect boundaries – or even language boundaries. 'What do you get if you cross a monkey with an Irishman?' (Answer: 'A stupid monkey') might be heard in any country where there is a traditional minority or enemy available to insult, and is doubtless told about the English in many parts of Ireland.

Word-play often relies on accent differences between social groups. The technique is the same, whether it is found in casual banter or a structured joke: a word spoken in one accent is interpreted as if it belongs to another, resulting in an incongruous effect or an unexpected meaning – or both. Here are four examples:

o Mick and Murphy were passing the employment exchange when they saw a sign outside saying: TREE FELLERS WANTED. 'What a shame', says Mick. 'There being only two of us'.

o A New Yorker was being shown Trafalgar Square by an upper-class Englishman, and was impressed by all the pigeons. 'Gee!', he exclaimed, 'Look at all dem boids!' 'Not boids', said the Englishman

3 DIALECT PLAY

This extract comes from the beginning of Sam Llewellyn's *Yacky dar moy bewty!* – subheaded *A Phrasebook for the Regions (with Irish Supplement)*. It illustrates the kind of conversation one might expect to encounter while travelling in the south-west of England.

Ear yoe!	Excuse me!
Ace?	Yes?
Can ee dellus the rawed vor Penzarnce?	Please tell me the way to Penzance.
Whoart?	I beg your pardon?
PENZARNCE!	PENZANCE!
This be Larnsen, nart Penzarnce.	But you are in Launceston.
Ace.	Precisely.
A! You'll be awantin the Mooderaway.	Proceed via the M5.
Wheer's the Mooderaway?	How do I reach the M5?
Juz vore the rawed.	It is ten miles away.
Durn leaft at the Jurch . . .	Left at the church . . .
raight at the wold howse . . .	right at the old house . . .
down the combe . . .	along the valley . . .
and orver the burge.	and across the bridge.

snootily, 'you should call them *birds*'. 'Well', replied the American, 'they sure choips like boids.'

o What did the Cockney barrow-boy say when a swarm of bees landed on his barrow? 'Why don't you "behave" yourselves.'

o A judge arrives at his chambers having left an important document at home. 'Fax it up', his clerk suggests. 'Yes, it does rather', replies the judge.

Zixty yaard leater, you're on the bype arse.	Sixty yards, and you're on the bypass.
Carnt miss ut.	The skeletons of your predecessors litter the verges.
Arl raight, me luvver?	Have you understood, sir?
Ace. Tar.	Yes. Thank you.

These jokes provide another example of the familiarity principle referred to earlier. They work only if you can internally 'hear' the accent contrasts: the Irish example depends on you knowing that *three* is pronounced [tree] by most Irish; the American example assumes that you can recognize at least one feature of a New York accent; the barrow-boy example depends on the fact that a Cockney pronunciation of *hay* would sound to non-Cockney ears as *high* (= *bee-hive*); and the legal example – how can I put this? – assumes that the two people were not pronouncing their front vowels in exactly the same way.

But at least these jokes can be written down. In other cases, it is impossible to use ordinary spelling without giving the game away. Some kind of phonetic transcription would have to be used, especially if there were major differences between the accents. This next story provides an example: it actually happened, and seems to have become a standard joke in medical circles. To see the point, you have to imagine the critical words (in square brackets) being pronounced with equal stress on each syllable (shown by ') – a rhythm widely used by foreign speakers of English.

o A South Asian woman goes to see her doctor about her husband. 'What's wrong with him?' asks the doctor. 'He's ['im'paw'tent],' says the woman. 'Yes, but what's wrong with him?' repeats the doctor. 'I've just told you,' replies the woman. 'He's ['im'paw'tent]!'

The woman says 'impotent', but because she stresses the second syllable – a pronunciation widely used by non-native speakers of English – the doctor hears the word as 'important'.

The variations between regional and class dialects have also fed another genre of language play – the dialect humour book. Tucked away in the 'local' section of bookshops all over the world will often be found a pamphlet or booklet illustrating 'the way we talk round here'. The idea is very simple: the author takes words or dialogues from standard English, and 'translates' them into local speech patterns, respelling the language to capture the phonetic effects. The humour lies in finding a 'serious' translation in standard English of what the local dialect is saying. The technique is immediately recognizable, locals readily identify with it, and the result can be huge sales. One of the earliest books in the genre, Afferbeck Lauder's *Let Stalk Strine* (= Australian), was published in 1962, and sold 100,000 copies in its first year. Since then we have had guides to several parts of the English-speaking world, such as South Africa (*Ah Big Yaws?* = 'I Beg Yours?'), Liverpool (*Lern Yerself Scouse*), London's West End (*Fraffly Well Spoken*), and Texas (*The Illustrated Texan Dictionary of the*

English Language). The whole of Britain has been covered in the elegantly named *Yacky Dar Moy Bewty!*[6]

In a sense, none of this is new. The representation of dialect speech for comic effect has a long history, and is well illustrated in many nineteenth-century novels, especially in the writing of Charles Dickens. Also, not all of the effects transcribed in the pages of such books are genuine dialect features. Often the transcriptions merely represent what happens when people speak quickly – a sound at the end of one word blends with the sound at the beginning of the next, one of the sounds is left out or a sound is articulated in a relaxed manner. There is actually nothing specifically Australian about the way *let's talk* is represented as *Let Stalk*. Exactly the same effect is heard in all varieties of spoken English – even including the prestige pronunciation in England known as 'received pronunciation'. And when we look through the dialect books from around the world, we find that all the authors are relying on the same sort of thing – as the use of *gorra* (= 'got a/to') below illustrates. The clever feature is not actually the regionalism at all, but the way in which the effect can be written down so as to remind the reader of something else. The humour relies entirely on the ingenuity of the transcribed words and on the translation equivalent in standard English.

o *Dijew gorra law since?* (from *Ah Big Yaws?*): an enquiry as to whether an activity has been accorded official sanction.
o *Av gorra gerroff, am goan to ado* (from *Lern Yerself Scouse*): I must leave, I have a party to attend.
o *Gorra loyt?* (Midlands, England, from *Yacky Dar Moy Bewty!*): Have you a light?
o *Egg-wetter Gree* (from *Fraffly Well Spoken*): an expression of concurrence and agreement.
o *Cheque etcher* (from *Let Stalk Strine*): did you obtain, as in: 'Where cheque etcher hat?'

Rather different in style and intention, but similar in its reliance on regional features, is literature which involves a 'translation' from one dialect into another. Consider Kel Richards' *Father Koala's Nursery*

Rhymes (1992). This is a collection of nursery rhymes, some indigenous to Australia, some a transculturation of rhymes indigenous to Britain – such as 'Swaggie Put the Billy On', 'Here We Go Round the Banksia Bush', and 'Sing a Song of Ten Cents'. All are excellent examples of localized language play.

> *Baa baa, black sheep,*
> *Have you any wool?*
> *Yes mate! Too right!*
> *Three bales full.*
> *One for the shearer,*
> *And one for the boss,*
> *And one for your pullover*
> *To stop you getting cross.*[7]

FUNNY SOUNDS AND VOICES

A common form of conversational language play involves the use of unusual voices which go well beyond the norms of conventional regional or social accents. Especially popular with the younger generation, the voice is simply 'funny' or 'stupid', maybe aping a cartoon voice, or a voice frequently used by some comedian of the moment, or some film or television personality – but often the speaker has no particular model in mind at all. Mock foreign accents are also popular, as are highly exaggerated regional accents. Many young people in fact achieve quite a presence among their peers through adopting an idiosyncratic 'silly' voice. A Donald Duck voice is a real winner, because it is so difficult to produce (you have to make use of air compressed within the cheeks). Such voices become a kind of vocal trade-mark, which delights friends and infuriates parents. The habit seems to emerge strongly in the early teens, but is heard among the members of any close-knit group when they are 'larking about', as the following examples show.

o A group of teenagers are being boisterous. One does something the others consider stupid. They all adopt a low, nasalized, drawling tone, imitative (as they imagine) of someone with a mental handicap, as they honk at the unfortunate one. A few minutes later, one of them threatens another with death and destruction, and puts on a heavy mock German accent, reminiscent of the Nazi interrogator of classic British war films. He frog-marches his friend around the room. 'Ve haff vays off making you valk,' he says, using a double deviation – departing from his normal voice, then departing from the standard cliché ('We have ways of making you talk').

o A man in his mid twenties enters a room and sees his brother. He addresses him in a high-pitched, querulous voice, somewhat reminiscent of the call of a seagull. The other immediately responds, using a similar voice. They exchange a number of remarks in this way, before lapsing into their normal voices.

o Several students in a pub are well into their evening. Someone brings a round of drinks, and one says 'Tanks' (= thanks) in a totally unbelievable Irish accent. A second student picks up the accent, saying 'No tanks in here, sure 'n' all'. A third begins to half-sing, 'Ta-a-nks for the memory . . .', and they then fall about, trying to out-pun each other, in the manner of Chapter 1. Eventually, the conversation collapses into general groaning, and a new topic emerges.

The range of abnormal voices adopted by speakers in informal settings is endless. A university linguistics lecturer sticks his head into a colleague's room, and calls 'Eeee – what's up, doc?', using the strident nasal tones of the cartoon character Bugs Bunny. (It should perhaps be made clear that, notwithstanding his profession, he does not normally talk like this.) A group of well-oiled Lions sitting around a table at their charter-night dinner suddenly decide to speak like Long John Silver (as portrayed by Robert Newton) and swap remarks in a bizarre West Country burr, adding 'oo-ar' at every available opportunity. A husband, mock-threatening his wife, switches into husky mafiosi, as learned from Marlon Brando in *The Godfather*. A wife, teasing her husband, comments on his 'nice car', but adopts the lilting, r-coloured voice of the woman in a British TV car advertisement

4 MOUTHPLAY

Putting on funny voices seems to be just one aspect of the general fascination we have with phonetic play. If it is physiologically possible for our mouths to produce a noise, then we like to make it. Why? The functions vary enormously, from the highly useful (whistling to grab attention over distances) to the totally pointless (making a 'birip' frog noise). Many show not so much a linguistic purpose as a general desire to imitate the sounds around us, which seems to be instinctive. From an early age (see Chapter 5), children copy guns, explosions, horns, passing vehicles (often with accurate Doppler effects – 'eeeiaowww'), animals and other environmental noises – a skill which adults retain (though usually manifested only when inhibitions have been left behind).

Here are some of the noises which people, from time to time, find linguistically useful.

o We need to sound hesitant. Aside from the conventional *er* and *erm*, we can make a rhythmical humming sound at the lips ('mumumu-mum'), click the tongue repeatedly, or flap the tongue between the lips.
o We need to make a strongly appreciative noise, such as after experiencing the first sip of a much-needed whisky or a particularly effective cocktail. Options include a hoarse, breathless, burning-throat effect ('What's in that thing?!'), a series of nasal noises made at the back of the mouth ('ang-ang-ang'), and a hissing or shushing noise around the sides of the tongue.
o We want to be rude. The classic noise is the raspberry, or Bronx cheer, made by putting the tip of the tongue between tightly closed lips and forcing air out; but it is possible to sound disgusting in many ways, using the vocal tract to make a wide range of simulated farts and burps.

Mock-animal noises seem to have a special attraction at certain times.

o We desperately want something from a person with whom we are intimate. The commonest noises are cute mock-puppy whinings, but some pleaders prefer a series of mock-kitten meows.

o We see someone at a party with whom we would very much like to be intimate, and let our friends (but not usually the object of our desire) know this by simulating the growl or bark of an eager dog (*r-r-ruff*) or an exaggerated panting.

o We are in a crowd, being all-too-slowly led in a certain direction (such as at a sports stadium exit, or while waiting to be let off a plane). Options here include mooing and bleating.

However, not every noise has a clear reason. For example, we can (with the judicious help of the index finger within the cheek) imitate the popping sound of a cork coming out of a bottle. I have heard people do this when they are trying to be offensive or cheeky, but as often as not it seems to be done just to pass the time. Then there is the remarkable rise of chicken behaviour in recent years. It is possible to release air compressed within the cheeks in a series of pulses, giving a hollow, mock-hen effect, sometimes written as 'bok-bok-bok'. Really expert mouth-players can also mimic the strangled hen squawk at the end of such a sequence – 'bok-bok-bok-bwaaak'. Why people do this, often accompanying it with a thumbs-in-armpits chicken walk, is one of life's great mysteries. It may be enough to accept that it is splendidly ridiculous, requiring no other reason. It is certainly highly contagious (I have observed a whole roomful of people being chickens together), and it has even been institutionalized in the form of a dance.

For people who are having difficulty mastering any of these sounds, it may be reassuring to know that there is a training guide (with record included): Frederick R. Newman's *Mouthsounds* shows you – tongue in cheek, as it were – how to make over seventy noises with your mouth. On the cover it is described as 'a practitioner's manual' – 'how to whistle, pop, click, and honk your way to social success'.[64]

of the mid 1990s which emphasized the sexual possibilities of good car-handling.

People will play with voices borrowed from any source that they think their listeners will recognize – characters from the Muppets, *Monty Python*, *The Goon Show*, *Star Wars* . . . The Swedish chef, Miss Piggy, and Kermit the Frog must have received millions of vocal rein-carnations around the English-speaking world. And everyday life is reflected back at us from the screen. Good-humoured 'buddy' TV sit-coms, such as *Friends*, present us with innumerable examples, as the participants chide and tease each other. It is also part of the stock-in-trade of stand-up comedians – well illustrated by the 'stupid person' voices adopted in sketches by British comedian Jack Dee. And some film stars – Robin Williams comes especially to mind – have devel-oped a remarkable ability to adopt a wide range of voices while play-ing a single character.

Recognition is everything. Choose an unfamiliar voice, and there is no effect. Worse, there can be an anti-effect. In one English house-hold, a father engaged in some banter with his teenage children pre-tended to be scared of them, and adopted the quavery falsetto of the 'Bluebottle' character (played by Peter Sellers) from *The Goon Show*, one of the most successful British radio comedy shows in the years after the Second World War (see p. 112). The effect was totally lost upon the children, who had never heard this show. They looked at each other in puzzlement, and asked if he was all right. He attempted to explain what he was doing, but – as anyone knows who has had to explain a joke, let alone a funny voice – his efforts were hopeless. He got into a tangle trying to describe the kind of over-anxious minus-cule being which Bluebottle was, then relapsed into silence, unable to compete with his children patting his brow and saying soothingly, 'Yes, Dad. Don't worry. It's all right, Dad.'

Why do we do it? Adopting bizarre voices seems to be a highly dis-tinctive way of achieving social rapport among the members of a group. They provide the group with a very simple means of bonding. They help to affirm group identity – and you can sometimes hear a teenage coterie using a particular funny voice as its own, to make itself sound different from others – a kind of ludic accent. There is a good example in Jack Rosenthal's TV play, *P'tang Yang Kipperbang*, where the teenage girls at one point express their contempt at the silly language used by their male counterparts in the classroom (which the title of the play reflects). But we must not look only at social explanations for unusual vocal behaviour. Some voices simply sound funny, and that's all there is to it. Comedy stars such as Peter Sellers, Kenneth Williams and Stan Freberg built their reputations on this fact, and the voices behind Goofy, Scooby-doo and hundreds of other cinematic cartoon characters continue to bear witness to it.

It is the same with individual sounds. In a particularly intriguing kind of play, just a part of a word is said in a deliberately silly way. A common example is *heffalump* for *elephant* – a child-based mis-articulation, eventually institutionalized by A. A. Milne (in *Winnie-the-Pooh*). Another (it was often used in *The Goon Show*) is to pronounce a word ending in *-ing* as if it rhymed with *singe*, as in 'pud-dinge'. Another is to impose this ending on a similar-sounding word, so that *sausages* comes out as 'sausinges'. To understand what is going on in cases of this kind, we need to study each instance individually, first by finding the words in the language which use the deviant sounds normally: which words usually end in *-inge*? It turns out that this cluster of sounds has some very distinctive resonances, for it is heard in only a dozen or so words in English, and these typically express a notion of smallness (*twinge, fringe, singe, hinge*) or some kind of inferiority (*winge, cringe, dinge*). To take a full-blooded noun or verb and change its *-ing* ending into *-inge* is thus to make it sound somehow feeble, inadequate, or puerile – and sounding childish is at the heart of language play.

The way in which individual sounds or sound clusters seem to have an intrinsic meaning or effect is studied in linguistics under the heading of *sound symbolism* or – especially when these effects are being used in poetry – *onomatopoeia*. I shall be looking at this phenomenon again in Chapter 4. Very few words in a language can be shown to have symbolic phonetic properties, but language play relies greatly on those sounds which can be used in this way. Absurdist poetry for children provides a convenient set of examples, in the names writers invent for their characters.

In John Foster's collection, *What a Lot of Nonsense!*, we find some extraordinary individuals: we encounter the Yellow Oozit, the Bongaloo, the Pobble and the Bumbly Boo; we are introduced to Clover McBeeze, Zonky Zizzibug and Nasty McGhastly; and we learn about Isabella McSpeet (who had very flat feet) and Millicent Millicheap (who gnawed her knickers in her sleep).[8] It is obvious which phonetic properties the writers are exploiting – vowels high up at the front of the mouth ('ee', 'i') or far back ('ah', 'oo'), consonants at the lips ('b', 'm', 'p') or towards the back of the palate ('ong', 'onk', 'ug'), lots of sonorant or liquid sounds ('z', 'l'), and lots of repetition (alliteration). Some authors, such as Edward Lear, James Thurber and Spike Milligan, are well known for their expert name-playing. The limerick heavily depends on it ('There was a young man called McJonk . . .'). And there are of course some highly respectable liter-ary antecedents, such as Richard Sheridan (many of whose characters have transparent surnames, such as Sir Benjamin Backbite and Lady Sneerwell) and Charles Dickens: *David Copperfield* introduces us (among many others) to Mr Creakle, Uriah Heep, and Thomas Traddles; and in *The Pickwick Papers* we meet Serjeant Buzfuz, Alfred Jingle, and Nathaniel Winkle.

NONCE WORDS AND MEANINGS

Another common form of conversational language play is the enthu-siasm with which we make up new words, as the *catfrontation* ex-ample in Chapter 1 showed. In cases of this kind, the speakers know that a word does not exist in the language, but they coin it none the less in order to make an impact on their listeners. There is no sugges-tion that the new word should become a part of standard English – and indeed it may never be used again after its first exposure in the conversation. The whole point of these words is that they are used just to capture the mood of the moment. They therefore fall into the category of 'nonce words' – a term whose history dates from the thirteenth century, where it is found in the phrase *for the nonce* mean-ing 'for a particular occasion'.

Nonce words can be coined for all kinds of purposes, apart from language play. For instance, they can help to get us out of a communicative jam. When a word is on the tip of the tongue, and despite our best efforts we cannot recall it, an invented word can get our meaning across. But in the following examples, the intention is entirely ludic.

o Two teenagers, Matthew and Ben, for several months got into the habit of adding the suffix -ness on to many nouns, in order to emphasize a particular abstract notion. *Look at the sizeness of it!*, Matthew might say. And Ben might echo with a double suffix, *Cor, the sizeness-ness!* Other examples included *bookness*, *upstairsness*, *wheelness* (at the sight of an enormous lorry), and *sadnessness*.

o A group of adults at a party were struck by one speaker's (perfectly normal) use of the prefix *neo-*, mocked him for being hyperintellectual, then carried on teasing him for several minutes by putting *neo-* before all kinds of inappropriate words – *neo-cake*, *neo-door handle*, and so forth. After a while, the joke faded, but it returned towards the end of the evening, when someone made

a further coinage, and a new 'round' of *neo*-isms was instituted.
o During a conversation before dinner, one person, asked if she were hungry, replied *hungry-ish*. For some reason this caught everyone's fancy, and they began to play with this suffix, adding *-ish* to their responses as much as they could. *I'm starving-ish*, said one. *I'm feeling ishy as well*, said another.
o Someone, struck by a description of one acquaintance as *uncouth*, drew a contrast with another by dropping the prefix and calling him *couth*. Several words in English exist only in their negative form, such as *inept*, *ungainly*, *disgruntled*, *unkempt*, and *dishevelled*, and it is fairly common to hear people playing with their non-existing opposites. Have you never felt *gruntled*?

These are all examples involving the ludic use of prefixes and suffixes. New words can also be created by splitting old words in half, quite arbitrarily. This was once a popular device in children's books, where a page might be cut in half horizontally, so that one of the sections could be turned separately while the other stayed the same:[9] in this way, we find pictures displaying, in addition to a *dachsund*, a *dachsaffe*, *dachstah*, and *dachsceros*; also, in addition to a *penguin*, a *monguin*, *gorguin*, and *kanguin*. The process can continue in real (almost) life, if this extract from the Ray Cooney and John Chapman farce *Move Over Mrs Markham* is anything to go by:

HENRY: *... Refresh my memory, what type of dog is Alistair?*
PHILIP: *Dirty.*
JOANNA: *No, no, he's er –*
ALISTAIR: *Er –*
JOANNA: *Labrador.*
    (Together.)
ALISTAIR: *Poodle.*
JOANNA: *Poodle.*
    (Together.)
ALISTAIR: *Labrador.*
JOANNA: *Half and half.*
PHILIP (sarcastically): *Very rare, labradoodles.*

Rather different are nonce-coinages where there is a deliberate intention to be ingenious, clever, or funny based on a perception that a word is missing from the language. We have all often felt that it would be nice if there existed a word for a certain notion which seems to have no lexical expression in English, and every now and then we may have a flash of inspiration, producing a new formation which we feel ought to be in the dictionary. *Fluddle* is one such, coined by someone to identify a pool of rainwater in the middle of a road which was larger than a puddle but smaller than a flood. The feeling that there are thousands of notions just waiting for their words to be invented has fuelled several humorous games and pastimes on radio and television. One American TV series, *Not Necessarily the News*, included a regular contribution by Rich Hall, who called them 'sniglets' – one of several terms which have been used for this type of coinage. An enthusiast, following in Hall's footsteps, supplied me with the sample on pp. 34–5.

There have been many variants of this kind of language play, some of which take us away from informal conversation into the world of puzzles and party games. One popular variant works the other way round: the player takes a standard English word and asks for a playful definition. Easy examples include *stalemate* ('an ex-husband or -wife') and *nitrate* ('the cost of off-peak electricity'). Rather more ingenious are *finesse* ('a female fish') and *semiquaver* ('half afraid'). Much cleverer, because they play with grammar, spelling rules, or regional accents, are *vixen* ('a female vicar'), *chinchilla* ('an icepack for the lower face'), *genealogy* ('allergic to denim'), and *reefs* ('objects placed around a coffin'). There is a close connection with certain kinds of crossword-puzzle clue: 'sounds like a wedding day' might generate *maritime*; 'male escort, perhaps' could lead to *mandate*. And the same source gives rise to the occasional publication of lists of student examination howlers:

An antibody is a way of dieting.
Bibliography is the study of the Old Testament.
A centimetre is an insect with a hundred legs.

Also working the other way round is the technique adopted by

5 NONCENESS

Following a programme on humorous nonce-words as part of the Radio 4 series *English Now* in 1988, several listeners sent me suggestions they had invented themselves. The following are selected from one of the best collections, by Neil McNicholas.

airogance n. The incomprehensible fact that an airline will keep a plane-load of passengers waiting for a handful of late arrivals.

archaesundheit n. The fraction of a second of history that passes without you when you sneeze.

bagonize v. To anxiously wait for your suitcase to appear on the baggage claim carousel.

blinksync n. The guarantee that, in any group photo, there will always be at least one person whose eyes are closed.

circumtreeviation n. The tendency of a dog on a leash to want to walk past poles and trees on the opposite side to its owner.

citrastreak n. The juice that squirts out when you eat an orange or grapefruit and which always hits other people no matter how far away they are.

coinsonance n. The ability of your telephone and doorbell to ring at the same time.

darnicity n. The mysterious force that changes a traffic signal to red just before you get to it.

elaversion n. Avoiding eye-contact with other people in an elevator.

emphasoids n.pl. Those people who, after you've quite obviously had a haircut, will say astounding things like, 'Oh, you've had your hair cut!'

envelip n. The papercut sustained licking the flap of an envelope.

hicgap n. The time that elapses between when hiccups go away and when you suddenly realize it's happened.

illuminotion n. The practice of switching on the bedside lamp to answer the phone in the mistaken belief that you'll be able to hear better.

illuminoyance n. Switching on a light only to find that the bulb has burned out.

inspectorate v. The habit people have of checking their handkerchief after they've used it.

kellogulation n. What happens to your breakfast cereal when you are called away by a fifteen-minute phone call just after you have poured milk on it.

lexikinesis n. The uncanny ability to open a dictionary at the exact page you were wanting.

missaisles n.pl. People in supermarkets who 'drive' their shopping carts in a reckless fashion.

pedicurious adj. The position you have to get into in order to cut your toenails.

potspot n. That part of a toilet seat which causes the phone to ring the moment you sit on it.

premavision n. The way a TV company knows you are about to switch on your set, and so you will be just in time for a commercial break.

reincaffeination n. The practice of coffee cups always being refilled in restaurants.

toilert n. Precautionary whistling when there's no lock on the bathroom door.

toiliterature n. The books and magazines that people keep in their bathrooms.

If some of these words don't one day enter the language, there's no justice.

Douglas Adams and John Lloyd in *The Meaning of Liff*. They find words which do exist, in the form of place names, and search out likely meanings for them – thus giving them temporary status as common nouns, verbs, or adjectives. Some examples from letter A give the flavour of the exercise:

Aasleagh (n.) A liqueur made only for drinking at the end of a revoltingly long bottle party when all the drinkable drink has been drunk.
Abilene (adj.) Descriptive of the pleasing coolness on the reverse side of the pillow.
Affpuddle (n.) A puddle which is hidden under a pivoted paving stone. You only know it's there when you step on the paving stone and the puddle shoots up your leg.
Ahenny (adj.) The way people stand when examining other people's bookshelves.
Amersham (n.) The sneeze which tickles but never comes.
Aynho (vb.) Of waiters, never to have a pen.[10]

In a prefatory comment, the authors point out that 'the world is littered with thousands of spare words which spend their time doing nothing but loafing about on signposts pointing at places. Our job, as we see it, is to get these words down off the signposts and into the mouths of babes and sucklings and so on, where they can start earning their keep in everyday conversation and make a more positive contribution to society.'

SOUNDS AND SPELLINGS

The alphabet, and the way letters are used to make up words (the spelling rules), can also provide a fruitful source of language play. This shouldn't be surprising, since we learn our alphabet at a very early age, and thousands of correct spellings are successfully instilled in most of us by the time we reach our teens. Indeed, the written form of a word becomes the norm, for many people, and is used to influence the way the word is pronounced: people often say they pronounce the 't' in *often* 'because it's there in the spelling', condemn the insertion of an 'r' in *draw(r)ing* or *law(r) and order*, 'because it isn't there in the spelling', or describe as 'lazy' the pronunciation of *February* as [febri] 'because letters have been left out'. With all this shared knowledge inside us, it would be surprising if we didn't put it to use in conversational language play.

A common device is to assume that English is a phonetic language, and then to pronounce letters which would normally have no separate value. Sometimes every letter in the word is affected – in this way, *phone* becomes 'puh-hon-ee'. Sometimes it is just a single letter combination – *fruit* becomes 'froo-it'. Silent consonants clamour for attention: *knife* becomes 'kuh-nif-ee', *scissors* 'ski-ssors', *knitting* 'kuh-nitting', *gnome* 'guh-nom-ee', *gnash gnash* 'guh-nash guh-nash'. Words with an unusual phonetic structure can be reversed: *banana* becomes 'nah-na-bah'. Even punctuation does not escape – though linguistic play in this domain is more likely to be heard only from professional comedians. The same phonetic principle is used, with a distinctive noise being given to each punctuation mark. The Danish-American comedian Victor Borge, in one of his most famous sketches, would generate uproarious sequences of sound effects by reading passages of trite dialogue with the punctuation marks sounded out in this way.

Some humorists stretch our intuitions about the links between sounds and spellings almost to breaking point. It would be hard to beat Ogden Nash for linguistic daring. He looks out for a word with an unusual spelling, then transfers that spelling to other words which rhyme with it. His poem, 'The Baby', is a pearl:

> *A bit of talcum*
> *Is always walcum.*

And in 'The Cobra' he gives us a double whammy:

> *This creature fills its mouth with venum*
> *And walks upon its duodenum.*
> *He who attempts to tease the cobra*
> *Is soon a sadder he, and sobra.*

Note that he also stretches the pronunciation in the process, thus playing with two levels of language at once – graphic and phonic.

Unusual spellings provide an endless source of fascination for the language player. Sometimes it is the esoteric spelling itself which is the attraction, as in these lines from the beginning of a children's poem by Charles Connell:

> Please ptell me, Pterodactyl,
> Who ptaught you how pto fly?
> Who ptaught you how pto flap your wings
> And soar up in the sky?[11]

Sometimes the attraction seems to lie in the potential of the language to permit weirdly spelled words that convey an impression of sound without actually being pronounceable. This is the technique beloved of comic-strip writers. Into the mouth of Desperate Dan, for example, is placed such vaguely phonetic locutions as *blargh*, *glumph*, *yeuch*, and *yeurgh*, as well as such recognizable (but totally unphon-

etic) expressions as *guffaw* and *snort*. Unphonetic? Thanks to our early exposure to children's comics, these expressions seem so familiar and natural that we can easily forget, as we scan the balloon speech of cartoon characters, that people don't go around actually saying *guffaw*, when they are laughing heartily. (And if someone does, it is an immediate signal that the guffawer is being ironic.)

Sometimes the humorist uses the spelling conventions of another language, to achieve an effect. American word enthusiast Bob Belviso is one who has taken this tack: his nursery rhymes are rendered in a weird mixture of phonetic and mock-Italian spelling and simplified Anglo-Italian grammar, as in this extract from *Di Tri Berrese*:

Uans appona taim uas tri berres: mamma berre, papa berre, e beibi berre. Live inne contri nire foresta. Naise aus. Uanna de pappa, mamma, e beibi go bice, orie e furghetta locche di dorra. Bai enne bai commese Goldilocchese. Sci garra natinghatu du batte meiche troble. Sci puscia olle fudde daon di maute; no live cromma. Den sci gos appesterrese enne slipse inolle beddse.[12]

Nursery rhymes have also attracted special attention, because they are so well known, as in the case of 'Et qui rit des curés d'Oc'. Say it aloud, and fairly quickly: it usually takes a moment before the penny drops.

> *Et qui rit des curés d'Oc?*
> *De Meuse raines, houp! de cloques.*
> *De quelle loques ce turque coin.*
> *Et ne d'ânes ni rennes,*
> *Écuries des curés d'Oc.*

This is close to the 'false French' (and other language) 'translations' which attract especially teenage foreign language learners, of which the following is a mercifully small selection:

coup de grâce	*lawn mower*
c'est à dire	*she's a dear*
pas de tout	*father of twins*

à la carte	served from the trolley
de gustibus	very windy
arriba	large stream
hasta la vista	you have very nice views

The alphabet itself, seen simply as a string of letters from A to Z, has also been a target of language play. Learning to recite it – usually forwards, occasionally (as a special challenge) backwards – has always been seen as an important stage in the 'serious' task of learning to read, write, and spell, and alphabet learning comes to the fore again when there is occasion for adults to learn a signalling system, such as semaphore or Morse Code. Wireless telegraphy early developed its own system of letter naming, and this came into its own during the First World War ('Ack, Beer, Charlie, Don, Emma . . .'). Later alphabets of this type are now widely recognized, through film and television, being a routine part of the unfolding dramas involving air traffic control or the emergency services ('Able, Baker, Charlie, Dog . . . ', 'Alfa, Bravo, Charlie, Delta . . .').

Perhaps because the task of learning the alphabet is so boring, authors and illustrators have worked hard at finding new ways of enlivening the first encounter with the world of letters, and all involve language play. Eric Partridge gives an enthusiast's account of the genre in *Comic Alphabets* (1961).[13] Rhyming alphabets, devised at first for educational or moral purposes, have an ancient history. Simple verse couplets, along the lines of 'A for an Apple, an Archer, an Arrow; B for a Bull, a Bear and a Barrow', can be traced back to the sixteenth century. By Victorian times, these had developed a wide range of variants, several of high moral tone ('A In Adam's fall, we sinnèd all . . .'), several intentionally humorous. *The Comic Alphabet* (1876), for example, begins:

> A is an ARCHER alarmed, for his arrow,
> Aimed at an antelope, stuck in a sparrow.
> B is a BUTCHER, both burly and bluff;
> Bob, his big bull-dog, is ugly enough . . .

This creation was anonymous, as was the contemporaneous 'The Siege of Belgrade', never surpassed for its awful alliterativeness:

> An Austrian army, awfully arrayed,
> Boldly by battery besieged Belgrade;
> Cossack commanders cannonading come,
> Dealing destruction's devastating doom . . .

Some alphabets were pedestrian, saved only by the quality of the illustrations. *A was an Apple-pie* is an example from around the turn of the century. It continues:

> *B bit it; C cut it; D dealt it; E eat it; F fought for it . . .*

and ends with

> *. . . V viewed it; W wanted it; X, Y, Z, and Ampersand / All wish'd for a piece in hand.*

Some were ingenious compilations – though always having to resort to devious stratagems to handle letter X – such as this 1871 compilation for the title-page of a book:

A Beautiful Collection, Delightfully Etched, Finely Grouped, Highly Imaginative, Jestingly Knavish, Ludicrously Mischievous, Notably Odd, Peculiarly Queer, Recreative, Sensational, Tittering, Unquestionably Volatile, Whimsically XYZite.

The latter, presumably, being an attempt at 'exquisite'.

This next example shows that some writers were ready to play with the conventions of standard spelling – this one, from 'Another Disappointed Author':

> A is an 'Andle to somebody's name;
> B's for the Book that's writ by the same.
> C's for the Cheque that the 'andle commands;
> D for the Difference left in my hands. . . .

6 THE FIRST COMIC ALPHABET?

The first Cockney comic alphabet to appear in print which Eric Partridge could discover was written by journalist R. Montague Smith in the *Daily Mail* on 22 December 1934 under the heading 'Try This New Game'. It contained fourteen letters (glosses are given below, if needed):

A for 'orses	N for a dig
B for mutton	O for a drink
C for get it	Q for dole
I for Novello	T for two
J for oranges	U for the high jump
L for leather	X for breakfast
M for sis	Z for effect

The first full alphabet didn't appear until nearly two years later, in the *Daily Express* on 20 June 1936.

Partridge makes the point that examples like this are an important stage in the emergence of the most famous twentieth-century comic alphabet of all, which begins 'A is for 'orses'. 'Hay is for horses' is in fact a catch phrase, attacking the use of *Hey* as an attention signal. Its typical use can be traced back to the early eighteenth century. It is reported in Jonathan Swift's *Polite Conversation* (1738):

MISS: *Mr Neverout.*
NEVEROUT: *Hay, madam, did you call me?*
MISS: *Hay! Why hay is for horses.*

Sometime during the 1920s it seems to have generated a following.

A for 'orses
B for mutton
C for thighlanders
D for dumb
E for brick
F fervescence
G fery Toye
H for retirement
I falutin
J affa oranges
K ferancis
L for leather
M phasis

N for a penny
O ver the garden wall
P for whistle
Q for seats
R for mo
S for you
T for two
U ferinstance
V for la France
W for a bob
X for breakfast
Y for heaven's sake
Z furbreezes

Glosses

1934: hay, beef, see, Ivor, Jaffa, (h)ell, emphasis, infra dig, oh, queue, tea, you, eggs, said

1936: hay, beef, Seaforth Highlanders, deaf, (h)eave a, effervescence, Geoffrey Toye (a contemporary impresario), age, highfalutin, Jaffa, Kay Francis, (h)ell, emphasis, in, over, pea, queue, (h)alf a mo(ment), as, tea, you for instance, viva, double you, eggs, why, zephyr

Partridge thinks it all started in the First World War, when Cockney signallers became so fed up that they started to 'play' with their phonetic alphabet, producing many unconventional and ribald versions. The genre would also have been fuelled by the linguistic creativity forced on telephone conversations at the time by poor communications. One caller is reported to have succeeded in passing the name *Ealing* over a bad line by shouting: 'E for 'eaven, A what 'orses eats, L where you're goin', I for me, N what lays eggs, and G for Gawd's sake keep yer ears open!'

Comic alphabets featured strongly in the music halls of the 1920s. In 1929, one version became especially well known when the cross-talk comedians Clapham and Dwyer broadcast a version on the BBC (the script was unfortunately destroyed during the War). A few years later, an alphabet – probably one of theirs – was published anonymously in the *Daily Express*, and this is reprinted on p. 43. In subsequent years, dozens of alternatives were invented, as times changed, and people tried to out-do each other in punning. Letter A was found in such guises as 'A for ism', 'A for disiac', 'A for gardener' (Ava Gardner) and 'A for mentioned'. Partridge collected over twenty alternatives for letter O, mainly punning on *over* or *Oh*:

O for and over	O for the garden wall	O for to you
O for one's shoulder	O for there	O for the wings of a dove
O for the top	O for goodness' sake	O for night
O for a beer	O for board	O for the rainbow
O for arm	O for the hill	O for we go

Comic alphabets are still recited, and are ever changing. The beginnings of one became a pop song: 'A you're adorable, B you're bee-

autiful, C you're a cutie full of charm . . .'. One can even imagine them entering the electronic era, and maybe something like the following already exists on the London Estuary Internet:

 A for 86, B for mat, C for Windows, D for ltoption, E for net, F for tran . . .[14]

LIMERICK LAND

The limerick is a perfect example of the way sounds and spellings interact in language play.[15] Limericks have had a mixed press, over the years, largely because of their risqué content. George Bernard Shaw was one who poured scorn on them; on the other hand, Dante Gabriel Rossetti was happy to try his hand at them, lampooning his friends into the bargain. Limericks were originally songs, popular at gatherings in early nineteenth-century Ireland, in which the exploits of imaginary people from different Irish towns were retold, with each line contributed by a different singer – the sort of thing you might find in a modern radio or TV improvisation show, such as the BBC's *I'm Sorry, I Haven't a Clue*. At the end, everyone sang a chorus beginning with the line, 'Will you come up to Limerick?' The genre was given some degree of prestige when Edward Lear published several in his *Book of Nonsense* (1846), though many of his limericks would now be considered rather poor examples, for often the end of the last line simply imitates the first.

> There was a young girl of Majorca
> Whose aunt was a very fast walker,
>   She walked sixty miles
>   And leaped fifteen stiles,
> Which astonished that girl of Majorca.

By the beginning of the next century, the limerick had become extremely popular, and never more so than during the great craze of 1907–8, when there were competitions in *London Opinion* and elsewhere, with large prizes: the first four lines of the limerick were given, and the punter had to compose a winning last line. There were soon 'limerick professors' advertising in the trade press, who (for a small fee) would provide you with a last line guaranteed to win.

So popular were these competitions that a speech made to the House of Commons in 1908 during the Post Office vote reported that the purchase of sixpenny postal orders (which happened to be the entrance fee for a limerick competition) had increased fourteenfold during the first half of the year, from around 800,000 to over 11 million. Nearly 6 million were sold in the month of August alone. And the craze was also fed by the advertisers, who set up competitions where the 'last line' had to extol the product. The first prize in the first major commercial competition of that time – for a brand of cigarettes – was an assured income of £3 a week for life! There was no entry fee, but competitors had to enclose a coupon proving they had bought half a crown's worth of the cigarettes.

The features of the limerick – its fantastic plot, catchy rhythm, ingenious rhymes, and climactic punch line – have maintained its popularity over the years. Here is one from Revd Charles Inge (the brother of Dean Inge):

> *A certain young gourmet of Crediton*
> *Took some pâté de foie gras and spread it on*
> *A chocolate biscuit*
> *Then murmured, 'I'll risk it.'*
> *His tomb bears the date that he said it on.*

Very ingenious. Indeed, the religious professions contributed greatly to the genre – perhaps most famously, Father Ronald Knox:

> *There was once a man who said, 'God*
> *Must think it exceedingly odd*
> *If He finds that this tree*
> *Continues to be*
> *When there's no one about in the Quad.'*

It was not long, of course, before the impulse to play with language turned its attention to the limerick itself. Here is W. S. Gilbert's famous rule-breaking contribution:

> *There was an old man of St Bees,*
> *Who was stung in the arm by a wasp,*
> > *When asked, 'Does it hurt?'*
> > *He replied, 'No, it doesn't,*
> *I'm so glad it wasn't a hornet.'*

And the introduction of irregular spellings for the rhymes, imitating the model introduced in the first line, proved remarkably popular. The more exotic the irregular spelling, the better.

> *There was a young lady named Psyche,*
> *Who was heard to ejaculate, 'Pcryche!'*
> > *For, when riding her pbych,*
> > *She ran over a ptych,*
> *And fell on some rails that were pspyche.*

Sometimes this would be done twice:

> *An unpopular youth of Cologne,*
> *With a pain in his stomach did mogne.*
> > *He heaved a great sigh*
> > *And said, 'I would digh,*
> *But the loss would be only my ogne.'*

And even further deviations could be introduced, involving mispronunciation and the loss of word boundaries:

> *A fellow who lisped went to Merthyr,*
> *To woo a young lady named Berthyr.*
> > *He asked, 'Have you been kitht?'*
> > *But when she said, 'Dethitht!'*
> *He murmured, 'She's false to me; curthyr!'*

Abbreviations were introduced, allowing a greater discrepancy between sound and spelling:

> *When you think of the hosts with out No.*
> *Who are slain by the deadly cuco.,*
> > *It's quite a mistake*
> > *Of such food to partake,*
> *It results in a permanent slo.*

And there were 'visual tongue-twisters' too:

> *A right-handed fellow named Wright,*
> *In writing 'write' always wrote 'rite'*
> > *Where he meant to write right.*
> > *If he'd written 'write' right,*
> *Wright would not have wrought rot writing 'rite'.*

Since this 'golden age' of the limerick, the genre has continued to appeal to the humorist. Competitions will still be found, and people continue to search for still more ingenious rhymes. Probably all the irregular words in the language have had their limerickability probed by now – including British English's least predictable proper names, both of places . . .

> *There was a mechanic of Alnwick*
> *Whose opinions were anti-Germalnwick;*
> > *So when war had begun,*
> > *He went off with a gun*
> *The proportions of which were Titalnwick.*

. . . and of people:

> *There lived a young lade called Geoghegan,*
> *The name is apparently Peoghegan,*
> > *She'll be changing it solquhoun*
> > *For that of Colquhoun,*
> *But the date is at present a veoghegan.*

For those not familiar with the phonetic peculiarities of British names, it is just about possible to work out the pronunciation of Alnwick [**an**ik], from the rhymes in the first example, and of [**gay**gan] from those in the second. However, the middle couplet in the second example could be a problem, if you didn't know that Colquhoun was pronounced [kal**hoon**]. It is not worth losing too much sleep over. It is, after all, largely nonsense. But it is enjoyable nonsense.

EVEN TOTAL NONSENSE

It would be difficult to think of a clearer case of ludic linguistic behaviour than the deliberate use of unintelligible speech; but it happens. Indeed, spoken nonsense, in one form or another, is quite common. Let us begin with the kind of nonsensical expression used to accompany a moment of sudden emotion, such as a shock or a pain. One person squealed 'iyiyiyiyiyiyi' after she pricked her thumb with a needle. Another was observed to utter an expletive, roughly transcribable as 'shplumfnooeeah', with a crescendo at 'fnoo', when he stood on a broom and the handle came up and hit his head. Quite possibly their vocalizations might have been more recognizable and unprintable if they had not been in company. As it was, both felt that their pain was eased by 'sounding off' in this way – and the latter, indeed, went so far as to say that he actually felt better, as a result. This was doubtless one of the reasons why the poet Robert Southey swore, it is said, by the 'great decasyllabon', *Aballiboozobanganovribo.*

Most people are happy to rely on conventional expressions – a standard 'four-letter' obscenity or curse – when they are giving vent to a sudden emotion. But even these do not escape the influence of language play. Indeed, the whole history of swearing provides evidence of the way people play with taboo words, turning them into nonsense in order to avoid the sanctions of a linguistically sensitive society – *drat* from *God rot*, *Jiminy Cricket* from *Jesus Christ*, *Heck* from *Hell*, and hundreds more. Many expressions in Cockney rhyming slang have the same origins: among the more obscure items are *bottle (and glass)* for *arse*, *Hampton (Wick)* for *prick*,

Cobblers (awls) for *balls*, and *Charley (Ronce)* for *ponce*; somewhat more transparent are *goose (and duck)* and *berk(eley hunt)*. In all such cases, the aim is to provide a code which avoids possible trouble, and the easiest form of code-making is language play.

Rhyming slang is a form of 'speech disguise' – a way of systematically hiding what the real meaning of a message is. The expressions make sense to the insider, but are nonsense to the outsider. People do this with varying amounts of sophistication, for all kinds of reasons, in all parts of the world. A group of criminals might exchange instructions about their activities, confident that casual listeners will not understand them. Much gangster slang arose in this way. Street traders might pass on innocent-sounding messages about the arrival of well-heeled customers or the location of nearby police. And parents have been known to resort to linguistic subterfuge (such as spelling out words) as they try not to give the game away in front of their children ('it's time for B-E-D') or pets ('I think he wants a W-A-L-K'). In many cases, it is simply not known why the use of a particular stratagem arose. Cockney rhyming slang, for instance, may have originated as a thieves' jargon, as Eric Partridge thought, but it soon came to be supplemented by a great deal of invention whose motivation was no more than innocent fun. Expressions such as *apples and pears* ('stairs'), *plates of meat* ('feet'), and *artful dodger* ('lodger') are today so well known that they have lost whatever secrecy value they may once have had. Rhyming slang none the less provides a good example of how quite complex systems of expression can be constructed out of apparent nonsense.

Another striking instance – because it is so widespread, cross-cultural, and international – is the insertion of nonsense syllables into the speech we use when we talk to babies or animals. As we shall see in Chapter 5, there is much more to baby-talk than the use of nonsensical expressions, but the fact remains that sequences such as 'wuzh-wuzh-wuzh' (the exact effect defies simplified phonetic transcription), said with protruded lips and a simpering mien, are a common part of the early linguistic experience of kittens, budgerigars, and newborn babies alike. Nor are adults excluded. We may call for a cat to come to us using a series of intrusive kissing sounds, or whispered shushing ('pshwhishwhishwhish'), but it is by no means unknown for adults to call to each other in precisely this way on occasions of, shall we say, special intimacy. Research surveys are unfortunately lacking on the topic, but I do seem to recall Peter O'Toole using the technique in the film *What's New, Pussycat?*

More complex and systematic levels of vocal nonsense exist – such as the remarkable phenomenon of jazz 'scat singing', where the voice is used to improvise meaningless lyrics in the manner of a musical instrument. This strange form of expression became known in the 1920s – an early recording by Louis Armstrong of 'Candy Lips' refers to a 'scat chorus' by Clarence Williams. Indeed, one story circulating about its origins suggests that it all began when Armstrong dropped his lyric sheet in a 1926 recording session, and had to improvise the words. If this is true, then Armstrong wasn't doing anything unusual at that point – for everyone scats, to some extent, when they forget the words of a song. What was remarkable was the sophisticated way in which he developed the form, and the creative complexity which it later achieved in the mouths of such experts as Leo Watson, Al Jarreau and Ella Fitzgerald (and not forgetting Baloo in Disney's *The Jungle Book*). American singer Slim Gaillard went so far as to invent a whole nonsense language for scat purposes, which he called 'Vout'.

Scat singing is a form of joyful language play which can be grouped along with the many other nonsense-syllable emissions which are part of the history of twentieth-century popular singing. It is in fact surprising just how much syllabic nonsense there is in modern pop songs. A quick stroll through my family's collective auditory memory produced 'Be-bop-a-loo-la', 'Ob-la-di, ob-la-da', 'Do-wah-diddy-diddy-dum-diddy-doo' ('Walking Down The Street'), 'Cutchy-cutchy-cutchy-coo' ('Has Anybody Seen My Girl?'), and 'Tutti Frutti' – whose vocal prologue, 'a-wop-bom-a-loo-mop-a-lop-bam-boom', according to *The Penguin Encyclopedia of Popular Music*, 'opened an era in popular music'.[16] Much of this is recapitulated at the end of *Grease*, when the friends fly off into the sunset ('We'll Always Be Together') following a chorus of nonsense lines that are impossible to spell. And when the Spice Girls burst upon the 1996 scene with their 'Wannabe!' hit, there was much debate about what the climax of their wanting, *zigazig ha!*, could possibly mean.

Clever nonsense regularly makes a hit record, whatever the musical style or period. Reigning supreme at Number 1 in the nonsense hit charts of all time would probably be the Goons' 'Ying-tong Song', for it contains little else other than splendidly silly syllables. Disney examples include 'Zippuhdeedoodah, zippuhdeeday' and 'Supercallifragilisticexpialidocious'. Several songs have made use of symbolic noises translated into conventional onomatopoeic words, such as 'boom-diddy-boom-diddy-boom . . .', representing the heartbeats of Peter Sellers and Sophia Loren in 'Goodness Gracious Me'. From an earlier era of hit records we have the 'folderee-folderah' chorus from 'I Love To Go A-Wandering' . . . and the highly successful wordplay, based on the natural assimilations of everyday speech, heard in 'Maisy Doats and Dozy Doats' (eventually explicitly glossed by the singer: 'mares eat oats and does eat oats'). And if we choose to look way back, we will find 'hey nonny nonny', 'fol-de-rol-de-rido', and many another (as the *Oxford English Dictionary* delicately puts it) 'meaningless refrain'. Indeed, a verb *to folderol* ('to sing unmeaning sounds') is cited in the *OED* from 1825.

You do not have to be a professional singer to achieve effective communication through lyrical nonsense. Scouts and guides have been bonding together for decades using it ('Ging-gang-goolie-goolie-goolie'). Adults have danced themselves into the small hours singing it ('Oh, hokey-cokey-cokey'). And parents have long entertained their children with it, both in nursery rhyme ('Hey-diddle-diddle, the cat and the fiddle', 'Diddle-diddle-dumpling, my son John') and in song ('Old Macdonald had a farm, e-i-e-i-o'). The children themselves relax within it, as we shall see in Chapter 5, both when they are playing with others and when they are alone – such as the ones (reported by Iona and Peter Opie) who bounced a ball against a wall while pun-chanting the film star's name: 'Shirley Oneple, Shirley Twople, Shirley Threeple . . .' and so on up to 'Shirley Nineple, Shirley Temple'.[17] And for generations, circus clowns have harangued each other and their audiences using it. All these people are doing something which is very simple, in their language play, yet so very profound. Ludic language seems to echo an ancient and deep-rooted element in the human condition. What it might be we shall also explore further in Chapter 5.

The aim of the present chapter has been to illustrate how language play is a common feature of everyday conversation in domestic settings. I claim that everyone does some of the things reported in this chapter. And I conclude that it is normal to be (linguistically) abnormal, by engaging in language play. Putting this another way, ludic linguistic behaviour is a sign that all is well with human relationships. And conversely, when a couple or a family begin to be irritated by each other's language play, or to stop using it, it is a sure sign that the relationship is breaking down.

Language play is pre-eminently an amateur, domestic matter – playable by all, regardless of sex, age, social background, or level of intelligence. All we need is an awareness of the rules, and this comes in the normal course of child development as we acquire our ability to listen and speak, and, much later, to read and write. But the references to pop-songs have introduced a change of direction. If the distinction between professional and amateur is that the former are paid for what they do whereas the latter are not, then the singers, and those who write their songs, have moved us firmly towards different areas of language play – areas which we will begin to explore in the next two chapters.

3

THE ENTHUSIASTS

Language play is infectious. It's like yawning. It only takes one person to make a pun, crack a joke, or engage in some silly vocal behaviour, and suddenly everyone else in the group feels the urge to do so. That is how pun-capping and joke-swapping sessions begin. The joy of participation lies largely in their spontaneity and unpredictability. It is a dynamic, exciting, anarchic, exploratory use of language, in which anything goes. And when it does go, it is usually in the relaxed atmosphere of our homes.

But there is another kind of domestic language play which, though in its own way just as enjoyable, exciting, and exploratory, is very different in character. It is steady, intense, serious, and regulated. It is no place for the flippant. Humour is not actually banned, but is only occasionally encountered. It is no laughing matter. It may take place at home, but it is often carried on between consenting adults in public. This is the world of the word game – and in this world, we need to go carefully, for there be enthusiasts.

THE LANGUAGE ENTHUSIAST

Language play enthusiasts are distantly related to language enthusiasts in general. There are many people who let their interest in language grow almost to the point of obsession. Some become furiously protective about their language and go to great pains to monitor changes in usage. One listener to Radio 4 once sent me a complete list of all the split infinitives he had heard in a day: it was four pages long, and each instance – there were over a hundred in all – was written out in full, giving its exact moment of occurrence, the name of the programme, and the name of the perpetrator. Whatever we think about the value or futility of such an exercise, one has to warmly admire the diligence. E for effort, undoubtedly.

There are enthusiasts who try to mimic accents and dialects. There are enthusiasts who collect irregular spellings. There are enthusiasts who learn languages. In this last respect, the 1997 edition of *The Guinness Book of Records* cites as a record holder Harold Williams, foreign editor of *The Times* in the early twentieth century, who spoke fifty-eight languages. He was apparently the only person able to converse with every delegate at the first League of Nations meeting in their own language. He died in 1928, but his total is already matched by Ziad Fazah, born in 1954 in Liberia, and now a Brazilian citizen – and there are several other linguists with totals not far behind.

There are enthusiasts who can think of no happier heaven on earth than to be studying the ways in which languages work. They are also called linguists – though in a very different sense from that used in the previous paragraph. These are practitioners of linguistics, the science of language. Linguists in this sense may speak very few languages fluently – perhaps only one – but they are highly skilled at techniques of comparing languages, analysing languages and generally getting to grips with what human language is all about. Some of them are so driven from within that they cannot stop writing about language, and have probably used up far too many trees by so doing. The present author falls into this category. Your readership's humble servant.

All these people have let their interest drive them – as I said above – almost to the point of obsession. Wordplay enthusiasts are different in one crucial respect: they have passed the point of obsession. No, I must not exaggerate. Some wordplay buffs are sane, gentle, balanced people. I would let my daughter marry one. Others give the impression of being quite the reverse. There is nothing personal about this, for I know none of them personally, but after reaching the end of this chapter, you must be the judge. Am I right or am I right?

MISSIONS IMPOSSIBLE

The impulse to play with words makes us behave in a truly bizarre way. What could be stranger than deliberately constructing a sentence which is difficult or impossible to pronounce – to try to say things that cannot be said? Such creations are known as 'tongue-twisters' – a not entirely accurate name, for many tongue-twisters focus on sounds that do not involve the tongue at all. The lips, for example, are at the heart of 'Peter Piper picked a peck of pickled peppers' – a sentence which has been known since the eighteenth century. But the best of them do juxtapose consonants and vowels that require disparate tongue positions, and thus present an articulatory nightmare.

Some tongue-twisters have had their moments of fame. 'She sells sea-shells on the sea-shore', for example, was made famous in a song by pantomime comedian Wilkie Bard in Drury Lane, London, in 1908, and it is still accurately remembered (if not accurately pronounced). The music halls were a particularly rich source of tongue-twisters – and the more risqué versions doubtless generated their share of uproarious laughter. But usually, successful articulatory acrobatics produce murmurs of admiration rather than outright merriment – as in several of the lyrics penned by W.S. Gilbert. For instance, the modern major-general serves up, in *The Pirates of Penzance*, a deadly fricassee of tongue-twisting rapid rhythm, rhyme and near-nonsense:

I know our mythic history, King Arthur's, and Sir Caradoc's,
I answer hard acrostics, I've a pretty taste for Paradox,
I quote, in Elegiacs, all the crimes of Heliogabalus!
In conics I can floor peculiarities parabolus.
I can tell undoubted Raphaels from Gerard Dows and Zoffanies.
I know the croaking chorus from the 'Frogs' of Aristophanes!
Then I can hum a fugue of which I've heard the music's din afore,
And whistle all the airs from that infernal nonsense, Pinafore! . . .
In short, in matters vegetable, animal, and mineral,
I am the very model of a modern Major Gineral.

Cue applause!

Now no one could possibly object to the occasional tongue-twister. But what are we to make of the monster creations which enthusiasts have compiled? Mark Cohen has collected a fine sample in his *Puffin Book of Tongue-Twisters* – a book which, as the publisher's blurb comments (in the manner of the joke books described in Chapter 2), 'ought to carry a government health warning'. There is space to give only the first part of one of the longer stories – a literal tongue-twister, for the focus is on 's' and 'sh', sounds which both use the front of the tongue. It is the story of 'Shrewd Simon Short':

Shrewd Simon Short sewed shoes. Seventeen summers saw Simon's small, shabby shop still standing, saw Simon's selfsame squeaking sign still swinging swiftly, specifying: Simon Short, Smithfield's Sole Surviving Shoemaker. Shoes Soled. Sewed Superfinely.

Simon's spouse, Sally Short, sewed sheets, stitched shirts, stuffed sofas. Simon's stout sturdy sons – Stephen, Samuel, Saul, Silas – sold sundries. Stephen sold silks, satins, shawls. Samuel sold saddles, stirrups. Saul sold silver spoons, specialities. Silas sold Sally Short's stuffed sofas . . .[1]

And so on for another 277 words – 351 in all. It is probably not a record for the longest story in which all the words begin with the same letter, but it is quite impressive.

Actually, there are no such things as sensible records in this business. If I were to suggest that the Simon Short saga *is* a record, I can guarantee that forever after, as people reached this point in the book, my postbag would be receiving manuscripts from readers who had taken the time and trouble to put together a tongue-twister consisting of 352 words, or 500, or 1000, or more. Ordinarily busy people somehow seem to find extraordinary amounts of spare time for language play. And no sooner is one record in place than it is broken, by adding another word or two. It isn't difficult, after all. It would be possible to almost double the length of the above extract just by repeatedly adding a few more adjectives and adverbs to it, such as *silly* or *stupid*. And it would hardly be possible to object that one shouldn't do this because it wouldn't always make sense!

7 ACROSTIC POETRY

Lewis Carroll wrote many acrostic puzzles and several times introduced them into his poetry. At the end of *Through the Looking-Glass*, he uses an acrostic to dedicate a poem to Alice Pleasance Liddell (the 'Alice' of *Alice's Adventures in Wonderland*), telling of the day it all started.

> A boat, beneath a sunny sky
> Lingering onward dreamily
> In an evening of July –
>
> Children three that nestle near,
> Eager eye and willing ear
> Pleased a simple tale to hear –
>
> Long has paled that sunny sky:
> Echoes fade and memories die:
> Autumn frosts have slain July.
>
> Still she haunts me, phantomwise,
> Alice moving under skies
> Never seen by waking eyes.
>
> Children yet, the tale to hear,
> Eager eye and willing ear,
> Lovingly shall nestle near.

In actual fact, much of Simon Short is hardly tongue-twisting at all – at least, not in the same league as 'The sixth sheikh's sixth sheep's sick', and the like. What we have here is more like alliteration – a use of language in which the words begin with the same initial sound/letter – though alliterative sequences never involve so many words at a time. The focus on initial letters does, however, move us in the direction of the acrostic – a type of language play in which a series of

In a Wonderland they lie,
Dreaming as the days go by,
Dreaming as the summers die:

Ever drifting down the stream –
Lingering in the golden gleam –
Life, what is it but a dream?

And, continuing this theme, he introduces *Sylvie and Bruno* with a short poem. This time, Isa Bowman is the name spelled out. (A *raree-show* is a 'peep-show' – a name, according to Dr Johnson, which came from travelling foreign showmen's mispronunciation of 'rare show'.)

Is all our Life, then, but a dream
Seen faintly in the golden gleam
Athwart Time's dark resistless stream?

Bowed to the earth with bitter woe,
Or laughing at some raree-show,
We flutter idly to and fro.

Man's little Day in haste we spend,
And, from its merry noontide, send
No glance to meet the silent end.

words, lines, or other units are manipulated so that their initial letters make up a message of some kind. The most familiar kind of acrostic is seen in a poem in which the choice of letter at the beginning of each line is controlled by some higher purpose – such as the need to make the letters spell out the poet's name, or some other 'secret' message. This kind of wordplay is known from ancient Greek and Roman times, it has been found in early Old English poems, and it has surfaced regularly in English literature throughout the ages. Not everyone has liked it. Joseph Addison (in *Spectator* no. 60) commented that 'The acrostic was probably invented about the same time with the anagram, tho' it is impossible to decide whether the inventor of the one or the other were the greater blockhead'. But the genre came into its own in Victorian times, where it proved to be a fashionable pastime – its appeal reinforced (if not caused) by the knowledge that it was frequently enjoyed by members of the royal family. Local acrostic clubs and societies were formed. There were hundreds of competitions and publications. And contemporary authors reflected the general interest – notably, Lewis Carroll.

The fascination with acrostics continued into the twentieth century. Word-game clubs and periodicals still publish new ones and launch competitions. American word-play enthusiast Ross Eckler reports such a competition in *Games* magazine for 1980–81, in which readers were asked to look for acrostics formed from the initial letters of successive paragraphs in a book. The longest word found was *synonyms*, in Elizabeth Graham's *Heart of the Eagle* (1978, p. 10). This was an accidental acrostic. Rather more interesting are the deliberate ones – or the apparently deliberate ones, as in the passage spoken by Titania to Bottom in *A Midsummer Night's Dream* (3.i.145):

> *Thou shalt remain here, whether thou wilt or no.*
> *I am a spirit of no common rate:*
> *The summer still doth tend upon my state;*
> *ANd I do love thee. Therefore go with me.*
> *I'll give thee fairies to attend on thee;*
> *And they shall fetch thee jewels from the deep.*

From *Word Ways* magazine in 1981 also comes this remarkable piece, in the Simon Short tradition, called 'An Allegory'. Its opening lines:

Adam and alert associate, agreeably accommodated, aptly achieved accord and amiability – ample ambrosias available, and arbors alone adequate against ambient airs. Ah, auspicious artlessness! Adversity and affliction attacked appallingly, as avowed antagonists, Adonai, almighty

Author, announced, and Apollyon, archangel-adder, asserted. 'Avoid apples and abide amid abundance,' admonished Adonai. 'Admire apples and acquire acumen,' advised Apollyon. Alas! Apollyon attained ascendancy. Ancestor Adam's attractive associate ate, arch and alluring against an antinomian apple-tree. Adam ate also, amoral although aware . . .

And afterwards, all abode 'appily? 'Ardly.

The question which comes to mind, after reading through hundreds of tongue-twisting and acrostic offerings of this kind must be – Why? Why do they do it? Why do we do it? And why do people enjoy it so? I read the Adam passage as part of a talk on language play to a tentful of people at the Hay Literary Festival in 1996, and everyone fell about.

Why do people engage in such bizarre linguistic activity? For this *is* bizarre behaviour, by any standards. Could there be anything more linguistically weird than trying to make every word begin with the same letter?

THE LUDIC TOWER OF BABEL

Well, yes. And before we start thinking about explanations, it would perhaps be as well to bring together a wider range of examples of just what it is we are trying to explain. The topics so far make up only a few of the blocks which form the ludic language enthusiast's Tower of Babel. You want more bizarre? Take these. In each case, the players obtain their pleasure by imposing increasingly savage forms of linguistic discipline upon themselves or their fellow-players. And the allusion is not far-fetched. It is the nicest possible kind of linguistic sado-masochism.

Make every word begin with the same letter? Easy. But what about making every word contain the same vowel – a *univocalic*? Short single sentences are not a problem, as can be seen from such off-the-cuff creations as 'I sit in this bin, idling, sighing, with bright lights visiting twilight hills'. The trick is to keep the language flowing, without allowing it to degenerate into total nonsense. And no cheating: every word must be in at least one standard dictionary.

In 1824, Lord Holland wrote a tragic piece using only 'e', called 'Eve's Legend'. Here is the first and the last paragraph. In between there are another 400 words or so.

Men were never perfect; yet the three brethren Veres were ever esteemed, respected, revered, even when the rest, whether the select few, whether the mere herd, were left neglected . . .

Her well-kempt tresses fell: sedges, reeds beckoned then. The reeds fell, the edges met her cheeks; her cheeks bled. She presses the green sedge where her cheeks bleed. Red then bedewed the green reed, the green reed then speckled her red cheek. The red cheek seems green, the green reed seems red. These were the terms the Eld Seer decreed Stephen Vere.
Here endeth the legend.

This is ingenious – even though at times it reminds me of the 'Run, pup, run' style of writing beloved of traditional reading schemes. But maybe not ingenious enough for our ludic masochist. Make every word contain the same vowel? Easy – in prose. Now if you could do it in poetry – with rhyme and a regular metre . . .

This is precisely what a Victorian wordsmith, C. C. Bombaugh, did in his book *Gleanings for the Curious* (1890). In a series called 'Incontrovertible Facts' he produces a univocalic for every vowel. My favourite is *O*, with line 7 surely getting the prize for univocalic poetry, and the whole thing the prize for linguistic surrealism.

No monk too good to rob, or cog, or plot.
No fool so gross to bolt Scotch collops hot.
From Donjon tops no Oronoco rolls.
Logwood, not Lotos, floods Oporto's bowls.
Troops of old tosspots, oft, to sot, consort.
Box tops, not bottoms, school-boys flog for sport.
No cool monsoons blow soft on Oxford dons,
Orthodox, jog-trot, book-worm Solomons!

Bold Ostrogoths, of ghosts no horror show.
On London shop-fronts no hop-blossoms grow.
To crocks of gold no dodo looks for food.
On soft cloth footstools no old fox doth brood.
Long storm-tost sloops forlorn, work on to no port.
Rooks do not roost on spoons, nor woodcocks snort,
Nor dog on snowdrop or on coltsfoot rolls,
Nor common frogs concoct long protocols.

No cool monsoons blow soft on Oxford dons. Ain't it the truth?

What about the opposite torture? To make no use of a particular letter – a *lipogram*. This genre of language play is one of the most ancient – known from classical Greek of the sixth century BC, and since practised in many languages. Here too there are gradations of linguistic pain. In English it would hardly cause a twinge to discipline oneself never to use the letter *Q* – or any other infrequent letter of the alphabet. But try doing without one of the more frequent ones, such as *e, t, a, i, n, o,* or *s*. Doing without *e* or *t* bans you from using the word *the*, for instance. Could any text sound natural without *the*? Bring on Ernest Vincent Wright!

In 1939, Wright published a 50,000-word novel called *Gadsby* which made no use of the letter *e* – probably the most ambitious work ever attempted in this genre. It was a serious effort, intended to paint a different picture of American society than the one presented by Scott Fitzgerald in *The Great Gatsby*. You can judge its style by this extract from the preface, and a fragment from the main text:

Upon this basis I am going to show you how a bunch of bright young folks did find a champion; a man with boys and girls of his own; a man of so dominating and happy individuality that Youth is drawn to him as is a fly to a sugar bowl. It is a story about a small town . . .

. . . Gadsby was walking back from a visit down in Branton Hills' manufacturing district on a Saturday night. A busy day's traffic had had its noisy run; and with not many folks in sight, His Honor got along without having to stop to grasp a hand, or talk . . .

8 MARY HAD A LIPOGRAM

Ross Eckler – the editor of *Word Ways* magazine and many other works on language play (notably, *Making the Alphabet Dance*) – in 1969 put together this splendid lipogrammatic sequence. Mary had a little lamb indeed, but in these versions she has it without S, H, T, E and A respectively. And at the end, by way of signing off, he gives us a version excluding half the letters of the alphabet.

Mary had a little lamb with fleece a pale white hue,
And everywhere that Mary went the lamb kept her in view.
To academe he went with her (illegal, and quite rare);
It made the children laugh and play to view a lamb in there.

Mary owned a little lamb; its fleece was pale as snow,
And every place its mistress went it certainly would go.
It followed Mary to class one day (it broke a rigid law).
It made the students giggle aloud; a lamb in class all saw.

It's cleverly done. And Wright isn't alone. Another novel which avoids *e* is Georges Perec's *A Void* (1995) – a translation by Gilbert Adair from a French work, *La Disparation* (1969), which also made no use of that letter. According to Ross Eckler, at least one reviewer took up the challenge, writing a review which made no use of the letter *e* either.

(Naturally it's difficult and limiting for authors to avoid using a linguistic form in this way, for a vast array of grammatical contrasts cannot play a part in what is said. Important stylistic modifications must occur. But it is indubitably a possibility for any author to carry on writing a work missing a particular symbol without producing a paragraph which is a total oddity. And you might not spot anything odd. Or again, you might.)

James Thurber introduced a fresh imaginative dimension to

Mary had a pygmy lamb, his fleece was pale as snow,
And every place where Mary walked, her lamb did also go.
He came inside her classroom once (which broke a rigid rule);
How children all did laugh and play on seeing a lamb in school.

Mary had a tiny lamb, its wool was pallid as snow,
And any spot that Mary did walk this lamb would always go;
This lamb did follow Mary to school (although against a law).
How girls and boys did laugh and play; that lamb in class all saw.

Polly owned one little sheep, its fleece shone white like snow,
Every region where Polly went the sheep did surely go;
He followed her to school one day (which broke the rigid rule);
The children frolicked in their room to see the sheep in school.

Maria had a little sheep, as pale as rime its hair,
And all the places Maria came the sheep did tail her there;
In Maria's class it came at last (a sheep can't enter there).
It made the children clap their hands; a sheep in class, that's rare!

letter loss. In his story, *The Wonderful O* (1957), pirates come to terrorize the island of Ooroo, and ban all words with an *O* in them. (Why? you ask. It turns out that Black, the pirate, has hated the letter ever since the night his mother became wedged in a porthole. 'We couldn't pull her in so we had to push her out.') The pirates begin their work.

And so language and the spoken word diminished and declined as the people were forced to speak without the use of O in any word. No longer could the people say Heigh-ho, Yoo-hoo, or Yo-ho-ho, or even plain Hello. The theater in the town was closed, for Shakespeare's lines without an O sound flat and muffled. No one could play Othello when Othello turned to Thell, and Desdemona was strangled at the start. Some sentences became so strange they sounded like a foreign tongue. 'Dius gre gling minus gress' meant 'Odious ogre ogling ominous ogress,' but only scholars knew it. Spoken words became a hissing and a mumble, or a murmur and a hum. A man named Otto Ott, when asked his name, could only stutter. Ophelia Oliver repeated hers, and vanished from the haunts of men.[2]

The islanders fight back, of course, placing their faith in four words which must not be lost – hope, valour, love, and – above all – freedom. And the story has a happy ending, with O eventually restored, and given its own monument.

But do I hear our ludic masochist asking for more? Univocalics? Easy. Lipograms? Peasy. Right, well how's about a pangram? Here, the target is to construct a meaningful sentence containing every letter ('pan' + 'gram') of the alphabet. The trick is to try to introduce each letter only once. The typist's *The quick brown fox jumped over the lazy dog* is a familiar, but very poor pangram, because it contains thirty-six letters. *D V Pike flung J Q Schwartz my box* contains only twenty-six, but is a bit of a cheat, as it contains proper names and initials – and it is not difficult to invent a series of names which eventually uses up each letter of the alphabet. *New job: fix Mr Gluck's hazy TV, PDQ* is far better, because it uses standard abbreviations. But you have to work quite hard to find a meaningful sentence which uses neither proper names nor abbreviations. (Remember that all the words have to be found in a major dictionary.) *Veldt jynx grimps waqf zho buck* is a winner, on this basis, as the following extracts from the unabridged *Oxford English Dictionary* show:

veldt In South Africa, unenclosed country . . .

jynx A bird, the wryneck . . .

grimp To cause to mount . . .

waqf In Islamic countries, land given to a religious institution for charitable purposes . . .

zho A hybrid bovine animal, bred from a yak bull and a common cow . . .

buck The male of several animals . . .

This is certainly grammatically and lexically plausible, though whether, in the real world, it is the case that a jynx living on the veldt has ever been observed to have cause to mount (or to cause something – or someone – else to mount) a zho buck in a waqf must be one of life's remaining empirical questions.

Enthusiasts are also very keen on constructing words or sentences which read the same way in both directions – *palindromes*. At word level, *Eve*, *madam*, and *level* are familiar, simple examples. *Deified* and *Malayalam* (an Indian language) are a little more complex. And, with a bit of cheating, through the judicious use of the hyphen, we can arrive at compound 'words' such as *name-garageman*, *sublevel-bus*, *trapeze-part*, and *retinue-reuniter*. Phrases and sentences offer more scope for ingenuity, and many of the best creations have been collected into books, such as Howard Bergerson's *Palindromes and Anagrams* (1973).[3] As with pangrams, the constructions must make grammatical and lexical sense. *Draw, O coward* works quite well, albeit archaically, as does *Was it a cat I saw?* and *Pull up if I pull up*, but these are amateurish by comparison with the following:

Di, did I as I said I did?
See, slave, I demonstrate yet arts no medieval sees.
Now ere we nine were held idle here, we nine were won.
Mother Eve's noose we soon sever, eh, Tom?
Anne is not up-to-date, godmother, eh? Tom, do get a dot put on Sienna.

As the last example suggests, it then becomes possible to begin telling a story, by stringing together sequences of palindromes, as in this extract from the opening of J. A. Lindon's 'In Eden' (1970), which takes the classic *Madam, I'm Adam* as a stimulus:

ADAM: *Madam* –
EVE: *Oh, who* –
ADAM: *(No girl-rig on!)*
EVE: *Heh?*

ADAM: *Madam, I'm Adam.*
EVE: *Name of a foeman?*
ADAM: *O, stone me! Not so.*
EVE: *Mad! A maid I am, Adam.*
ADAM: *Pure, eh? Called Ella? Cheer up.*
EVE: *Eve, not Ella. Brat-star ballet on? Eve.*
ADAM: *Eve?*
EVE: *Eve maiden name. Both sad in Eden? I dash to be manned. I am Eve.*

And the story eventually reaches a climax with the undeniably palindromic *Mmmmmmmmmmmmm!* Palindromic stories can continue in this way until their creators decide that they (or their readers) have had enough. But enough can be a long time coming, when you're an enthusiast. Lawrence Levine's palindromic novel, *Dr Awkward and Olson in Oslo*, contains 31,954 words.

Anagrams, one of the oldest forms of linguistic manoeuvring, are another example of a ludic pastime which brings out both the best and the worst in people. They are often encountered in children's word-game books, party games, and crossword-puzzle cryptic clues, where their role is occasional and innocent enough. But for language-play enthusiasts, the aim is not simply to reorder the letters in a word or phrase in order to find any other word or phrase – *rail* and *lair*, for instance. That is far too straightforward. The true aim is to find a transposition which relates *in meaning* to the original – whether serious, or ironic, or jocular – as the following examples illustrate:

the eyes	*they see*
negation	*get a 'no' in*
endearment	*tender name*
cabaret	*a bar, etc*
desperation	*a rope ends it*
sexual intercourse	*relax, ensure coitus*
received payment	*every cent paid me*
total abstainers	*sit not at ale bars*

Even proverbs can be given this treatment:

Absence makes the heart grow fonder.	*He wants back dearest gone from here.*
Rome was not built in a day.	*Any labour I do wants time.*
A stitch in time saves nine.	*This is meant as incentive.*

From a committed anagrammatist's point of view, of course, the more anagrams that can be generated by a single source, the better. *William Shakespeare* has yielded several, of varying quality, such as the pedestrian *We all make his praise*, the questionable *I am a weakish speller*, and the semantically (but not grammatically) unarguable *I ask me, has Will a peer?* One may increase the difficulty of the task by looking for anagrams of similar as well as different meaning (*astronomers – moon starers* alongside the 'antigram', *no more stars*). Or by requiring – in the manner of the crossword's 'cryptic clue' – that pairs of words in a solution must be anagrams of each other: in this way *drink fit for a king* yields *regal lager*, and *object in outer space* yields *remote meteor*. Extra constraints can be added for further difficulty, as the many anagram competitions illustrate – for example, finding anagrams from a fixed list of sources, such as the titles of Shakespeare's plays, or the names of American presidents.

Proper names always seem to generate special interest, as can be seen from these fine examples:

Florence Nightingale	*flit on, cheering angel*
Dwight David Eisenhower	*he did view the war doings*
Clint Eastwood	*old West action*
Arnold Schwarzenegger	*he's grown large 'n crazed*
Manchester United	*nice team thunders*

People generally enjoy discovering the words which emerge when the letters of their name are reordered. Some, having found a character-enhancing discovery, will go to any length to drop news of it into a conversation or text. Not the sort of thing I'd do myself, but – I might

as well mention it, in passing, as we're talking about these things – *David Crystal* transposes into *add vast lyric*.* Likewise, many people derive malicious pleasure from discovering the hidden 'meaning' within the name of a politician or organization they particularly dislike.[4] Lewis Carroll used to think up anagrams when unable to sleep: *Wilt tear down all images?* was one he devised for *William Ewart Gladstone*, along with *Wild agitator! Means well* and *A wild man will go at trees*. Whole books have been compiled, to feed this pleasure – though regrettably few are capable of providing quotations that aren't libellous. Computer programs are now available which will take your name (or any other input) and print out all the word-sequences it will yield. Of course, in a totally fair world, a name would yield two readings, one positive and one negative – but this feat is rarely achieved. Gladstone was one exception (cf. also *At will, great wise old man*); Margaret Thatcher was another (*Meg the arch tartar* alongside *That great charmer*).

But in former times, fairness had nothing to do with it, nor was

*But also, *avid lard cyst*.

letter transposition thought to be merely a game. The rearrangement of the letters in a name was thought to have great significance. The oracles and advisors of ancient Greece and Rome would regularly find omens in anagrams. Flatterers would present them to monarchs. It was well known in the court of King James I that the letters of *James Stuart* would transpose into *A just master*. Some monarchs went out of their way to find anagrams: Louis XIII of France actually appointed a Royal Anagrammatist. And there are many reports of people living their lives according to their anagrams: a famous case is the Frenchman André Pujom who, having learned that his name could be turned into *pendu à Riom* ('hanged at Riom' – a town in Auvergne where the law courts were located), committed a murder so that the 'prophecy' would come true. During the seventeenth century the fashion to look for anagrams reached unprecedented levels in Britain, Jonathan Swift being one of many who satirized those who unthinkingly relied upon them: in *Gulliver's Travels* he reports on the inhabitants of the kingdom of *Tribnia* ('Britain') who employed 'the anagrammatic method' to discover plots even in the most innocent of messages. And indeed, using anagrams it is possible to show almost anything you want – that the Bible contains prophecies of twentieth-century disasters, or that Bacon (or anyone else) wrote Shakespeare.[5] All kinds of hidden meanings have been derived from the words on Shakespeare's tomb. And could there be anything more convincing than the discovery, in 1901, that the last two lines of *The Tempest* can be anagrammatized as follows (assuming that *u* and *v* are alternative forms of the same letter)?

> As you for crimes would pardon'd be,
> Let your indulgence set me free.

> 'Tempest' of Francis Bacon, Lord Verulam.
> Do ye ne'er divulge me, ye words!

It does make you start to ponder – until you realize that Bacon was not created Lord Verulam until 1618 – several years after the play was written.

BUILDING HIGHER TOWERS

The ludic tower reaches higher and higher, as people strive to find fresh ways of playing with language, almost to the point of perversity. Ask the question, 'What could be crazier than trying to do X with language?' – and you will always find someone ready to provide an answer. It would take a large encyclopedia now to bring together all the variations which ludic ingenuity has devised. Here are just a few to illustrate the range of possibilities. Some play with the written language; some with the spoken; and some with both.

o You can replace syllables with numbers (e.g. *weight* is written *w8* and *tent* appears as *10t*) and see how many you can get into a sentence, or into unexpected places. Children's rebuses have long made use of this kind of strategem. *Rebus* comes from Latin, meaning 'by things'. It refers to any kind of representation where words or syllables are replaced by pictures of objects, or by other symbols (such as numerals), whose names phonetically resemble the sound of the original forms – for example, *bean* might be shown by a picture of a *bee* plus the letter *n*. Here is a fairly ingenious numerical example quoted by Willard Espy in *An Almanac of Words at Play (1975)*:

> *I'm very sorry you've been 6 o long;*
> *Don't B disconsol8;*
> *But bear your ills with 42de,*
> *& they won't seem so gr8.*

o Rather more difficult are substitution-games in which the nature of the substitution is not at all obvious. All you know is that you have to find a well-known word, phrase, or saying. How do you say *potooooooooo*? 'Potatoes.' What is *fecpoxtion* telling you? 'Smallpox infection.' In some professionally produced word games (such as *Dingbats®*, a board game devised in 1987), this kind of 'lateral thinking' is taken as far as it will go, as the following examples illustrate:

MAUD	*mad about you*
noos	*back soon*
CAR JACK TON	*Jack in the box*
02 EMOH	*nothing to write home about*
ev en	*break even*

o Everyday conversation is not safe from the enthusiast either. A popular game on radio and television improvisation shows, such as *Whose Line Is It Anyway?*, is to construct a dialogue in which each person is limited to one sentence, and each sentence must be a question.

A: *Are you ready to go out?*
B: *Do you doubt it?*
A: *How was I to know?*
B: *Haven't you any imagination?*
A: *Are you trying to be rude?*
B: *Why should I be rude?*

Alternatively, you can construct a dialogue in which each person is limited to one sentence, and each sentence must begin with a successive letter of the alphabet.

A: *Are you ready?*
B: *Better believe it.*
A: *Can we get a taxi?*
B: *Do you think that'll be easy?*
A: *Easy?*
B: *Finding taxis here is never easy.*
A: *Gosh!*

o Back with the written language, you can try composing a paragraph (e.g. of 100 words) in which every word is a monosyllable.

The task now is to write a piece in which each word has just one beat or pulse of sound in it. This is not too hard, for a tongue like ours, where there are lots of small words to use. It would be hard to

9 PLAYING AT QUESTIONS, STOPPARDLY

A famous literary piece of language play occurs in Tom Stoppard's *Rosencrantz and Guildenstern Are Dead*. The two players take it in turns to ask questions, and try to win by making the other reply with a statement, repeat a previous question and generally break various rules which they refer to as they go along.

ROSENCRANTZ: We could play at questions.
GUILDENSTERN: What good would that do?
ROSENCRANTZ: Practice!
GUILDENSTERN: Statement! One-love.
ROSENCRANTZ: Cheating!
GUILDENSTERN: How?
ROSENCRANTZ: I hadn't started yet.
GUILDENSTERN: Statement. Two-love.
ROSENCRANTZ: Are you counting that?
GUILDENSTERN: What?
ROSENCRANTZ: Are you counting that?
GUILDENSTERN: Foul! No repetitions. Three-love. First game to . . .
ROSENCRANTZ: I'm not going to play if you're going to be like that.
GUILDENSTERN: Whose serve?
ROSENCRANTZ: Hah?
GUILDENSTERN: Foul! No grunts. Love-one.
ROSENCRANTZ: Whose go?
GUILDENSTERN: Why?
ROSENCRANTZ: Why not?
GUILDENSTERN: What for?
ROSENCRANTZ: Foul! No synonyms. One-all.
GUILDENSTERN: What in God's name is going on?
ROSENCRANTZ: Foul! No rhetoric. Two-one.
GUILDENSTERN: What does it all add up to?
ROSENCRANTZ: Can't you guess?
GUILDENSTERN: Were you addressing me?

ROSENCRANTZ: Is there anyone else?

GUILDENSTERN: Who?

ROSENCRANTZ: How would I know?

GUILDENSTERN: Why do you ask?

ROSENCRANTZ: Are you serious?

GUILDENSTERN: Was that rhetoric?

ROSENCRANTZ: No.

GUILDENSTERN: Statement! Two-all. Game point.

ROSENCRANTZ: What's the matter with you today?

GUILDENSTERN: When?

ROSENCRANTZ: What?

GUILDENSTERN: Are you deaf?

ROSENCRANTZ: Am I dead?

GUILDENSTERN: Yes or no?

ROSENCRANTZ: Is there a choice?

GUILDENSTERN: Is there a God?

ROSENCRANTZ: Foul! No non sequiturs, three-two, one game all.

GUILDENSTERN (*seriously*): What's your name?

ROSENCRANTZ: What's yours?

GUILDENSTERN: I asked you first.

ROSENCRANTZ: Statement. One-love.

GUILDENSTERN: What's your name when you're at home?

ROSENCRANTZ: What's yours?

GUILDENSTERN: When I'm at home?

ROSENCRANTZ: Is it different at home?

GUILDENSTERN: What home?

ROSENCRANTZ: Haven't you got one?

GUILDENSTERN: Why do you ask?

ROSENCRANTZ: What are you driving at?

GUILDENSTERN (*with emphasis*): What's your name?

ROSENCRANTZ: Repetition. Two-love. Match point to me.

GUILDENSTERN (*seizing him violently*): WHO DO YOU THINK YOU ARE?

ROSENCRANTZ: Rhetoric! Game and match![G9]

do this in a tongue such as French, where there are lots of words which have two or more beats in them. Some think, with good cause, that this is one of the nice things to do with the way we speak – that there are lots of short words, which help to make up a style that is neat, crisp, terse, and to the point. But some do not find this a plus. They want big words – or at least, words which have more weight, and which can help to make a text (or a speech) which has great strength. Yet we must bear the fact in mind that there are lots of words which are quite long, though they still have just one beat. I can think of stretched and shrugged, scrounged and screeched, spoiled and strapped. Note that lots of these long words start with *s*, and end in a past tense.

That's already over 200. But by all means carry on, if you feel the need. Do no violence to yourself.

o If you need something more challenging, then try composing a paragraph of 100 words in which no word is used twice. It seems easy enough – to begin with.

The task is to write a paragraph in which no individual word turns up more than once. Beginning that kind of absurd composition doesn't present many intractable difficulties, but after about two sentences big problems emerge, because common items start being needed, yet they cannot, given such constraints as have been mentioned above. Inevitably, grammatical constructions get very stilted, or artificial, and stylistic naturalness proves almost impossible. Nonetheless, exercises like this can succeed, although maintaining momentum successfully must become increasingly hard when totals pass beyond ninety-nine. There are probably theoretical limits, though I don't know what these might be.

o You can make a sentence in which each word begins with a successive letter of the alphabet. It has to be grammatical – though examples usually wouldn't gain high marks for plausibility.

A bronzed cowboy, dancing elegantly for grand hotels in Jersey, knitting lovely mittens nicely on prettily quilted rubber shoes, thought untrained vets would X-ray your zebra.

Alternatively, you can make up a text in which each word must have at least one letter in common with the previous word (a *homoliteral* text):

This sentence illustrates some words which have at least one letter shared.

The opposite procedure is also possible, and rather more tricky – *no* two consecutive words can have any letter in common (a *hetero-literal* text):

This example shows ten words that follow this procedure vigilantly.

Or – to illustrate the almost unending possibilities – the final letter of a word must be the same as the first letter of the following word (a kind of *word-chain*). The sentence must be grammatical and make (a sort of) sense. It gets harder as the sentence gets longer.

The escaping gangster ran next to old deserted docks.

And if this is too easy – make it: the final *two* letters of each word must be the same as the initial two letters of the next:

The head adjudicator organized educational alienation on one network.

The alphabetic constraints could continue indefinitely – words which must contain no more than one of any letter (famously illustrated by *ambidextrously*), words which must contain two (or three, or four . . .) instances of a letter, hunting down the maximum possibilities (such as the seven *i*'s of *indivisibilities*), words which must begin and end with the same letter (including *octavo* and *xerox* – but can you find examples for every letter of the alphabet?),[o] words which end in a q, or a vowel, or two vowels . . .

o You can make up sentences in which each word contains one letter or one syllable more than the previous word (a *rhopalic* – a Greek term for a club which thickens from the handle to the head). It is very

10 TRANSPOSITIONAL POETRY

If it is a really empty day, you can compose transpositional poetry, in which all the words of an original poem are used to create a new poem. A famous example is Wayne Carlson's 'translation' of Wordsworth's 'Upon Westminster bridge'.

> Earth has not anything to show more fair:
> Dull would he be of soul who could pass by
> A sight so touching in its majesty:
> This City now doth, like a garment, wear
> The beauty of the morning; silent, bare
> Ships, towers, domes, theatres, and temples lie
> Open unto the fields, and to the sky;
> All bright and glittering in the smokeless air.
> Never did sun more beautifully steep
> In his first splendour, valley, rock, or hill;
> Ne'er saw I, never felt, a calm so deep!
> The river glideth at his own sweet will:
> Dear God! the very houses seem asleep;
> And all that mighty heart is lying still!

difficult to get as far as twenty. Here is an example of Dmitri Borgmann's, which just about manages it:

I do not know where family doctors acquired illegibly perplexing hand-writing; nevertheless, extraordinary pharmaceutical intellectuality, counterbalancing indecipherability, transcendentalizes intercommun-ications' incomprehensibleness.

It would be ultraconscientiousness to go further.
o Finally (insofar as 'finally' has any meaning at all, in this section)[7] – and only if you still have unused mental energy – you can (try to)

A city is lying still, asleep in the dull morning;
A steep hill towers more unto the smokeless sky,
Touching the heart and soul of God.
Bare fields doth lie in the valley,
Like ships that glideth, all silent in the river.
I saw all His own houses, now temples to the sun;
Sight at first has never felt more dear.
Who would not wear His garment, open to the calm air?
Could anything be so beautifully bright and glittering?
He will never show its theatres and domes;
Or pass by this fair Earth; a mighty rock,
Of very deep beauty, splendour, and majesty
Ne'er did seem so sweet!

Because the same words are being used, some of the ethereal resonances of the original work inevitably transfer; but the transposition
makes no claims to poetic merit. Some people find such exercises scan-
dalous – taking unacceptable liberties. 'Wordsworth must be turning
in his grave!', said one person to whom I showed the above. And yet
that same person was fascinated, and couldn't resist the temptation to
check the words, to see if the author had really done it. There is nothing more compelling than someone else's obsession.

make a 'sonic alphabet', by finding a sequence of words which (when
said aloud) will allow you to hear the sound of the names of the letters. The words must all be legitimate, and ideally the sequence
should be grammatical and make sense. Here is one phonetically
plausible offering, from Harry Matthews, though its grammar deteri-
orates towards the end:

*Hay, be seedy! He-effigy, hate-shy jaky yellow man, O peek! You are
rusty, you've edible, you ex-wise he!*

GEMATRIA, AND ITS LEGACY

Yet more domains of language play appear when people add a numerological dimension to their games. There are many such practices, and some have an ancient pedigree. *Gematria* (pronounced [gi-**may**-tree-a]) is one of the most influential. This was a medieval mystical technique, devised to investigate the Hebrew scriptures, with the aim of bringing to light the secret messages God was thought to have hidden within the letters of the words. One way of applying it to modern English is like this. You take the letters of the alphabet, and assign them numerical values from 1 to 26, in serial order. You then take a word, and obtain a total by adding up the values of the letters it contains. If two words have identical totals, gematria practitioners would consider this to be highly significant. Other significant relationships are when two words have adjacent totals (such as 62 and 63), reverse totals (62 and 26), or totals separated by 100 (62 and 162). In one booklet which appeared a few decades ago, *God Proved in Words and Figures*, 'ABC Arithmetic' of this kind was used to demonstrate that a divine revelation had been offered to those who speak English in the twentieth century.[8]

The authors made their case by finding as many religious pairings as they could. For example, the numerical total for *man* is 28; so is *Eden*. The total for *Adams rib* is 67, and for *woman* it is 66. The total for *Bible* is 30, and *Holy Writ* is 130. *Annunciation* is 135, *Virgin Mary* is 136. *Jesus, Messiah, cross, parables, gospel*, and *son God* (though not, regrettably, *son of God*) each adds up to 74. A whole string of correspondences to do with this total emerge if you parse *Gospel / according / to St / John* at the points marked by the slashes – 74, 74, 74, 47. These relationships are thought to be beyond coincidence. Moreover, it is possible to find support for them by plotting the patterns which God has introduced into the language as a whole. If you add the numerical value for *arm* to that for *bend*, you get the total for *elbow* (57). *King + chair = throne* (80). *Keep + off = grass* (64). Identical totals are found in *back* and *ache* (17), *bird* and *seed* (33), *lay* and *eggs* (38), and *girl* and *guide* (46). Adjacent totals are there in *film* and *camera* (40 and 41), *tick* and *clock* (43 and 44), *cut* and *knife* (44 and 45), and *nut* and *shell* (55 and 56). Reversals are there in *judge* and *jury* (47 and 74) and *cork* and *bottle* (also 47 and 74) – those numbers again, though what the association with lawyers and drink does to the character of St John remains somewhat unclear. Some sequences in the *God Proved . . .* booklet yield quite lengthy chains of events: *December two five* (155) is the day, the *twentyfifth* (156) of *December* (55) when *Santa* (55) *Claus* (56), aka *Father* (58) *Xmas* (57), arrives. *Santa* (55) and *December* (55) together make up *Christmas* (110). Which Santa? *The* Santa Claus (144), of course, aka *Saint Nicholas* (144). Can it be true? The whole story is confirmed by the link between *Santa Claus* (111) and *December twenty-fifth* (211).

The whole thing, of course, is indeed just a string of coincidences, partly influenced by the way letters are not used randomly in words, within a language, but reflect certain regular distributions and frequencies of occurrence. In any case, there will always be hundreds of numerical correspondences, if any sample is large enough, and the fact that some words display semantic links is not at all surprising. I used a computer program (devised by Tony MacNicholl) to sort the 2 million words in *The Cambridge Encyclopedia* database and add up their letter values. If we look at the words for the apparently significant 74, we find that there are 1050 of them (there would be over five times more if we included the related totals for 73, 75, 47, and 174). Here is a selection from those beginning with *A*:

abominable, accursed, additive, adequate, advocacy, aerobatic, agonised, ailment, allergen, angular, antennae, anyone, artefact, audibly, audits, audrey, aurora, avoidance, aztecs

All kinds of intriguing correspondences emerge when we scan such lists, and many options open up if we choose to live our lives by them. Let us imagine that *Audrey* is at the beginning of her career. If she is to take 74 seriously, then she must plan to become a *ballerina* or a *bagpiper*, watch out for *dandruff*, certainly learn *English*, always fly on *holiday* from *Gatwick*, be prepared to encounter a *sailor* from *London* – or perhaps from *Sheffield* – named *Eustace*, surname probably *McGough*, or maybe find a partner who is a *widow* called *Winnie*. The

occurrence of a verb like *diagnose* makes the task of finding correspondences especially easy: there is bound to be something in the list which can plausibly be diagnosed – and, indeed, as we scan the columns for 74, we encounter *measles*, *melanoma*, and *goitre*. The list will inevitably contain cases of semantic links which practitioners of gematria would seize upon as significant, such as *Jewish* and *menorah*, but these tend to be lost to view within the plethora of links which have no such significance. Everything is eventually put in its place, when a sample of words is large enough. *Jesus* and *Messiah* may both be 74; but so is *Lennon*. And *Lucifer*.

Gematria has to be a non-starter as a source of religious inspiration; but its techniques make a fine source for contemporary language play. It is possible to give a considerable lift to a flagging after-dinner speech by demonstrating, for example, that the letters in the surname of the host, or a well-known guest, produce the same total as those in *Rambo*, or *Tarzan*, or whoever; or that the first names of a bride and groom add up to the total for *eternal happiness* (or something naughtier). It doesn't take long to find some links: simply write out the letters of the alphabet with their numbers alongside, and do some quick computations of the words and names which are most closely involved in an event. When I was giving a paper to a Round Table in Linguistics conference at Georgetown University, Washington, in 1996, I discovered in about half an hour that *Round Tables* (131), *Washington* (130), and *Georgetown* (129) made a nice series, that linguistics must be getting some hidden presidential (and vice-presidential) support, as the surnames of *Clinton* and *Gore* totalled 132, and that Clinton must have a real interest in the subject, as his surname makes 87, the same total as for *languages*. They say that even a specialist in syntactic theory, who had found himself in the audience by mistake, was observed to laugh.

What a waste of time! Or is it? I have always enjoyed the few hours I've spent over the years trying to find amusing numerological equivalences, and most people appreciate the results. I don't suppose people these days try to live their lives by these coincidences, as happened in medieval times – only travelling on days whose value was felt to be auspicious, for example, or arranging marriages on the basis of numerical identity – but it wouldn't surprise me to learn that there are those who still do so. I expect I shall hear, in due course.

GRID GAMES

Undoubtedly the most widely practised form of language play – though whether its practitioners realize that this is what they are doing when they practise it – is the grid game, more familiarly known through its chief incarnation, the crossword puzzle. Grid games come in all shapes and sizes, and present a wide range of challenges to the ludic intuition. Word squares are one of the oldest manifestations: the aim is to produce a square of words in which each column and line forms an intelligible word.

Here are two examples: the first is a simple four-letter square, in which the words read the same in both directions; the second is the famous Latin palindromic square found in various locations from as early as the first century AD;[9] and the third is an example of a 'double square', in which the horizontal words are different from the vertical ones:

```
L A N E        S A T O R        O R A L
A R E A        A R E P O        M A R E
N E A R        T E N E T        E V E N
E A R S        O P E R A        N E A T
    R          O T A S
```

The aim, of course, is to make larger and larger word squares, and over the years the size of the square has gradually increased. Several nine-letter squares are now known – most generated with the aid of a computer, and needing a goodly array of archaic words, compounds, place names, and other forms to succeed. In this 1993 example, by Chris Long, all the words are in the *Oxford English Dictionary*:

```
W O R C E S T E R
O V E R L A R G E
R E C O I N A G E
C R O S S T I E D
E L I S I O N A L
S A N T O N A T E
T R A I N A G E S
E G G E A T E R S
R E E D L E S S E
```

Proposals for ten-letter squares have been made, but are so full of artifice that they strain one's intuitions as to what counts as a legitimate word in English.

Many variants of the grid game exist. One of the most popular among children is Word Search – with several examples always provided in any book of word games bought by parents to keep their progeny occupied on long train journeys or wet Saturdays. Here, the scrutiny of a square of apparently randomly distributed letters brings to light hidden words, discovered by finding strings of adjacent vertical, horizontal, or diagonal letters. No letter should be used twice. In the following example, the grid hides a six-word proverb (the answer is given in the note).[10]

```
T  O  E  E  I  R  L  R  J  L
U  H  M  T  A  M  E  Y  B  O
A  L  V  N  I  H  N  S  E  C
X  S  T  Q  C  T  A  S  I  N
B  A  I  T  D  I  V  E  N  E
W  L  E  W  A  R  M  I  A  T
T  O  O  M  O  N  Y  O  S  I
A  E  L  L  I  E  S  T  U  P
Y  R  O  D  N  G  O  N  E  G
R  E  H  W  O  N  U  S  T  E
```

But there is no doubt that the crossword puzzle is the king of grid games, attractive to millions for its convenience (it can be played alone, in virtually any situation) and its ability to operate at several levels of difficulty.

The history of the crossword puzzle has often been recounted. It was devised by a US journalist, a Liverpudlian emigré called Arthur Wynne, who was trying to think up something new for the puzzle page of the 1913 Christmas edition of the New York Sunday newspaper, *World*. Beginning with the idea of a word square, he hit on the idea of making the words across different from the words down, and slotted them into a diamond-shaped grid, calling it a 'word-cross'. The new game was an immediate success. A month later, he changed the name to a 'cross-word', and – much later – the hyphen was dropped. The grid gradually standardized into a square, though there have always been many variants, including diamonds, crosses, hexagons, and all kinds of 'real world' shapes. For over a decade the *World* was the only newspaper using crosswords, then things changed following the totally unexpected success of the first crossword book in 1924 – a compilation of fifty of the paper's best puzzles published by the Plaza Publishing Company (alias Simon and Schuster, who adopted the pseudonym because they were fearful that their newly

11 THE FIRST CROSSWORD

This is Arthur Wynne's first crossword puzzle. The word FUN appears at the top because it was the title of the newspaper's comic section in which the puzzle appeared. The solution is given in note G11. (Two of the answers are identical – something which would not be allowed now.)

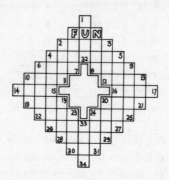

Clues

2–3.   What bargain hunters enjoy.
4–5.   A written acknowledgment.
6–7.   Such and nothing more.
10–11.   A bird.
14–15.   Opposed to less.
18–19.   What this puzzle is.
22–23.   An animal of prey.
26–27.   The close of a day.
28–29.   To elude.
30–31.   The plural of is.
8–9.   To cultivate.
12–13.   A bar of wood or iron.
16–17.   What artists learn to do.
20–21.   Fastened.
24–25.   Found on the seashore.
10–18.   The fibre of the gomuti palm.

6–22.   What we all should be.
4–26.   A day dream.
2–11.   A talon.
19-28.   A pigeon.
F-7.   Part of your head.
23–30.   A river in Russia.
1–32.   To govern.
33–34.   An aromatic plant.
N-8.   A fist.
24–31.   To agree with.
3–12.   Part of a ship.
20–29.   One.
5–27.   Exchanging.
9-25.   To sink in the mud.
13–21.   A boy.

The first crossword published in Britain, in the *Sunday Express*, in November 1924 – also one of Wynne's, with some US spellings changed.

Clues

Horizontals

1. A coin (slang).
4. A tree.
7. Period.
8. Through.
9. Counters of votes.
11. Cosy little room.
12. Drainages.
16. Meaning three (prefix).
17. Snake-like fish.
18. An oriental coin.
19. Parched.

Verticals

1. Wager.
2. Mineral substance.
3. Eminent political figure.
4. Inflicted retribution.
5. A title.
6. Possesses.
10. Grassland.
12. Home of a certain animal.
13. Before (poetic form).
14. Always (poetic form).
15. Cunning.

launched publishing house would be harmed if it took on a flop). Other volumes followed, and sales soon reached over half a million. Crosswords became a national craze in the USA, an obligatory piece of travellers' luggage (especially across the Atlantic), the subject of many national tournaments and – as US humorist Gelett Burgess commented in a newspaper of the time – of many domestic trials:

> *The fans they chew their pencils,*
> *The fans they beat their wives.*
> *They look up words for extinct birds –*
> *They lead such puzzling lives!*

There were crossword costumes on sale in the fashion shops; crosswords were brought in to fuel missionary campaigns in churches; doctors expressed their anxiety over the eye-strain being caused by excessive solving. The craze reached Britain by the end of the year, with Queen Mary and the Prime Minister both among the early enthusiasts. All kinds of organizations suddenly found themselves involved – acting as potential sources of information when solvers could not find an answer using conventional dictionaries and thesauruses. At one point, it is reported, the officials at London Zoo had to make an announcement refusing to answer any more telephone enquiries about the gnu, the emu, or any other three-letter creature.[11] By the time of Wynne's death, in 1945, crosswords were being solved, in a variety of languages, all over the world. A Gallup report in 1959 found it to be America's top pastime.

Nothing has beaten the crossword for popularity – but Scrabble comes close, the Queen to crossword's King. Scrabble, for example, is now thought to be the most widely played board game in the world, available in many languages, with a formal competitive dimension, a world championship, and associated books of commentary, all in the manner of chess. And it illustrates very well the bizarre nature of what we are doing when we play language games. In Scrabble, someone has given us a physical limit (a grid on a board), assigned numerical values to letters (based on their intuitions of the frequency with which the letters turn up in the language), and then forced us to hunt out and use the most obscure (because highly scoring) words in the language. Now this is not rational linguistic behaviour. Words don't normally 'score' anything. We do not listen to a sentence, then hold up score cards, as in an ice-skating competition. Moreover, in Scrabble it is not even necessary to know what the words mean: all we need to know is that they exist. There are many publications which list all the words in English consisting of two letters, of three letters, and so on, or those which are most useful because they are highest scoring (such as *xebec*, *qaid*, and *hajj*). None of them say what the words mean. If challenged, we look them up in a dictionary – and if we are playing 'professionally', in the game's official dictionary (*Chambers*). In a market survey of dictionary use a few years ago, most people said they used their dictionaries most often when they were playing Scrabble.

Some people get very serious about word games. For instance, you don't mess with crossword enthusiasts. I know a man who gets very nasty if he can't complete his *Times* crossword in fifteen minutes. And it is perhaps no coincidence that so many of the famous crossword compilers, such as Ximenes and Torquemada, chose as their pseudonym the name of a practitioner of the Spanish Inquisition. (No-o-one expects the Spanish Inquisition: see p. 111.) But most of us appreciate the fun involved in playing with our language, manipulating letters, searching for coincidences, and looking for the unexpected links between words. Look on the walls of many a subway and you will find thousands of examples of vernacular linguistic ingenuity – a topic we shall explore further in the next chapter. It is all around us.

AND FINALLY . . .

The media are a mirror in which we see ourselves. We would therefore expect language play to be well represented in the press, and on radio and television – and so it proves to be. Crosswords and other word-play puzzles are now routine in most newspapers. And when a few years ago I analysed all the game shows I could find on British radio and television, over half turned out to be language based. They

12 TOM SWIFTIES

In 1910 the firm of Grosset and Dunlap published the first book in a new series introducing a new boy hero: *Tom Swift and His Motorcycle*. The story outlines were created by Edward Stratemeyer, and the first thirty-five books in the series were written by Howard Garis under the pseudonym of Victor Appleton. The series became the best-selling boy adventure series of its day, with over 30 million copies sold. It ended in 1941, but a second series began in 1954, telling the adventures of Tom Junior, and there were attempts at launching a third and fourth series in the 1980s and 1990s, before a halt was called in 1993.

It isn't known who first played 'Tom Swifties', but this name has been used to identify a special kind of punning at least since the 1960s, and the kind of wordplay involved probably antedates Tom himself. The game is a pastiche of the style of the Tom stories, in which brave Tom's verbs of speaking would tend to be accompanied by a dramatic, atmospheric adverb – 'Tom said quietly', 'Tom laughed harshly', and the like. The genre appeals especially to professional writers of fiction, who are daily faced with the uphill task of finding interesting ways of saying 'he/she said', and it has since been extended to other parts of speech. But anyone can play it, and some of the creations have been highly ingenious.

Adverb puns
'Can I get you something?' Tom asked fetchingly.
'Try that direction,' Tom said pointedly.
'We're out of whiskey,' Tom said dispiritedly.
'My electrocardiogram's fine,' Tom said wholeheartedly.
'Wouldn't you prefer a poodle?' asked Tom's father doggedly.
'It's the maid's night off,' said Tom helplessly.

'The needle has reached zero,' Tom said naughtily.

'We like fairy tales,' said Tom's brothers grimly.

And some verbs and adjectives . . .

'Let's get on with the operation,' the surgeon cut in sharply.

'I used to be a pilot,' Tom explained.

'Your visits to the psychiatrist have been helpful,' Tom reminded him.

'I'm quite disconcerted,' said the conductor.

'We've been discharged,' said the electricians.

'I'm nonplussed,' said the mathematician.

'We'll arrest the president,' the soldiers cooed.

'You must look after your spaniel,' Tom dogmatized.

included games in which the aim was to guess a word in a well-known phrase (*Blankety Blank*), to distinguish between real and false etymologies (*Call My Bluff*), and to talk for a minute without hesitations or repetitions (*Just a Minute*), as well as several which built up words using randomly generated sequences of letters. Open the published broadcasting guides, and you would see such programme titles as *My Word*, *Catch Phrase* and *Chain Letters*. The names vary from country to country, but the topics do not.

Why are there so many such games? My feeling is that language-based games are so popular because everyone who has learned their language can play them without further training. Once you have learned to talk (or, for the writing-based games, to read and spell), you need no other special skill. It is not like *Mastermind*, a question-and-answer game where you have to remember a great deal of general knowledge as well as have the ability to master a highly specialized topic. Nor is it like *Gladiators*, a physical participation game where you need above-average strength and athleticism if you are to survive. To play a game like *Blankety Blank*, all you need is your linguistic intuition about what word is most likely to fill the blank in such a phrase as, say, *life and* — . Is it *limb*, or *soul*, or *death*? Choose one, and if you're lucky, your choice will match the choice previously made by a celebrity guest – and then you win! We all know the options, intuitively, and we all have the same chance of guessing which one is likely to make the correct match. In such games, therefore, we are all equal. Whether we are in control of our ludic obsession, whether it controls us, or whether we have no language obsessions at all, is no longer the issue.

The domain of language play, from this point of view, is the most democratic of worlds. And it is perhaps precisely because we have such a world of equal linguistic opportunities that so many people have found a comfortable home in it.

4

THE PROFESSIONALS

The weird and wonderful linguistic behaviours brought together in the last two chapters support the view that language play is natural, spontaneous and universal. It is practised in some shape or form by everyone, whether they are born jokers or people who would never receive an Oscar for their sense of humour. It is not solely a matter of humour, after all, but involves notions of enjoyment, entertainment, intellectual satisfaction, and social rapport. Although patterns and preferences vary greatly, the phenomenon of language play seems to cut across regional, social and professional background, age, sex, ethnicity, personality, intelligence and culture. People are very comfortable with it. It seems to meet a need. (Where this need comes from will be the subject of the next chapter.)

But any account of those who engage in language play would be seriously incomplete if it did not devote a chapter to the people who make a living from it – or (to avoid begging any questions about levels of income) whose reputation is partly or wholly dependent on a professional ability to work with it. For it is here that we see the linguistic manipulations involved in language play achieve some of their most complex and effective manifestations. And it is also here that we encounter the need to broaden the notion of language play to include some unexpected domains of language use. Were you expecting some theological reflections, when you first picked up this book? Read on.

THE ADVERTISERS

But first, some domains where you would expect language play to be conspicuous. And advertising is an obvious place to start. Language play is part of the essence of advertising. While it is perfectly possible to present a product without any verbal language at all, relying entirely on a visual association of ideas, virtually all advertisements do have a linguistic component, and in a good number of these – chiefly the commercial and public service ads – there is use of language play. This is probably not surprising, as a general observation. It has often been suggested that the first task of advertising is to get you to *notice* the ad, and then to register the identity of the product – so that when you actually arrive in the market-place you are capable of singling out that product from the array of similar products on display.[1] It is also essential to arouse the interest of the readers/viewers, to convince them that the product will satisfy some need and to persuade them that this particular product is superior to others. To help meet all these demands, language play provides an invaluable resource. Not only does it generate sentences which are distinctive and memorable in their own right, its conventions are so familiar – they are, as we have seen, used routinely and domestically by the target audience – that they immediately enable readers or viewers to identify with the situation presented in the ad and thus promote a receptive frame of mind in those whom the advertiser is hoping to persuade to become purchasers.

It hardly seems worthwhile devoting a great deal of space to illustrating a linguistic point which everyone can see just by picking up a daily paper or turning on the television. Five successful specimens of the genre can act as a quick reminder.

o The slogan advertising milk on British television in the 1960s, 'Drinka pinta milka day', was so effective it became a catch-phrase. It is a fine example of language play, here operating at three levels simultaneously – in pronunciation, through the unexpectedly metrical rhythm; in orthography, through the losing of expected word spaces; and as a consequence, in the lexicon, providing us with potentially new words – one of which, *pinta*, did actually join the language for a while, as an informal equivalent of *pint*.

o In Australia in 1997, a billboard advertisement for a certain brand of chocolate dip biscuits contained the slogan, 'Never Unfun' – a daring lexical creation, whose impact can be judged by comparing it with the clichéd effect generated by its orthodox equivalent: 'Always Fun'.

o In the UK in 1996, a full-page ad for P & O Cruises shows a cruise-ship resting peacefully on a flat blue sea. Across the middle of the sea we read: 'BE CALMED'. This is an unusually effective interaction between grammar and lexicon. There are only a few words in the language which allow the first syllable to double as an imperative use of *be*, and hardly any of those allow a similar semantic relationship – though one might be able to work up something with *beloved* or *berated*. *Be wildered* might just work as advice to see a show starring US actor Gene Wilder, and *Be witched* might possibly be construed as advice to buy the consumer magazine, *Which?* But I am scraping the

13 ADS AT PLAY

Here is a selection of word-coinages found in advertisements in recent years.

Coinage	Product
biteables	snacks
choysa (= choicer)	tea
exschweppesionally	soft drink
lushus (= luscious)	jelly
lotsa	bananas
nu plastik	paint
orangemostest	soft drink
peelability	oranges
sea-esta	air bed
temptational	chocolates

A selection of alliterations:

all the fun of the fare
built better
carefree cruising
dazzling discount deals
delightfully delicate
delights of the Danube
dramatically different
extra economy
fabulous furnishings
fuller flavour

golden goodness
luscious lingerie
pampered to perfection
perfect present
ship shape shopping
spring into style
super snack
superb smoothness
silken soft
temptingly tasty

bottom of a rather small barrel. That is why 'BE CALMED' has such an impact: it cannot be easily copied. The best ludic linguistic ads discover a barrel which has just one item in it.

o Next, a piece of grammatical play: a 1977 British ad for Pyrex casserole

And a few rhymes:

Don't be vague – ask for Haig (*whisky*)
What a lot I got (*Smarties*)
You know what beanz meanz (*Heinz beans*)
Take the waiting out of marinating (*sauce*)
Hey Mabel! Black Label! (*beer*)
Go to town with Crown (*wallpapers*)
Grace . . . Space . . . Pace . . . (*cars*)
Go go go for Eskimo (*fishsteaks*)
Clunk, click, every trip (*seat-belt advice*)
Once you pop, you can't stop (*crisps*)
Get the train to catch the plane (*rail travel*)
Twice as nice, not twice the price (*furniture*)
Durability, reliability, desirability (*cars*)
Affordable, washable, desirable (*sofas*)
Safety, economy, flexibility (*cars*)
It's not only coughs and sneezes that spread diseases (*toothbrush cleanser*)
Sprinkle the wrinkles (*raisins*)
Great floors like these don't grow on trees (*carpets*)
Drivers to Spain choose the right lane (*car ferries*)
I'm only here for the beer (*beer*)
A Mars a day helps you work, rest and play (*chocolate bar*)

dishes shows a picture of an old-fashioned housemaid under the headline, 'Before Pyrex casseroles, it was Ethel what made life simple'. Playing with nonstandard grammar is always eye-catching. The body-copy of the ad adds a further grammatical trick, changing Ethel into a countable noun: 'if you owned an Ethel . . .' , but stays with standard grammar until the very end, when it reprises the headline: 'It was Ethel what had to go. And Pyrex casseroles what stayed ever after.'

o Finally, a television ad for Crazy Cow breakfast cereal, used on US television in 1978. This shows a typical use of pronunciation play – rhythm, rhyme and alliteration – here extending over several conversational turns and including some singing:

BOY (singing): *My best friend is a cow.*
CRAZY COW (singing): *And how.*
VOICE OVER (adults, singing): *How now Crazy Cow.*
CRAZY COW (singing): *That's me.*
VOICE OVER (adults, singing): *Makes chocolate milk – wow!*
GIRL: *Wow!*
VOICE OVER (adults, singing): *How now Crazy Cow.*

This last example is an ad aimed at children, and we shall see examples of similar word-play when we investigate children's language in the next chapter; but the linguistic strategies used are by no means restricted to young people. In the world of advertising, we stay children for a long time.

The Crazy Cow example also illustrates another important feature of language play in advertising: the way it relies on proverbs, catchphrases and other well-established expressions in the language – in the present case, 'How now brown cow' and 'A man's best friend is his dog'. Often, indeed, the ad engages in an incestuous relationship with other ads – assuming a knowledge of a previous slogan. I saw in London in 1997 an advertisement by a sea-ferry firm which drew attention to the merits of travelling by catamaran – *cat*, for short. The text read: 'Take a Break. Have a Quick Cat.' The full effect is obtained only if you recognize the allusion to a much earlier advertisement for Kit-Kat chocolate bars, where the slogan was: 'Have a Break. Have a Kit-Kat'. The original ad was already a fine example of language play, with its bouncy rhythm, repetitive syntax and unexpected spelling of *Kat*, and it achieved catchphrase status in several countries. The new ad borrows the syntax and rhythm, and plays again with the spelling – but this time, returning *cat* to its normal form, a nice instance of language play 'in reverse'. Of course, if you don't know the original ad, the new one will be a puzzle. Relying on the public's memory of the genre is always a risky business, especially if earlier ads have not been used worldwide.

Another case of reminiscence appears within a 1997 ad for the British superstore chain, Sainsbury's. The heading is a straightforward pun: 'Sainsbury's have eight kinds of onion. And that's shallot'. The body copy goes on to explain, mock seriously, that a shallot isn't technically an onion, but an *Allium ascalonicum*; then, having slipped the technical term in, they defuse its effect by playing with it, in a supremely cheeky piece of borrowing.

As far as we know, Sainsbury's offer more kinds of alliaceous vegetables (onions, shallots, garlic, leeks and chives) than any other supermarket.
Which must make Sainsbury's the most supercalifragilisticexpialliaceous supermarket in the country.

One subgenre of language play playing with another. It only works if you know your Disney – but then I suppose most people do.

In my favourite example of this kind of linguistic risk being taken, the advertising campaign was not simply incestuous, it was positively narcissistic. This is the series of poster and television ads for Heineken lager, introduced by the Whitbread Beer Company in the UK in 1974, which created a slogan and then, once it had become well established, began to manipulate its language in strange ways. The creative brief was the theme of refreshment and emphasized the restorative abilities of the drink; and the slogan devised by Terry Lovelock was still part of adult British public consciousness over twenty years later: *Heineken refreshes the parts other beers cannot reach*. At the outset, the different advertisements introduced variations on the idea 'When something isn't right, Heineken puts it right'. We would see a situation which was unsatisfactory in some respect – a person who could not do something well, perhaps, or a machine which would not work efficiently. After ingesting a quantity of the lager, the person (or the machine) would then proceed to function with super-efficiency. In a typical three-part ad, the first frame might show a lawn-mower (the person, not the machine) unable to make progress in the task; in the second frame, the machine would be given some of the lager; and in the third frame, we would see the mower (the machine, not the person) mowing the lawn all on its own.

To this point, such advertisements could only be described as instances of situational ingenuity, not language play. The linguistic element emerged later, when the advertisers felt they could take the original slogan for granted, and embarked on a long series of word substitutions, in which *parts* was replaced by other words with a similar phonetic shape, such as *pilots, parrots, pirates, poets* and *partings*. As usual, each ad introduced a failed visual situation which the lager was able to turn into an immediate success. In one case, a dilapidated Long John Silver character, with a wooden leg, crutch, eye-patch and apparently moribund parrot, is miraculously rejuvenated – appearing with two wooden legs, two crutches, two eye patches, a hook in place of his right hand and his parrot turned into a vulture. The slogan? *Heineken refreshes the pirates other beers cannot reach.* In another case, we see a woodland scene and hear a male voiceover incoherently trying to tell a story about his visit to the place; we hear the sound of a can of lager being opened and drunk; and then we hear: 'I wandered lonely as a cloud, which floats on high o'er vales and hills . . .' The slogan, of course: *Heineken refreshes the poets other beers cannot reach.*

A risky business, indeed. I recall having to explain at great length what one of these slogans meant to a group of Japanese teachers of English. *Heineken refreshes the poets other beers cannot reach*? What on earth was going on? They knew what the sentence meant, as a string of words, but not why anyone would ever want to say it. Not being part of the culture, they had no linguistic memory to which they could relate the language play – or even recognize that it *was* language play. I did my best, and the teachers politely nodded, but the explanation probably only confirmed them in their impression that the British were several sandwiches short of a picnic.

A footnote to this section: does advertising work? In my case, yes. I am incapable of telling the difference between the various kinds of lager on sale in a bar, but this series has given me such linguistic joy that whenever I am asked which lager I want I always make my first choice Heineken.

THE HEADLINE WRITERS

Newspaper subeditors all over the English-speaking world devise headlines or subheadlines with great ingenuity. Like advertising, the aim is to catch the reader's attention – and apparently one of the best ways of doing this (in addition to using the conventional methods of increasing the size of the type, and summarizing the content of the piece in a succinct, telegraphic style) is to introduce an element of language play. Some newspapers use language play more than others; and within these newspapers, some sections make more frequent use of it than others. In Britain, for example, the *Guardian* in particular achieved a reputation for the ingenuity of its headline punning. But all newspapers do it to some extent – though in the more 'serious' papers, the language play is often restricted to the more populist sections, such as sports, entertainment, cookery and diary columns. Ludic headlines, moreover, turn up in all English-writing countries, and in many other languages, using the same basic repertoire of strategies – puns, word-play, hidden allusions and deliberate misquotation. Here is a small selection of examples taken from some 1993 newspapers:

Pandamonium (heading a story about zoos, *Los Angeles Times*)
Bladerunner (heading a sports story about fencing, *Vancouver Sun*)
Pain Stops Play (heading a story about a cricketer bitten by an adder, *Sun*)
Pork Chop (heading a story on meat banned from a pub, *Sun*)
A Roo Awakening at the Table (heading a story on gourmet kangaroo meat, *Sydney Morning Herald*)
Where's There a Will? (heading a story on looking for evidence of Shakespeare, *Guardian*)
A Suitable Case for Placement (heading a story on social care, *Guardian*)
Manufacturers Seek Peace of the Action (heading a story on military technology, *South China Morning Post*)

14 NEWSPLAY

The following set of headlines (1–12) were encountered in some 1997 UK newspapers. To the right, but in a different order, are summaries of the stories which they relate to (A–L). Sorting out the pairs is relatively easy (though some rely on a specifically British intuition more than others). Explaining how you did it to someone who isn't a native speaker of English is more difficult. Explanations are given in note G14. The jokey allusion rarely has any semantic relationship at all to the point of the article.

1 Common scents on the buses
2 The pain in Spain lies mainly in the hills
3 A bird in the hand
4 The kooky crumbles
5 Ab fad
6 Where there's a wheel
7 Let's face it, villains ain't wot they used to be
8 Pull the wool over your eyes
9 Pay as you learn

Several of these examples are straightforward puns, the point sometimes being made through the spelling (*peace, pandamonium*), sometimes through the different senses of a word (*pork chop*), and sometimes by relying on the reader's awareness of an idiom (*roo/rude awakening*) or proverbial expression (*Where there's a will, there's a way*). Other examples are more sophisticated, asking us to tap into intuitions which are part of a cultural linguistic heritage. To appreciate the play in *Bladerunner*, we need to know that there was a film called *Blade Runner*; similarly, the social care story reminds those who know of the film *A Suitable Case for Treatment*. If we don't know, the point will, quite simply, be missed, and the headline will become obscure.

Part of the sub-editorial skill is in judging the level of intuitive cul-

10   The Web of intrigue
11   Here comes the judge
12   The best things since slice bread

A   A biopic of the chair of a book awards panel.
B   Students at university need to know more about their tax liabilities.
C   Men are increasingly trying to reduce the risk of developing a paunch.
D   As part of an advertising campaign, washing powder fragrance is being added to London bus tickets.
E   A group of inventors talk about their new creations.
F   A new television show mixes comedy and cooking.
G   Balaclavas are coming into fashion this winter.
H   Falconry is more popular today than it has been for decades.
I   A review of a new gangland movie set in London's East End.
J   There is to be a sale of collectors' vehicles.
K   Finance houses are increasingly using the Internet to promote their products.
L   A national cycle race is in its final stages.

tural knowledge which can be relied upon in this way. To make the allusions too arcane runs the risk of putting readers off – like a too-difficult crossword puzzle. That is why most of the jokes in headlines are towards the 'more obvious' end of the spectrum. But even that end can be surprisingly culturally restricted. We need to know that there is a tradition of saying 'Rain stops play' at cricket matches before we could possibly 'get the joke' in *Pain Stops Play* – and is there any adult in Britain who would not know this? But during a lecture to non-native English-language teachers, I once asked the 200-strong audience whether they recognized the allusion in *Pain Stops Play*: nobody did. There is, it seems, a huge gap between native and non-native intuitions, when it comes to language play. I also asked a group of American students: same result. How much do the British miss when they read newspapers from other parts of the English-speaking world, I wonder?

And in cartoon captions, too – which in their succinctness, graphic autonomy and collaborative status are plainly related to headlines. There is a fine cartoon drawn by Bestie and published in an issue of the new series of *Punch* (18–24 January 1997), which illustrates the same kind of linguistic dependence. It shows a grocer's shop: a badger is serving behind the counter, and a bear, a weasel and a rabbit are queuing up. The bear is saying to the badger: 'Half a pound of tuppenny rice and half a pound of treacle please'. The caption reads: 'Weasel didn't like the sound of this' – and poor weasel's facial expression helps to make the point. You need to know the nursery rhyme 'Pop Goes the Weasel' to know what must be passing through his mind; if you don't, no amount of poring over the cartoon will ever enable you to decode its meaning.

Ludic captions and headlines also provide us with a very clear instance of the general point made in Chapter 1 – that language play has little or nothing to do with the transmission of information. We might be tempted to ask: 'What extra information do we obtain about fencing once we know that *Blade Runner* is the title of a popular film?' And the answer would surely have to be, 'Not a lot'. The writer is not suggesting that there is some analogy between the fencing article and the plot of the film – a futuristic detective story which has nothing to do with fencing at all. Indeed, the newspaper story itself is so minimalist that it is difficult to read any kind of extra meaning in:

Jean-Paul Banos of Montreal posted Canada's best ever result in sabre as he finished 10th at the 60-country world fencing championships in Essen, Germany.[2]

That's it. The best we might argue is that the excitement of the film is adding some additional atmosphere to the newspaper story through a kind of loose association – but this is hardly 'information'. Evidently this is not the way to look at it. A more plausible account is to recognize the role of language play in headlines of this kind. The writers are appealing directly to our ludic sensibilities. They are simply 'being clever', and asking us to admire their verbal ingenuity. The ingenuity is not without purpose: the unexpected language attracts our attention, making us read a piece which we might otherwise have passed over. But it does something more, offering us an extra dimension of enjoyment. We expect news, when we read the paper. Ludic headlines are a bonus, no extra charge.

THE COMEDIANS

Professional comedians come in many linguistic shapes and sizes. All at some point in their performances rely on language play, and some choose to specialize in it. It's important not to overstate the matter, of course: vast tracts of vocal humour, whether on radio or television, stage or night-club, use language in a perfectly ordinary way (many jokes, as we have seen in Chapter 2, rely on absolutely conventional language), or do not play with language at all. The humour might be slapstick or situational, relying on bizarre settings, ridiculous clothing, eccentric characters, the unexpected behaviour of inanimate objects, or a thousand other things that do not depend on language for their effect. When Norman Wisdom falls, or Lucille Ball reacts to a crazy domestic crisis, or Eric Morecambe gives Ernie Wise a slap, we are not dealing with language play. Language is unnecessary for Mr Bean to work his magic – indeed, it came as a surprise to everyone that he proved able to speak so much, in the film *Bean* – and Rowan Atkinson's comic creation falls into line behind a long list of other comic characters and clowns whose humour comes from how they look and the chaos they cause – Jacques Tati, Charlie Chaplin, Frankie Howerd ... But when Peter Sellers or Stan Freberg adopt a funny voice, or Rowan Atkinson, in a different comic persona, reads out a list of pupils' unusual surnames in a mock serious tone, or Ronnie Barker presents a monologue in which words get jumbled up at high speed, or Peter Cook and Dudley Moore exchange pleasantries in pastiche accents, or impersonators and satirists exaggerate their targets' vocal traits, then we are entering the domain of professional language play.

Sometimes, the forms of language are themselves the focus of the humour. A character is presented who has some unfortunate linguistic trait, such as a difficulty with certain sounds, an inability to get grammar right, or an obsession with certain words. British actor/comedian 'Professor' Stanley Unwin was rightly given his title, in this respect; as he once said, in an address to the United Nations:

O joyful peoplodes! Quick vizzy intercapitoles, round table and freedom talkit with genuine friendly eyebold gleam . . .[3]

Really skilful language players, such as British comic Ronnie Barker, are able to say words and sentences backwards, mix up sounds, add syllables, change word order and carry out a variety of other deviant linguistic tasks at high speed to great effect. In Barker's case, it almost seemed at times as if the scriptwriters were testing how far he could go before he would explode in a tangled mass of consonants and vowels.

Although there is always a vocal performance, the written language is also tapped as a source of effects. For instance, in the British television series *The Two Ronnies*, the stars (Ronnie Barker and Ronnie Corbett) are seen interacting in a restaurant solely through the medium of letters of the alphabet and number names – presented to us as a new method of English teaching. The name of each letter is articulated carefully and separately: 'L' sounds like 'ell', 'O' like 'oh', and so on. The viewers are first taught how to interpret this language: Ronnie 1 gives the target form, along with a picture, and Ronnie 2 supplies the translation. Both are speaking in pastiche foreign accents, which allows them to take considerable liberties with the pronunciation of the letters.

R1: L.O.
R2: Hello.
R1: P.T.
R2: Pity.
R1: C.T.
R2: City.

R1: *T.T.*
R2: *(No comment, as the picture speaks for itself.)*

The lesson then begins (for slow learners, a gloss is given on p. 231):

CUSTOMER: *L.O.*
WAITER: *L.O.*
CUSTOMER: *R.U.B.C?*
WAITER: *S.V.R.B.C* ...

And after a while:

CUSTOMER: *F.U.N.E.X?*
WAITER: *S.V.F.X.*
CUSTOMER: *F.U.N.E.M?*
WAITER: *9.*[4]

By the end of the sketch, some quite complex pieces of syntax have been built up, such as *I F C D M* ('I have seen the ham') and *Y F N U N E X* ('Why haven't you any eggs?'). The studio audience roars with laughter.

In the world of *Monty Python*, no area of language is sacrosanct. Although many of the sketches are based on absurd situations, a large number gain their effect only through the use of funny voices, exaggerated regional accents, deliberately inappropriate lexicon, the excessive use of a single sentence pattern – or just breaking the normal rules of linguistic interaction. Playing with lexical repetition is the hallmark of the famous 'Spam' sketch. A man enters a café and asks the waitress what's on the menu. She replies (with a Viking chorus singing in the background, for good measure):

Well, there's egg and bacon; egg sausage and bacon; egg and spam; egg bacon and spam; egg bacon sausage and spam; spam bacon sausage and spam; spam egg spam spam bacon and spam; spam sausage spam spam bacon spam tomato and spam; spam spam spam egg and spam; spam spam spam spam spam spam baked beans spam spam and spam ...

The sketch continues in this vein for quite a while – and lives on in the term *spamming*, now used on the Internet for the unwanted sending of junk e-mail.

The Python team specialized in bizarre linguistic interactions. In the 'Argument Clinic' sketch, a man walks into an office, wanting an argument. The receptionist directs him to a room where he sees a man behind a desk:

MAN: *Is this the right room for an argument?*
OTHER MAN (pause): *I've told you once.*
MAN: *No you haven't!*
OTHER MAN: *Yes I have.*
MAN: *When?*
OTHER MAN: *Just now.*
MAN: *No you didn't!*
OTHER MAN: *Yes I did!*
MAN: *You didn't!*
OTHER MAN: *I did!*
MAN: *You didn't!*
OTHER MAN: *I'm telling you, I did!*
MAN: *You didn't!*
OTHER MAN (breaking in): *Oh I'm sorry, is this a five minute argument, or the full half hour?*
MAN: *Ah!* (takes out his wallet and pays) *Just the five minutes.*
OTHER MAN: *Just the five minutes. Thank you. Anyway, I did.*
MAN: *You most certainly did not! . . .*

The 'Contradiction' sketch uses a similar conceit:

HOST: *With me now is Norman St John Polevaulter, who for the last few years has been contradicting people. St John Polevaulter, why do you contradict people?*
POLEVAULTER: *I don't!*
HOST: *But you . . . you told me that you did.*
POLEVAULTER: *I most certainly did not!*

HOST: *Oh. I see. I'll start again.*
POLEVAULTER: *No you won't! . . .*

Sometimes, an established speech style is the target, as in the 'Banter' parody of RAF slang. The scene is a wartime RAF station:

JONES: *Morning, Squadron Leader.*
IDLE: *What-ho, Squiffy.*
JONES: *How was it?*
IDLE: *Top-hole. Bally Jerry, pranged his kite right in the how's-your-father; hairy blighter, dicky-birded, feathered back on his sammy, took a waspy, flipped over on his Betty Harpers and caught his can in the Bertie.*
JONES: *Er, I'm afraid I don't quite follow you, Squadron Leader.*
IDLE: *It's perfectly ordinary banter, Squiffy . . . [He says it again.]*
JONES: *No, I'm just not understanding banter at all well today. Give us it slower.*
IDLE: *Banter's not the same if you say it slower, Squiffy . . .*

As for a prime example of lexical play, the popular vote would probably go for the thesaurus sequence in the 'Dead Parrot' sketch. A customer enters a pet shop, complaining that the parrot he has just purchased is dead. The denials of the pet-shop owner leads the customer into one of the most famous rhetorical climaxes of contemporary comedy:

CUSTOMER: *'E's bleedin' demised!*
OWNER: *No, no! 'E's pining!*
CUSTOMER: *'E's not pinin'! 'E's passed on! This parrot is no more! 'E 'as ceased to be! 'E's expired and gone to meet 'is maker! 'E's a stiff! Bereft of life, 'e rests in peace! If you 'adn't nailed 'im to the perch 'e'd be pushin' up the daisies! 'Is metabolic processes are now 'istory! 'E's off the twig! 'E's kicked the bucket! 'E's shuffled off 'is mortal coil, run down the curtain and joined the bleedin' choir invisible! This is an ex-parrot!!*

Even language games themselves can be the focus of language play, as in the 'Hate Anagrams' monologue. This begins:

Hello, and welcome to a page written entirely for people who dislike anagrams. Hi, anagram-haters everywhere! . . .

The presenter guarantees no anagrams on the page at all, but after a while . . .

Don't you just hate those bores who can crack an anagram faster than they can pour the irate? I'm sorry. That wasn't an anagram. It was a typing error. It should of course have read 'I rate her pout'. Oh dear. I'm sorry again. That wasn't a typing error. It was a printer's slip. The phrase 'heat our tripe' should have read 'I rape her tout'. Oh golly. Sorry . . .

There is a sequel, which begins:

Because of the anagrams dispute, it has been decided to devote the rest of this space to a page specially written for people who like figures of speech, for the not a few fans of litotes, and those with no small interest in meiosis, for the infinite millions of hyperbole-lovers, for those fond of hypallage, and the epithet's golden transfer, for those who fall willingly into the arms of the metaphor, those who give up the ghost, bury their heads in the sand, and ride roughshod over the mixed metaphor, and even those of hyperbaton the friends . . .

And on another occasion:

PALIN: *. . . But first on the show we've got a man who speaks entirely in anagrams.*
IDLE: *Taht si crreoct.*
PALIN: *Do you enjoy it?*
IDLE: *I stom certainly od. Revy chum so.*
PALIN: *And what's your name?*
IDLE: *Hamrag – Hamrag Yatlerot.*
PALIN: *Well, Graham, nice to have you on the show . . .*

A successful series like *Monty Python* in fact generates many catch-phrases, which in turn are used in popular language play by its devotees. *Ex-parrot* produced a rash of *ex*-usages. Sudden changes of topic can still be heard from time to time being introduced by *And now for something completely different. Spam* continues to intrude. I was in a London restaurant not so long ago, and there were two respectable middle-aged couples falling about at the next table – adding *spam* to the items as they reflected on the menu. And, in the world of *Monty Python* freaks, it is no longer possible to refer to the Spanish Inquisition in a sane tone of voice. (No-o-one expects the Spanish Inquisition!) To the insider, this is all normal behaviour. To the outsider, it is at best ridiculous and puerile. But interrogate those who condemn, and sooner or later their own bizarre worlds will come to light, peopled by the linguistic creations of their favourite (and often long-dead) comedians. Can I do you now, sir?

For an earlier British generation, it was radio rather than television which provided the source of much daily humour – *The Goon Show* most of all.[5] This show was heavily dependent on funny voices and sound effects, as can now be seen from the published scripts, where many of the lines are flat without the force of the eccentric voice quality behind them. But the material is also permeated by verbal language play, and the two dimensions usually complement each other. The high-pitched querulous tones of the 'schoolboy weed' Bluebottle, for example, are matched by his baby-talk – he uses the verb-patterns of a four-year-old – and some of his phrases achieved catch-phrase status at the time: *He has deaded me, I don't like this game, Let justice be doned, You rotten swine, I have been hitted on my bonce.* The slow, imploded tones of the idiot Eccles are supported by simplified pronunciation (*Who's dat?*) and disregard of the rules of normal conversation:

SEAGOON: *Shut up, Eccles.*
ECCLES: *Shut up, Eccles.*

Major Bloodnok, the blustering old soldier with the gravelly, raucous voice, relies heavily on nonsense expletives: *Flatten me Cronkler with Spinachmallets!, Great thundering widgets of Kludge!*

Nonsense, indeed, is conspicuous throughout, as the following selection of exclamatory outbursts illustrates:

> *Ying tong iddle I po!*
> *Needle nardle noo!*
> *Sapristi Knockoes!*
> *Shot in the kringe!*

Names are twisted, and even the name of the show is not exempt: *Florence Nightengoon, The Grune Show.* Words are given mock endings, such as *-ule* – *jungule* (for *jungle*), *jokule* (for *joke*) (see p. 29). Mock foreign languages are much in evidence, especially in the pastiche accents, but also in the words, as in this 'Spanish' example: *Heavens-o! El knocko on the door-o. Come in-o.* And national stereotypes are wildly exaggerated, even affecting animals, seen in this Welsh sequence:

SEAGOON: *Puss, puss, come here, puss bach.*
SPIKE: *Meiouw, meiouw bach.*

Allusions are often being made to the conventions of written language, as in this extract:

SEAGOON: *Can I help you, sir?*
CRUN: *Are you a policeman?*
SEAGOON: *No, I'm a constable.*
CRUN: *What's the difference?*
SEAGOON: *They're spelt differently.*

Bluebottle regularly talks in a written commentary style, in the manner of a stage script, as if reading instructions from his brain about what to do next:

BLUEBOTTLE: *I heard you call, my Capatain – I heard my Captain call – waits for audience applause – not a sausage – puts on I don't care expression as done by Aneurin Bevan at Blackpool Conservative Rally.*

He also makes repeated use of the speech-bubble, *Thinks*, to precede what he thinks – and sometimes this convention is extended throughout a dialogue, becoming increasingly surreal as it proceeds:

SEAGOON: *Lad, lad, lad, tell me, what speed does Mr Crun's organ do?*
BLUEBOTTLE: *No, I shall not telle-d, I have been sworn to secrecy by Mr Crunge.*
SEAGOON: *Lad lad lad, tell me, and these two ounces of cardboard brandy balls are yours.*
BLUEBOTTLE: *Coo, brandy balls. Thinks, with those-type sweets my prestige will increase at school. Eh, thinks again, if I gave one of them to Winnie Henry it might act like a love philtre on her. And then – o ehhhh ehh.*
SEAGOON: *Thinks. You dirty little devil.*
BLUEBOTTLE: *Thinks. Are you referring to me?*
SEAGOON: *Thinks. Yes I am.*

15 GOONPLAY

The balance between situational and language play can be judged from this extract from one of *The Goon Show* scripts, 'The Silent Bugler' (recorded in 1958):

SEAGOON: Before my departure for Russia, I took one final test.

BROLLICKS: We want you to identify objects that will be held up in rapid succession. Sergeant Eccles, do your duty.

ECCLES: OK. The first object I hold up is *this*.

SEAGOON: It's a banana!

ECCLES: Good, good. (*Eats it.*) Dat got rid of dat. Now then, what's this?

SEAGOON: A pencil.

    FX Sound of man eating pencil.

ECCLES: Good. (*Gulps*) And dat got rid of dat! What's this (*grunting and straining*) that I'm holding?

SEAGOON: Er, let me see . . .

ECCLES: Hurry up – I can't hold it up all day! *Come on!* Look at the shape.

    FX Creaking noises as of something about to give way.

SEAGOON: Yes. I've seen one like it. Er – no, I'm not quite sure. I give up. What is it?

ECCLES: It's an elephant.

    FX Eccles drops elephant.

SEAGOON: Ah, of course – he was the big one.

BLUEBOTTLE: *Thinks. You big fat steaming nit you.*
SEAGOON: *Thinks. Take that.*
F.X. WALLOP.

As with *Monty Python* later, so much of the humour depends on an exaggerated or inappropriate use of a conventional expression, such as the melodramatic *Little does he know*:

ECCLES: Ohh. I didn't know he had a big one.

BROLLICKS: Now, Seagoon, just one more small thing. Private Bluebottle.

BLUEBOTTLE: Sir! I heard you call, sir Captain, I heard you. Hello, everybody and sir. Like a jelly baby?

BROLLICKS: No thank you, baby.

SEAGOON: I understand you have a secret weapon for me.

BLUEBOTTLE: I have it, I have. Unscrews false kneecap, takes out secret gun. Am in agony, as I have not got false kneecap. Puts on bold face. It still hurts, though.

SEAGOON: Oh what is it?

BLUEBOTTLE: It is my backshot pistol.

SEAGOON: You mean, whoever fires the pistol gets killed himself?

BLUEBOTTLE: Yes. You just give it to the enemy, he aims at you, and then – bang! – he gets deaded himself! He he he!

SEAGOON: How does it work?

BLUEBOTTLE: I'll show you. I just point the gun at you, then I pull the trigger and – ah hah! no! *You* point it at *me*, and *you* pull the trigger.

SEAGOON: So. I point it at you like this.

BLUEBOTTLE: No! Don't point it at *me*, point it at *yourself* – I think –

SEAGOON: But you said –

FX Gunshot.

BLUEBOTTLE (*screams*): You rotten swine you – right in my hat, look at the hole! People can see in now and laugh at my school hair cut!

SEAGOON: . . . *I must think quick. Little does he know I suspect him of foul play.*

MORIARTY: *Little does he know I've never played with a fowl in my life.*

SEAGOON: *Little does he know that he has misconstrued the meaning of the word foul. The word foul in my sentence was spelt F-O-U-L not F-O-W-L as he thought I had spelt it.*

MORIARTY: *Little does he know that I overheard his correction of my grammatical error and I am now about to rectify it – aloud. (Ahem)*

So, you suspect me of foul play spelt F-O-U-L and not F-O-W-L.
SEAGOON: *Yes.*

And, as also with *Python* humour, the team is prepared to play with the very conventions of language play. A really awful pun might be followed by an explosion or a badly played orchestral chord:

SEAGOON: *Eccles! Stop that! Where did you get that saw?*
ECCLES (big joke): *From the sea – it's a sea-saw.*

And an expected response might be disregarded:

GRIPTYPE-THYNE: *I thought I saw a Greek urn buried in the sand.*
MORIARTY: *What's a Greek earn?*
GRIPTYPE-THYNE: *It's a vase made by Greeks for carrying liquids.*
MORIARTY: *I didn't expect that answer.*
GRIPTYPE-THYNE: *Neither did quite a few smart alec listeners.*

One test of the professional comedians' successful use of language play is to see the way in which their coinages turn up in other ludic contexts, such as newspapers and advertisements. Liverpool comic Ken Dodd, having created a world in Knotty Ash (a suburb of the city) peopled by 'Diddymen', thereby offers sub-editors extra scope for language play when writing a story about him or where he's from. 'He's a Diddy genius,' said a rave review of one of his one-man shows, using the phonetic pattern of *bloody* to coin a new intensifier. It is unintelligible to all except the Doddy-aware, and most of those must be in Britain. The stand-up comedians' language play rarely survives the crossing of national boundaries.

THE COLLECTORS

And now for something completely different. Language play, by its nature, is occasional and idiosyncratic. If we all played with language all the time, it would become the norm and cease to be noticed. The domain is therefore ideal for the attentions of the professional collector – the enthusiast who amasses examples of a particular feature and then publishes them. Nigel Rees is a leader in this field, known especially for his books collecting examples of graffiti.[6] By its nature, graffiti inhabits a rule-breaking, anarchic world, and we would expect to find in it many kinds of language play, alongside the political, lavatorial, absurdist and other forms of situational comment which the genre invites. Here are some examples:

Don't cut hire education
Emmanuel Kant but Genghis Khan
T S Eliot is an anagram of toilets
There was no way. Zen there was
There are Pharaohs at the bottom of our garden (written in Cairo)
I'm a fairy. My name is Nuff. Fairynuff.

Linguistic manipulations are especially noticeable over a period of time, as different writers bounce off each other's creations.

ORIGINAL: *Be alert. Your country needs lerts.*
LATER: *No, Britain has got enough lerts now. Be aloof.*
LATER STILL: *No really, be alert. There's safety in numbers.*

They are often reactions to already existing signs and notices:

ORIGINAL: *THINK!* (Wayside Pulpit)
ADDITION: *or thwim*

ORIGINAL: *Avenue Road*
ADDITION: *What's wrong with the old one, then?*

ORIGINAL: *To do is to be – Rousseau*
LATER: *To be is to do – Sartre*
LATER STILL: *Dobedobedo – Sinatra*

We would also expect to find the same kind of culture-dependence as we have seen in newspaper headlines and advertisements. To

16 RULES RULE, OK

The origins of this simple pattern are obscure. Known since the 1960s, it may have begun as a soccer fans' boast or as a political statement (e.g. *Arsenal Rules*), with *OK* sometimes following a comma, and thereby acting as an assertive tag (= 'I'm telling you'), and sometimes preceded by no comma, yielding an adverbial sense (= 'rules very well'). Whatever the origins, the formula has become one of the most productive sources of graffiti, and a perfect illustration of the ludic intuitions which are the subject of this book. Although the original formula is still used in a non-ludic form – a football fan writing simply 'MY TEAM rules OK', for example – true graffiti artists would nowadays consider such emanations to be distinctly amateur. The following selection of examples relies heavily on the compilations of Nigel Rees, whose first book on this topic carried the appropriate title, *Graffiti Lives OK* (1979). Some are linguistically quite straightforward, relying on a simple change of spelling or pronunciation; others are much more complex, playing with the meaning of words and idioms, and often reflecting a sophisticated level of linguistic, technical, or cultural awareness.

Slide rules, OK
Saliva drools, OK
Einstein rules relatively, OK
Heisenberg probably rules, OK
Procrastination will rule one day, OK?
Cowardice rules – if that's OK with you
Schizophrenia rules, OK, OK
Sceptics may or may not rule, OK
James Bond rules, OOK
Anarchy, no rules, OK?
Pessimists rule – not OK
Rooner spules OK
Gershwin rules – oh Kay

OK sauce rules – HP?

Shaking it all about rules – Hokay Cokay

Absolute zero rules O^0K^0

The law of the excluded middle either rules or does not rule OK

Examples rule, e.g.

Bureaucracy rules – OK? OK? OK?

Persuasion rules OK – just this once!

Sausage rolls, OK

Royce Rolls, KO

Town criers rule, okez, okez, okez

French dockers rule au quai

French diplomats rule au Quai

Spanish punks rule, olé

Archimedes rules, Eurekay!

Synonyms govern, all right

Roget's Thesaurus dominates, regulates, rules, OK, all right, adequately

Pedants rule, OK – or, more accurately, exhibit certain of the trappings of traditional leadership

Jargon rules, ongoing agreement situation

Mallet rules croquet

Flower power rules, bouquet

Scots rule, och aye

The King of Siam rules Bangk, OK

Anagrams – or luke?

Rogers and Hammerstein rule, Oklahoma

Dyslexia lures, KO

Queen Elizabeth rules UK

Queensbury Rules, KO

Amnesia rules, O . . .

Lethargy rulezzzzzzzz

Apathy ru

understand these, you need to know your literature (the first three), your philosophy (the next two) or your UK television commercials for building societies (the last two):

Oedipus was a nervous rex
Tolkien is Hobbit-forming
Back in a minute – Godot
Coito ergo sum
I'm pink therefore I'm spam
Get the Abbey habit – go to bed with a monk
Jesus saves – with the Woolwich.

And of course, other subgenres of language play are a fair target.

Beanz Meanz Fartz (cf. p. 97)
Hook Norton Ale reaches the parts Heineken daren't mention (cf. p. 99).

Apart from graffiti, there are dozens of language play topics which have resulted in book-length collections. Here is a small selection:[7]
o 'Wellerisms' are named after the kind of expression used by Sam Weller and his father, in Dickens's *The Pickwick Papers*. A wellerism consists of a statement (often proverbial in character), an identified speaker and a situation, which adds a humorous twist, usually in the form of a pun. Children have played with them probably for centuries, usually crudely constructed contradictions such as 'I see, said the blind man to his deaf daughter.' Adults employ more sophisticated crudity, turning innocent utterance into something risqué by the simple addition of 'as the actress said to the bishop', or some such phrase. Wolfgang Mieder and Stewart Kingsbury have edited a 150-page collection of them (1994), including these specimens:

'We are not what we seam,' as the sewing machine said to the needle.
'I'm labouring under a false impression,' as the die said to the counter-
    feiter.
'That's the spirit,' cried the medium, as the table began to rise.
'Eaves dropping again,' said Adam, as his wife fell out of a tree.

o 'Unusual names' is the chief topic in John Train's *Remarkabilia* (1984). This is a surreal, Happy-Families-type world: there really is (or, at least, there was at the time) an undertaker called Mr Bones in Glasgow, a venereal disease counsellor called Mr Clapp in California, a pathologist called Dr Deadman in Ontario, a singing teacher called Mrs Screech in British Columbia and a dentist called Dr Fang in Massachusetts. There is a Father O'Pray working in a church in New York City. This is where we learn of the existence of a tax collector in Brazil called Cardiac Arrest Da Silva, a lady called Constant Agony in New York and of a man called Iccolo Miccolo who played (I kid you not) the piccolo with the San Francisco Symphony Orchestra. And we learn of people with such first names as Tarantula, Urine, Fartina, Vaseline and Earless.

o In *Bizarre Books* (1985), Russell Ash and Brian Lake have collected an extraordinary number of strange titles, authors' names and publishing eccentricities. In many cases, the humour relies on a *double entendre*: thus we encounter *How to Enjoy Intercourse With Your Unfriendly Car Mechanic* (1977), *Memorable Balls* (1954), and *Joyful Lays* (1886). In others, it is the author's name which is the butt, such as those which suit their subjects: *A Treatise on Madness*, by William Battie (1758), *Criminal Life* by Superintendent James Bent (1891), and *The Encyclopaedia of Association Football* by Maurice Golesworthy (1967). But most of the sections are simply lists of obscure or unlikely book titles, such as *Cooking With God* (1978), *I Was a Kamikaze* (1973) and *Life and Laughter 'midst the Cannibals* (1926).

These last two cases fall into the category of inadvertent humour, which is a fruitful domain of language play. It is probably best illustrated from the collections of misprints which people have found in publications, especially the press. One of the earliest British compilations was Fritz Spiegel's *What the Papers Didn't Mean to Say* (1965); in the USA, there was Earle Tempel's *Press Boners (1968)* and Kermit Schafer's series of 'blooper' books derived from human errors made on radio, on television and in the press.[8] Some are simple but unfortunate typesetting errors, such as the wrong letter or an omitted word; others are ambiguities, double entendres, or just plain stupidities which weren't spotted by the editors. *FLIES TO HAVE TWINS IN IRELAND*? Even the headlines aren't safe.

In Chicago five men were accused of bride taking. (Chicago News)

To the ringing cry of 'Hi-yo Silver!' the Lone Banger rides again. (TV Guide)

About one third of all passengers flying between London and Paris travel by air. (Cleveland Plain Dealer)

The higher register found the sopranos still pure and unsqueezed (Daily Telegraph)

Not thrice but three times has lightning struck the barn on the Henry Summer farm. (Santa Cruz News)

WOMEN LAY OBSERVERS AT COUNCIL (The Times)

It is easy to point the finger, to condemn such things as 'sloppy practice'; and there is nothing more sobering than the discovery that there is just such a rich vein of linguistic humour awaiting discovery in your own work. In my case, the discovery came while editing an encyclopedia.

It happened like this. In 1986 I took on the job of editing the first edition of *The Cambridge Encyclopedia*. This was being planned as a single-volume general reference work, with its entries organized on an A-to-Z basis. There were over 30,000 entries in all and they came from a team of specialist contributors, each responsible for a topic area, such as music, space exploration and natural history. As the entries came in I would edit them, then pass them over to a group of inputters, who would add them to our computer database. Every so often I would read a print-out of the newly typed entries to check that all was well. It didn't take long to see that all was not as well as it should have been. The material was being input at speed and there were a fairly large number of typographic errors. The inputters had checked the entries on screen, of course, but – as everyone who writes with a computer knows – you can read through a piece of text on a VDU, find it perfect, print it out and only then see the typos. So it was in this case.

This routine exercise became a source of language play when it transpired that the typos weren't random. There was the occasional *teh* and *langauge*, of course, but the majority proved to be of the kind that no spelling checker would ever pick up – the typo resulting in a different and often plausible English word, as when *best* comes out as *bet*. It was as if there was some mischievous gremlin inside the inputters – or perhaps even inside the computer (as we shall see) – which forced their fingers to opt for a perverse reading. But, whatever the reason, the result was at times so delightful that I started to keep a note of them – and before I knew it, I had become a collector. Ten years on, and I can testify that there is nothing which can liven up a lecture on encyclopedia construction more than to include some examples of the typos which were caught (fortunately) before the books went to press. Moreover, once the members of an audience realize what is going on, they prove very ready to join in – providing examples of imaginary typographical errors in imaginary encyclopedias, and generating a game in which the aim is to create a bizarre element within an otherwise sober, factual encyclopedia style. As so often happens, a chance phenomenon is seized upon, and used as an excuse for language play. It is the publishing equivalent, I suppose, of the cinematic out-takes which have fuelled such TV programmes as Denis Norden's *It'll be All right on the Night*.

It only takes a single letter to go wrong for interesting things to start happening.

o Sometimes one letter replaced another, with potentially disastrous results:

Beethoven was handicapped by deadness.
The country obtains most of its income from oik refining.
The dominant theory of the origins of the universe, known as the Bog Bang . . .
From 1800, until his retirement through ill-health in 1928 . . .

It was the making of substitutions of this kind, involving adjacent keys on the keyboard, which nearly introduced the world to the

Brutish Broadcasting Corporation and also to the great actor (and, presumably, screenplay writer), *Robert de Biro*.

However, there was no such easy explanation for substitutions when the keys are well away from each other:

Carthage was refounded by Julie Caesar.
Tubular balls are commonly found in the percussion section.
Indo-European languages must have been spoken 3000 years BT.

(It's always been good to talk.)[9] And I remain intrigued about the nature of the unconscious processes which led our inputters to invent the *Puking Opera*, the *Society of Fronds* and *telebonking*, let alone the well-known children's author, *Lewis Carrott* (a relative of Jasper?).

Sometimes, it was a letter omitted which introduced us to a Great New Truth:

God was discovered in California in 1848.
Through his wok, the Cavendish became a major research institution.
Such works of art were intended to appal in their own right.
The machine also contains a vice synthesizer.
A famous teacher, he provided the basis of a new approach through his
 systematic codification and groping . . .

And in such ways, the world was nearly informed about the *Index of Prohibited Boos*, the grammatical fact that there are *proper and common types of nuns* and the new olfactory means of linking Britain and France, the *Chanel Tunnel*.

A habitual letter omission could even produce a theme. One inputter had particular problems with the word *West*, with the result that it seemed to be raining everywhere:

the Wet Bank of Israel; the Wet End of London; Wet Sussex
the demise of Wet Germany; Wet Virginia; Wet Glamorgan
the Economic Community of Wet African States.

Another was unable to type *public* without omitting the *l*, thus presenting us with fresh fantasies over the social roles of the *Pubic Record Office*, the *Director of Pubic Prosecutions* and the *pubic sector borrowing requirement*.

o Sometimes the fantasy was caused through the addition of a letter. One wonders, for example, what might have been going on within these institutions:

... formed a new political party, the Social Demoncrats
... the Imperial Wart Museum.

And how was it that *The Cambridge Encyclopedia* knew, in a certain country, that *there will be fresh elections in the year 1995*?

Phonetic factors accounted for some of the extra letters. A sensitivity to regional accents surely explained the spellings of *Oirish Republic* and the Scottish town of *Perrrth*. And how else to explain the

AFRICAN LION
(*Panthera leo*)
THE LION IS AFRICA'S LARGEST MAT-EATER.

Bettle of Spion Kop, if not by its apparently South African pronunciation? Nor were social accents ignored: witness *art gellery*. And a desire to be phonetically accurate must have motivated *stutttering* and the fact that *Pergolesi wrote muuuch church music.*

o Sometimes, the transposition of letters produced special results:

. . . at this place of pilgrimage, where there is a statue of a scared bull.

Likewise, the Vatican was also, temporarily, *a scared city.* The South Pacific was evidently explored by *Catpain Cook.* And there were many things we might have learned about *the beauty of Carolingian rat.*

o But it was not only the individual letter which could produce an effect. On several occasions, the omission of a word, or of a major part of a word, completely changed the sense. There was a well-known physicist whose role in the laboratory was forever altered through the inadvertent omission of the word *research*:

He then moved to Cambridge, where he carried on in physics.

Similarly, all kinds of innocent individuals could have their characters fundamentally changed (I give the omitted portion in parentheses):

She is now a successful broad. (-caster)
A gribble is a small, boring crustacean. (wood-)
A kea is a large, dull parrot. (-coloured)

Finally, we need to note the cases where the computer itself took over, introducing glitches into the production process which, if we were in the right frame of mind, we would humbly accept as opportunities for Great Insight. For instance, the computer would occasionally print out the beginning of one entry and the end of the next, omitting everything in between. It happened with the entry on *Nigel Lawson*, who was UK Chancellor of the Exchequer at the time. His entry began well enough, but inexplicably jumped to the final sentences of the following entry, on *laxative*, so that the account of this respected figure concluded:

a drug which causes emptying of the bowels. Except when medically recommended, does more harm than good.

THE COMIC WRITERS

And now for something completely different: comic writers whose reputation rests entirely on the way they handle the written language. We have already seen some examples of written language play in Chapter 2, where there were extracts from humorous dialect books, comic alphabets and deviantly spelled poems. But these items were occasional in character. Are there cases where somebody's identity as an author is *totally* dependent on their abilities in language play?

The late nineteenth century in the USA provided two fine examples, in the form of Josh Billings (real name, Henry Wheeler Shaw) and Artemus Ward (real name, Charles Farrar Browne). These writers were in the forefront of a comic-spelling genre which swept the nation, providing an appealing mix of homespun wit and down-to-earth sentiments, expressed in a style which seemed to reflect the sounds and rhythms of local, rural speech. The use of nonstandard spelling and grammar was the key to its success. Translate the language into Standard English, and most of the effect of the rustic philosophizing is lost. Here are some of Billings' proverbs:

When yu korte a widder, yu want tu du it with spurs on.
Man was kreated a little lower than the angells and has bin gittin a little lower ever sinse.
When a feller gits a goin down hil, it dus seem as tho evry thing had bin greased for the okashun.
He who skorns to be inflooensed at tall by fashun is a wize fool.
When a man dies the fust thing we talk about iz hiz welth, the nex thing hiz failings, and the last thing hiz vartues.

17 ESSA ON THE MUEL

The mule is haf hoss, and haf Jackass, and then kums tu a full stop, natur diskovering her mistake. Tha weigh more, akordin tu their heft, than enny other kreetur, except a crowbar. Tha kant hear enny quicker, nor further than the hoss, yet their ears are big enuff for snow shoes. You kan trust them with enny one whose life aint worth enny more than the mules. The only wa tu keep them into a paster, is tu turn them into a medder jineing, and let them jump out. Tha are reddy for use, just as soon as they will du tu abuse. Tha haint got enny friends, and will live on huckel berry brush, with an ocksional chanse at Kanada thissels. Tha are a modern invenshun, i dont think the Bible deludes tu them at tall. Tha sel for more money than enny other domestik animile. Yu kant tell their age by looking into their mouth, enny more than you kould a Mexican cannons. Tha never hav no dissease that a good club wont heal. If tha ever die tha must kum rite tu life agin, for i never herd nobody sa 'ded mule.' Tha are like sum men, very korrupt at harte; ive known them tu be good mules for 6 months, just tu git a good chanse to kick sumbody. I never owned one, nor never mean to, unless there is a United Staits law passed, requiring it. The only reason why tha are pashunt, is bekause tha are ashamed ov themselfs. I have seen eddikated mules in a sirkus. Tha kould kick, and bite, tremenjis. I would not sa what I am forced tu sa again the mule, if his birth want an outrage, and man want tu blame for it. Enny man who is willing tu drive a mule, ought to be exempt by law from running for the legislatur. Tha are the strongest creeturs on earth, and heaviest, ackording tu their sise; I herd tell ov one who fell oph from the tow path, on the Eri kanawl, and sunk as soon as he touched bottom, but he kept rite on towing the boat tu the nex stashun, breathing thru his ears, which stuck out ov the water about 2 feet 6 inches; i did'nt see this did, but an auctioneer told me ov it, and i never knew an auctioneer tu lie unless it was absolutely convenient.

The essay which made Josh Billings's name

*Don't let us forget that the higher up we git the smaller will things look
   tew us here belo.*[10]

And here is an extract from one of Artemus Ward's stories. The character is the manager of an itinerant sideshow who has just made a
troublesome visit to the southern states, where some of his belongings
had been confiscated:

*I had a narrer scape from the sonny South. 'The swings and arrers of
outrajus fortin,' alluded to by Hamlick, warn't nothin in comparison to
my trubles. I come pesky near swearin sum profane oaths more'n onct,
but I hope I didn't do it, for I've promist she whose name shall be nameless
(except that her initials is Betsy J.) that I'll jine the Meetin House at
Baldinsville, jest as soon as I can scrape money enuff together so I can 'ford
to be piuss in good stile, like my welthy nabers. But if I'm confisticated agin
I'm fraid I shall continner on in my present benited state for sum time.*

Just as famous in Britain was Edmund Clerihew Bentley, born in
1875, chief leader-writer on the *Daily Telegraph* for over twenty
years, novelist (beginning with *Trent's Last Case*, 1912), and inventor
of a ludic verse form which was eventually named after him, the
clerihew. He began to write them when he was sixteen, as a relaxa-
tion from school work, first publishing them in 1905 under the
pseudonym of his mother's maiden name, E. Clerihew. Each
item consists of four lines, organized as two rhyming couplets, but
without any particular metrical rhythm. Clerihews are always
pseudo-biographical, always absurd or zany, often anachronistic.
They typically begin with a name which is hard to rhyme, introducing it at the end of the first line, and conclude by using another
unexpected rhyme to make a succinct and punchy point. It only
takes one example to see what is happening, but here are six of (to
my mind) Clerihew's best:

> *Lewis Carroll*
> *Bought sumptuous apparel*
> *And built an enormous palace*
> *Out of the profits of Alice.*

> *The people of Spain think Cervantes*
> *Equal to half-a-dozen Dantes:*
> *An opinion resented most bitterly*
> *By the people of Italy.*

> *Dante Alighieri*
> *Seldom troubled a dairy.*
> *He wrote the Inferno*
> *On a bottle of Pernod.*

> *Edward the Confessor*
> *Slept under the dresser.*
> *When that began to pall,*
> *He slept in the hall.*

> *It is curious that Handel*
> *Should always have used a candle.*
> *Men of his stamp*
> *Generally use a lamp.*

> *Henry the Eighth*
> *Took a thuctheththion of mateth.*
> *He inthithted that the monkth*
> *Were a lathy lot of thkunkth.*[11]

Comic writers these days tend not to put all their eggs into a single linguistic basket. The versatility is all. But it isn't difficult to find authors who devote a considerable proportion of their comic oeuvre to language play. Here are two modern examples.

o Alan Coren regularly explores the possibilities of language play in his writing and pieces for radio. In one of his *Punch* pieces (21 August 1985), he is struck by an article he read in the *Daily Telegraph* that volunteers who fear they may be losing their memory are being sought by a Manchester University professor for research into absent-mindedness. He decides to write to the professor:

I do hope you will forgive my writing to you out of the, without prior, out of the, we have not met, but I saw the item in the Daily, blue, out of the blue, but I saw your item in the Sunday, in the, I heard the item on the car, unless it was News at, um, you see a picture of Old Ben, the big hand is on the, on the, or to put it another way, the little hand is, the little hand is, anyhow you hear the pips, the chimes, and they go one, two, three, God Almighty, do you know, Geoff, I have been watching that programme for he past, for the past, since we lived in, since we lived at number, since we, large block of flats, next to the, small block of flats, next to the Tube at, at, there was a Sainsbury's across the, there was a Sainsbury's on the corner.
Or a Tesco.
My wife will remember. She's out in the, she's up on the . . .

o Miles Kington is known for his forays into the world of *Franglais* – a subgenre of language play par excellence. Here is his complete translation of *20,000 Leagues Under the Sea*, par Jules Verne, which he describes as 'un rip-roaring, rollicking yarn de underwater football!':

C'était Cup Final jour, dans le Premier Underwater League.
'Heads ou tails?' dit le referee.
'Heads,' dit Captain Nemo.
'Heads it is,' dit le referee. 'Choisissez.'
'Nous jouons droit à gauche, avec l'incoming tide,' dit Captain Nemo.
Actually, ce qu'il dit était un peu comme ceci:
'Noodle joodle droidle a gaudle, addle l'incuddle tidle.'
Underwater speaking, c'est difficile.
Underwater football, c'est même difficile.
Et c'est pour cette raison, je crois, que la game était une total failure.[12]

Ludic language mixing of this kind shouldn't be confused with the real code-switching which is to be encountered in many parts of the world, as people cope with the realities of languages in contact. The kind of code-mixing which is heard in parts of south-eastern USA, for example, based on Spanish and English, is often called Spanglish (also Tex-Mex and other names); it tends to be dismissed as 'sloppy', but linguistic analysis has shown it to be a complex and systematic phenomenon, in which speakers use the two languages to express a wide range of meanings, attitudes and social relationships. Similarly, you could encounter a genuine Franglais in a part of the world where French and English were routinely in contact, such as parts of Africa. Kington's Franglais cleverly alludes to some of the linguistic features of real code-mixing, but actually inhabits a quite different world.

The same point applies to those comic authors who parody non-standard English grammar and vocabulary, whether produced by native speakers or by foreign learners.

o The former category can be illustrated by the variety of nonstandard London speech used by Keith Waterhouse in his saga of the Laggard Bros, in a series for *Punch* in 1996. This firm will fix anything in your home, bearing in mind that the customer is always wrong. The Laggard brothers especially disapprove if customers have tried to do some building work themselves, as this extract from 'The Log of the Laggard Bros', Part 3 (23 November 1996), indicates:

Some punters, though, they would not take the hint, bigheads that they are. Bloke coupla weeks ago, simple grouting job it says on the worksheet. I thought to myself, Half an hour at most, Derek, so what I will do, I will get Eric to drive us round in the van, then he can wait while I knock off the job, after which we will have it away on our wheels to the big loft conversion what we should of started last week, only something cropped up, didn't it?

o Collections of nonstandard utterances made by foreign learners of a language have been around a long time. A particularly famous instance is the nineteenth-century Portuguese–English phrase-book, *O Novo Guia da Conversação*, parts of which have been reprinted at various times under such titles as *English as She is Spoke*. It was originally a Portuguese–French book, published in 1853 by José da Fonseca. Pedro Carolino then arranged for the French sections to be translated into English, and the book eventually appeared under his name in 1869. To capture the flavour of the book, here are a few of the translated proverbs and an extract from one of the dialogues:

A necessidade não tem lei.	*The necessity don't know the low.*
As paredes teem ouvidos.	*The walls have hearsay.*
Está como o peixe n'agua.	*He is like the fish into the water.*
Pedra movediça nunca mofo a cubiça.	*The stone as roll not heap up not foam.*

Para fazer uma visita de manha.	For to make a visit in the morning.
Têu âmo está êm cása?	*Is your master at home?*
Sím, senhôr.	*Yes, sir.*
Já sê levantôu?	*Is it up?*
Não, senhôr, índa dórme.	*No sir, he sleep yet.*
Vôu acordál-o, ê fazêl-o erguêr.	*I go make that he get up.*

133

Pósso entrár? Quê é isso!   *It come in one's? How is it, you are*
  aínda nâ câma?   *in bed yet?*
Hôntem á nôite deitêi-me tão tárde, *Yesterday at evening, I was to bed*
  quê não púde levantár-me   *so late that I may not rising*
  cêdo ésta manhã.   *soon that morning.*[13]

Magazines and newspapers regularly reproduce examples of 'fractured English' brought back by tourists from abroad. Doubtless similar examples can be found in any language where the need to communicate with foreigners results in amateur and inadequate translations; but English, being so widely used around the globe as a foreign language, has proved to be a major source of comic examples. Some are very likely mythical. Vintage examples such as 'The water in this hotel has been personally passed by the manager' may have once existed; or they may have been the creations of a group of inebriated tourists. But it is not difficult to find genuine examples on any trip abroad:

Photographer executed.
Specialist for the Decease of Children.
The wines shall leave you nothing to hope for.

There are even some distinguished literary precedents for fractured English. The conversation between Alice and Katherine in Shakespeare's *Henry V* (III.iv) must be one of the most famous – 'De nails, de arma, de ilbow . . .' – with the wooing scene between Catherine and Henry (V.ii) including examples of Henry's fractured French as well as Catherine's 'broken English':

HENRY: . . . *Come, your answer in broken music – for thy voice is music and thy English broken. Therefore, queen of all, Catherine, break thy mind to me in broken English: wilt thou have me?*
CATHERINE: *Dat is as it shall please de roi mon père.*

Leo Rosten's Hyman Kaplan gets into innumerable linguistic scrapes during his language classes in New York City, as this extract from 'Christopher K*A*P*L*A*N' illustrates:

'. . . Class, let's not guess. What date is tomorrow?'

'Mine boitday!' an excited voice rang out.

Mr Parkhill ignored that. 'Tomorrow,' he said firmly, 'is October twelfth. And on October twelfth, 1492 –' He got no further.

'Dat's mine boitday! October tvalf! I should live so! Honist!' It was (but why, oh why, did it have to be?) the proud, enraptured voice of Hyman Kaplan.

Mr Parkhill took a deep breath, a slow, deep breath, and said cautiously, 'Mr Kaplan, is October twelfth – er – really your birthday?'

Mr Kaplan's eyes widened – innocent, hurt. 'Mister Pockheel!'

Mr Parkhill felt ashamed of himself.

Stanislaus Wilkomirski growled, 'Kaplan too old for have birtday.'

'October tvalf I'm born; October tvalf I'm tsalebratink!' Mr Kaplan retorted. 'All mine life I'm hevink boitdays October tvalf. No axcep-tions!'[14]

Much of the humour in Malcolm Bradbury's *Rates of Exchange* (1983) lies in the fractured English used by the inhabitants of the fictitious country of Slaka. His hero, Dr Petworth, on a British Council tour, arrives at his first hotel accompanied by his guide:

There is a girl behind the desk in blue uniform, with dark red hair, spread fanlike from her head in lacquered splendour; she looks at them without interest. 'Hallo, dolling,' says Lubijova, 'Here is Professor Petwurt, reservation of the Min'stratii Kulturi, confirmation here.' 'So, Petvurt?' the girl says, taking a pen from her hair and running it lan-guidly down the columns of a large book, 'Da, Pervert, so, here is. Pasipotti.' 'She likes your passport, don't give it to her,' says Lubijova. 'Give it to me. I know these people well, they are such bureaucrats. Now, dolling, tell me, how long do you keep?' 'Tomorrow,' says the girl, 'it registers with the police.' 'No, dolling, this is much too long,' says Lubijova. 'I do not love you. You can arrange, do it for me tonight. Tomorrow he goes to the Min'stratii Kulturi, and they don't let him in without it.' 'Perhaps,' says the girl, 'I try.' 'Comrade Petwurt, remember, come back in three hour and ask it from her,' says Lubijova. 'Remember, here if you do not have passport, you do not exist. And I expect you like to exist, don't you? It is nicer.' 'Here, Pervert,' says the lacquered-haired girl, pushing a form across the desk, 'I need some informations . . .'

And when Petworth arrives at one of his hotels, he encounters a card on the dressing table which reads: 'Please tickle one: [ ] I like very much my stay; [ ] It is all right; [ ] I disappoint.'[15]

But even Slaka doesn't reach the linguistic depths of the deformed Salvatore, in Umberto Eco's *The Name of the Rose*, who is described as speaking 'all languages, and no language'. This is how he greets the visitors to the monastery, when they encounter him for the first time:

Penitenziagite! Watch out for the draco who cometh in futurum to gnaw your anima! Death is super nos! Pray the Santo Pater come to liberar nos a malo and all our sin! Ha, ha, you like this negromanzia de Domini Nostri Jesu Christi! Et anco jois m'es dols e plazer m'es dolors . . . Cave el diabolo! Semper lying in wait for me in some angulum to snap at my heels. But Salvatore is not stupidus! Bonum monasterium, and aquí refectorium and pray to dominum nostrum. And the resto is not worth merda. Amen. No?[16]

It was left to *Monty Python* to take the genre to absurdist extremes, inventing a publisher who has deliberately introduced wrong translations into an edition of a phrase book (though the man actually pleads incompetence when later brought before a Pythonesque court). In the sketch, a Hungarian tourist approaches the clerk in a tobacconist's; the tourist is reading haltingly from a phrase book:

HUNGARIAN: *I will not buy this record, it is scratched.*
CLERK: *Sorry?*
HUNGARIAN: *I will not buy this record, it is scratched.*
CLERK: *Uh, no, no, no. This is a tobacconist's.*
HUNGARIAN: *Ah! I will not buy this* tobacconist's, *it is scratched.*
CLERK: *No, no, no, no. Tobacco . . . um . . . cigarettes.* (He holds up a pack.)
HUNGARIAN: *Ya! See-gar-ets! Ya! Uh . . . My hovercraft is full of eels.*
CLERK: *Sorry?*

HUNGARIAN: *My hovercraft* (mimes puffing a cigarette) . . . *is full of eels.* (He pretends to strike a match.)

CLERK: *Ah, matches!*

HUNGARIAN: *Ya! Ya! Ya! Ya! Do you waaant . . . do you waaant . . . to come back to my place, bouncy bouncy?*

CLERK: *I don't think you're using that thing right.*

HUNGARIAN: *You great poof.*

CLERK: *That'll be six and six, please.*

HUNGARIAN: *If I said you had a beautiful body, would you hold it against me? I . . . I am no longer infected.*

CLERK: *Uh, may I, uh* (takes phrase book, flips through it) . . . *Costs six and six . . . ah, here we are.* (Speaks Hungarian words.)

Hungarian punches the clerk.

THE AUTHORS

Shakespeare, Rosten, Bradbury, Eco . . .? We have entered a different area of professionalism now: the world of the 'author' – poets, playwrights, novelists, essayists and others whose writing has been accepted as reaching a level of excellence that allows us to refer to them as 'literature'. This is hardly the place to engage in a discussion of the nature of literature and of literary language; but it is the place to make two relevant points. First, that a considerable proportion of the language used in literature is indeed ludic, in the sense of this book (some, indeed, might argue that all of literature, by definition, is ludic); and second, that there is no clear boundary between the way in which 'authors' play with language and the way everyone else does. Indeed, from time to time we even find examples where the link between these two worlds is prominent, with authors explicitly incorporating the language play from some non-literary domain into their writing. We have just been discussing fractured English. Robert Graves once wrote a parodic poem based entirely on this kind of English, using as a stimulus the language he encountered in a guide-book description of the caves of Arta, Mallorca ('. . . a suporizing infinity of graceful columns of 21 meter and by downward, which prives the spectator of all animacion and plunges in dumbness. The way going is very picturesque, serpentine between style mountains . . .'):

Such subtile filigranity and nobless of construccion
    Here fraternise in harmony, that respiracion stops.
While all admit thier impotence (though autors most formidable
    To sing in words the excellence of Nature's underprops,
Yet stalactite and stalagmite together with dumb language
    Make hymns to God wich celebrate the stregnth of water drops.

¿You, also, are you capable to make precise in idiom
    Consideracions magic of ilusions very wide?
Already in the Vestibule of these Grand Caves of Arta
    The spirit of the human verb is darked and stupefyed;
So humildy you trespass trough the forest of the colums
    And listen to the grandess explicated by the guide.

¡Too far do not adventure, sir! For, further as you wander,
    The every of the stalactites will make you stop and stay.
Grand peril amenaces now, your nostrils aprehending
    An odour least delicious of lamentable decay.
It is some poor touristers, in the depth of obscure cristal,
    Wich deceased of thier emocion on a past excursion day.

A thorough study of the ways in which professional authors manipulate the rules of the language to suit their purpose ('bend or break' them, as Graves once put it) would be a very large work indeed. Virtually the whole of poetry would be encompassed. As soon as we accept the facilitating constraint of a poetic structure, such as a line length, a rhyme-scheme, a verse pattern or a graphic design, we have begun to play with language. The 'bending and breaking' appears in the contrasts of rhythm and pause, of alliteration and rhyme, of word order and lexical choice, and in the many other effects which lie dormant in the storehouse of language. Anything can be bent or broken, for special effect, and it is usual for several things to be broken at once. In the non-literary world, this tends not to happen: most of the effects are the result of the breaking of a single rule – a particular point of pronunciation, spelling, or syntax, or a simple play on words. In the literary world, by contrast, we must be prepared to encounter multiple effects, where sounds, grammar and vocabulary collaborate to produce a level of linguistic expressiveness which ranges from playful and intriguing to moving and profound. Graves's 'Arta' poem manages to be both playful and moving at once.

Throughout this book I have drawn attention to such effects as rhyme, alliteration and wordplay in a wide range of non-literary settings, and the shortness of my extracts does these subgenres of language play no harm. There are no layers of meaning to be unravelled in ping-pong punning (Chapter 1). Works of literature, however, inevitably suffer from such selective quotation, especially those where the nature of the language play is cumulative or where a pattern of play is evident only over long stretches of text. What extract from James Joyce's *Finnegans Wake*, for example, could sensibly represent the ludic vastness of that work? Never have so many linguistic rules been so bent and broken at the same time – and, of course, the more

18 POETIC PLAY

The distinctive typographical and phonological properties of poetry make this genre stand out, as a domain of language play. Not that the genre can be easily defined by these properties, as generations of discussion on the differences between poetry and prose have shown. But it is certainly easier to illustrate language play at work in poetry, because of the way some authors go in for rule-breaking and bending with especial diligence – E. E. Cummings, for example, exploring the possibilities within typographical play, or many of the concrete poets. The example below is a personal effort, which I use in order to illustrate the use within a single work of more than one kind of language play, without fear of contradiction from the author.

From a ludic point of view, the poem operates on three levels. First, and most obviously, there is the manipulation of meaning conveyed by the line and verse divisions, the setting up of a four-line verse norm in the first half of the poem, and the departures from this norm at various points. At a second level, variations in typography and spacing highlight certain points in the narrative. At a third level, a number of playful allusions are made to other texts.

VOICES

Chester station
On a Saturday night
Waiting for a connection
A new sense of eternity.

London 165 miles, that way.
Holyhead 85 miles, that way.
And miles to go before I sleep
And miles to go before I sleep.

85 of them.

The distant roar of passing traffic
The dusty rattle of diesel trains
And then on to my platform
A deafening riot of Homo footballiens.

Li-ver-pool clap-clap-clap
Li-ver-pool clap-clap-clap
Leeds are shite, mate, aren't dey?
Yes, yes, Leeds are shite.

The Liverpool train pulled in
And its engine drowned the fans
(Oh, I wish)
And when it pulled out
They were only a distant rhythm
Above the clacking wheels.

Li-ver-pool clap-clap-clap
Clackety-clack clackety-clack
Li-ver-pool clap-clap-clap
Li-ver-pool clap-clap-clap

NO, LEEDS AREN'T SHITE!

The station quivered
Got over its huff
At having its silence interrupted
And settled down to being empty again.

Time passed.
I listened.
Time passed.

Then into the listening
Came the gentle sound of a flute.
An Irish lilt I'd heard before
But never knew the name.

I couldn't see who the player was
Or who he was, or why
He was playing such a haunting tune
On Chester station.

The melody echoed along the platform
Like wisps of musical mist
Rubbing its back along the window panes
And I shivered in the warm night
As into my mind tumbled
Fragments of past poems.

Then it stopped.
I waited for more, but none came.
And after some minutes I wondered
Did I really hear it?
Gone is that music.
Did I wake or sleep?

Keats
Was never at Chester station
On a Saturday night
Nor Robert Frost, and I suppose
Neither Thomas nor Eliot,
But that unknown fluting player
Brought me an unexpected
And welcome connection
With their sense of eternity.

THE PROFESSIONALS

this happens, the more difficult it is to reconstruct a coherent meaning. Take this passage from the *Wake*, where Earwicker is making his defence against the pub customers who are going to tear him apart:

Missaunderstaid. Meggy Guggy's giggag. The code's proof! The rebald danger withthey who would bare whitness against me I dismissem from the mind of the good. He can tell such as story to the Twelfth Maligns that my first was a nurssmaid and her fellower's a willbe perambulatrix. There are twingty to twangty too thews and leathermail coatschemes penparing to hostpost for it valinnteerily with my valued fofavour to the post puzzles deparkment with larch parchels' of presents for future branch offerings.

As Anthony Burgess remarked, in his insightful appreciation of Joyce's language, *Joysprick*: 'To attempt a close analysis of this, a typical passage, is to invite madness.'[17] We could indeed investigate the elements which produce the neologistic blends, and track the semantic associations which they convey, and a great deal of ongoing Joycean research does precisely that. For present purposes, though, it is simply the ludic nature of the language itself, rather than its meaning, which needs to be recognized. Burgess makes the same point: 'like music, this passage is finally to be accepted as what it is, not what it is about. And, of course, so is the whole book.' That could also be the epitaph for the entire world of ludic language.

A less aggressive kind of language play is present throughout the work of Dylan Thomas – at times sharp and satirical, at times comically nostalgic, at times lyrical and romantic. Lyrical playfulness is very much the tone of the opening scene of *Under Milk Wood*, for example, where a steady flow of metaphors is underpinned by a network of sound associations, chiefly involving the repeated use of /b/ and /s/, to produce a vivid and sonorous description of the sleeping town:

It is spring, moonless night in the small town, starless and bible-black, the cobblestreets silent and the hunched, courters'-and-rabbits' wood limping invisible down to the sloeblack, slow, black, crowblack, fishingboat-bobbing sea . . .

In his poetry, Thomas has long been recognized as someone who routinely breaks quite basic rules of grammar and semantics, in ways that have fuelled many a linguistic article and dissertation. Here is a fragment from 'Poem in October':

> *My birthday began with the water-*
> *Birds and the birds of the winged trees flying my name*
> *Above the farms and the white horses . . .*

It runs so smoothly, especially when read aloud in a flowing, declamatory style such as the one Thomas himself used, that we can easily miss the rule-breaking: the water-birds, split by a line-break; and the trees winged, rather than the birds. Thomas cannot resist playing with language. It pours out of him, even in his letters:

My dear John,

This pig in Italy bitterly knows – O the tears on his snub snout and the squelch in the trough as he buries his fat, Welsh head in shame, and guzzles and blows – that he should have written, three winevats gone, a porky letter to Moby D. two-ton John; but with a grunt in the pines, time trottered on! The spirit was willing; the ham was weak. The spirit was brandy; the ham was swilling. And oh the rasher-frying sun! . . .

My dear Margaret, . . .

Oh, oh, oh, the heat! It comes round corners at you like an animal with windmill arms. As I enter my bedroom, it stuns, thuds, throttles, spins me round by my soaking hair, lays me flat as a mat and bat-blind on my boiled and steaming bed. We keep oozing from the ice-cream counters to the chemist's. Cold beer is bottled God . . .

Nothing is clear. My brains are hanging out like the intestines of a rabbit, or hanging down my back like hair. My tongue, for all the ice-cold God I drink, is hot as a camel-saddle sandily mounted by baked Bedouins. My eyes like over-ripe tomatoes strain at the sweating glass of a Saharan hothouse. I am hot. I am too hot. I wear nothing, in this tiny hotel-room, but the limp two rivers of my Robins'-made pyjama trousers. Oh for the cyclonic Siberian frigidity of a Turkish bath![18]

Language play permeates poetry, and is often present in prose, as the above examples show – but in drama? Obviously, when plays are written in verse, they will display a comparable range of linguistic effects to those found in poetry, in addition to whatever linguistic consequences may follow from the creation of individual characters. But there is plenty of scope for language play in prose drama too – as illustrated by the Stoppard questions game already quoted (p. 74), or Lucky's 'thinking' monologue in Beckett's *Waiting for Godot*:

Given the existence as uttered forth in the public works of Puncher and Wattmann of a personal God quaquaquaqua with white beard quaquaquaqua outside time without extension who from the heights of divine apathia divine athambia divine aphasia loves us dearly with some exceptions for reasons unknown but time will tell and suffers like the divine Miranda with those who for reasons unknown but time will tell are plunged in torment plunged in fire whose fire flames if that continues and who can doubt it will fire the firmament that is to say blast hell to heaven so blue still and calm so calm with a calm which even though intermittent is better than nothing but not so fast and considering what is more that as a result of the labours left unfinished crowned by the Acacacacademy of Anthropopopometry of Essy-in-Possy of Testew and Cunard . . .[19]

Then there is this kind of example, from Pinter's *The Birthday Party*. Two strangers, Goldberg and McCann, have arrived at the boarding-house where Stanley Webber is staying, and have begun to interrogate him. By the end of the scene, the previously cocky and verbal Stanley is reduced to inarticulateness through their linguistic onslaught. Here, language play has a prominent role and a serious edge. Asking an unanswerable question is usually a joke; not so here, in the middle of the interrogation:

MCCANN: He's sweating.
GOLDBERG: Is the number 846 possible or necessary?
STANLEY: Neither.
GOLDBERG: Wrong! Is the number 846 possible or necessary?

STANLEY: *Both.*

GOLDBERG: *Wrong! It's necessary but not possible.*

STANLEY: *Both.*

GOLDBERG: *Wrong! Why do you think the number 846 is necessarily possible?*

STANLEY: *Must be.*

GOLDBERG: *Wrong!*

Or here, at the end:

GOLDBERG: *Speak up, Webber. Why did the chicken cross the road?*

STANLEY: *He wanted to – he wanted to – he wanted to –*

MCCANN: *He doesn't know!*

GOLDBERG: *Why did the chicken cross the road?*

STANLEY: *He wanted to – he wanted to . . .*

GOLDBERG: *Why did the chicken cross the road?*

STANLEY: *He wanted . . .*

MCCANN: *He doesn't know. He doesn't know which came first!*

GOLDBERG: *Which came first?*

MCCANN: *Chicken? Egg? Which came first?*

GOLDBERG and MCCANN: *Which came first? Which came first? Which came first?*

Stanley screams.[20]

Not all writers of prose play with language in such noticeable (albeit different) ways as do Joyce, Thomas and Beckett – dramatically altering word forms, breaking the usual associations between words, manipulating sound patterns and deviating from norms of spelling. Novelists and short-story writers on the whole bend rules, rather than break them – making a more natural use of words and sentence patterns, but probably using some of these patterns with a greater frequency and in less predictable contexts than would be the case in everyday conversation or domestic writing. The style of a novelist is something which emerges gradually, as we read; its effect is cumulative. Often, we read a paragraph without realizing there is any linguistic artifice in it at all. Our attention is wholly taken up by the story, the characters, the settings, the descriptions, the conversations and other matters of content; the language, like the typography, is virtually invisible. Joyce is very much the exception, in his major works: you cannot miss the linguistic artifice there. But pull down several novels from your shelves, turn to any page and try to 'spot the language play'. In most cases, it would take a stylistician to define it.

A typical example, chosen at random (almost – see the last sentence of this chapter) from my bookshelves, is Margaret Drabble's splendid final paragraph in *The Radiant Way* (1987):

At the top of the last steep, homeward ascent, they pause for breath, leaning on a gate. Below them lie the deep wood, the grove, the secret valley, the cottage, the wooden table, the cherry tree. Beyond are the hills, and beyond the hills, the sea. Where they stand it is still, but above their heads, high in the broad leaves of the trees, a high wind is passing. It shakes the leaves, the branches. The leaves glitter and dance. The spirit passes. The sun is dull with a red radiance. It sinks. Esther, Liz and Alix are silent with attention. The sun hangs in the sky, burning. The earth deepens to a more profound red. The sun bleeds, the earth bleeds. The sun stands still.[21]

Where is the language play here? It is there, all right. Ask the question: in what ways does this passage differ from the kind of unpremeditated language we would use in everyday conversation? You would note the use throughout of the 'commentary' present tense with the simple present tense (very unusual in everyday speech); the piling up of simple noun phrases without *and*; the use of short, simply structured clauses; the variation in rhythmical pace achieved by the judicious siting of very short sentences; and the controlled deceleration of narrative speed as the book 'winds down'. The vocabulary is, for the most part, everyday, but there are a couple of dramatic figures of speech towards the end. There is some mutual reinforcement of meaning through alliteration. And that is more or less it – though of course there might be further elements of language play here which are not noticeable from this paragraph alone – such as the use of a phrase or word which was of importance earlier in the novel.

These more subtle aspects of language play are not the focus of the present book. To engage with them would be to turn the book into an account of stylistics – the study of the properties of language which identify *any* situationally distinctive use of language, whether it be the language of law, of science, of religion or of individual authors. It is of course possible to extend the notion of language play in that direction – and even to go beyond it, adopting broader and broader conceptions of language play, but if we do this, we shall end up defining the whole of language as language play. From that point of view, as soon as we open our mouths to speak or pick up our pens, we are 'playing with language', engaging in a 'language game' for which we need to follow the rules. This would be a very different notion of language play from the one presented in this book. For me, it is the way we *break* the rules, and not the rules themselves, which is the focus. It is a much narrower conception of language play – perhaps of less interest to those, shall we say, of a French philosophical persuasion – but it is this conception which has been so badly neglected, in accounts of language, and the one which this book seeks to remedy.

THE ARTISTS

In the present context, 'artist' means anyone who introduces a playful linguistic element into a painting, drawing, design or sculpture. This definition thus includes a wide range of specializations, including graphic designers, typographers and concrete poets, as well as artists in the traditional sense. In the history of art, language play is one of the distinctive features of the twentieth century. The Cubists put letters and words into their paintings – such as Picasso's use of 'Le Journal' in several works, in whole or in part – and in due course the letters themselves became major elements of the composition, often using stencils, as in Fernand Léger's designs for Blaise Cendrars's *La Fin du Monde* (1919), one of the earliest to put letter forms and colour in a collage. Later, language play emerged as a major element in Pop Art, with advertisements, newspaper fragments, journal covers, product labels, dollar bills and other verbal paraphernalia incorporated

into a work. Insofar as these elements were being faithfully reproduced, as in some of Andy Warhol's paintings, with no linguistic rules
being broken, it is a debatable point whether we would want to
include them under the heading of language play (as in the literary
example discussed in the previous paragraph). But in many cases, the
language was certainly being manipulated, often to make a (not
always clear) point: to distort the typography of a Coca-Cola label or
a dollar bill was to offer a comment of some sort on America, or perhaps the materialistic world. A small selection of works illustrate a few
of the possibilities which artists have explored:[22]

o One of the most famous examples is Robert Indiana's *Love Rising*
(1968, Museum Moderner Kunst, Vienna). The source of this picture
is a design in which the four letters of the word LOVE, in capitals, are
displayed with the L and O above the V and E, with the O set at an
angle, leaning away from the L. In *Love Rising*, this becomes the lower
left quadrant of a four-quadrant picture. The lower-right quadrant
shows this image reversed; and the upper two quadrants show this
pair of images inverted. The picture became one of the favourites of
the hippie generation.

o In Joe Tilson's reliefs, pictorial elements are combined with the
typographic, including words like *Oh!* and *Vox*, to express the power
of the human voice and the nature of vocal reactions. For example, in
Vox Box (1968, Tate Gallery, London), exclamation marks in a mouth
become teeth.

o Roy Lichtenstein's comic-strip works make frequent use of ono-
matopoeic words in large cartoon lettering – such as BRATATATA-
TA for the sound of a machine-gun (*As I Opened Fire*, 1964, Stedelijk
Museum, Amsterdam). Other examples are *Whaam* (1963, Tate
Gallery, London) and *Takka Takka* (1962, Museum Ludwig,
Cologne).

o The 'neo-pop' artist, Kenny Scharf, presents a light-hearted array of
linguistic images in *Speak* (1988, Akira Ikeda Gallery, Tokyo). Words
and phrases in English or Italian, with an accompanying translation and
semi-phonetic transcription, are scattered across the painting, vying
for attention with strongly delineated outline heads and other shapes.

If language play is so pervasive in society, as I am arguing in this book, then we would expect it to become a legitimate subject, in its own right, of Pop Art – and so it is. A good example is Jim Eller's *Scrabble Board* (1962, collection of the artist), in which we see a Scrabble grid, empty apart from the letters RAT glued on in the centre. This is the lowest possible score, for such a word; and it is an anagram of ART. What is going on? The real discussion would need to begin now – but not in this book.

Typography as such is an obvious domain for language play. Although for most purposes textual typography needs to be 'invisible', so that it does not obscure the message, there are many occasions where the issue is one of identity (of a product, an organization, a newspaper . . .) rather than intelligibility, and here the choice of a particular typeface is critical, as are such factors as choice of colour and the layout of a page. Some products are chiefly identified by their typography, such as the distinctive red *K* of *Kellogg's* and the yellow *M* of *McDonald's*. And once a conventional association is established, it then proves possible to play with it – as when the *K* (in the Kellogg's cereal *Special K*) transforms itself in a television advertisement into the shape of a red-clad woman leaning back against a rock. There is no shortage of products, but there is no shortage of fonts either. Hundreds of amusing and ingenious typefaces have now been devised, in which the letters resemble faces, people, animals, objects, geometrical shapes, handwritten shapes and other phenomena: examples are Peter Warren's appropriately named 'Amoeba', Alessio Leonardi's 'Priska Serif Little Creatures', Tim Donaldson's 'FancyWriting', and John Critchley's 'Child's Play'. Experiments are always in progress. In some cases, typographers have even tried to see how far it is possible to obscure or distort letter shapes while still retaining graphic identity, as in Pierre di Sciullo's 'ScratchedOut Book', or 'YouCan ReadMe', which omits the lower parts of most letters.[23]

The use of typographic play to reinforce a message can be seen in the large capital letters which greet the visitor to *BRISBANE INTERNATIONAL AIRPORT* – where the letters are slanted forwards, conveying an appropriate suggestion of onward movement.

Other examples are the use of elegant, consistent lettering in a product called *Harmony*; the bold black lettering in a sign saying *Undertakers*; and the use of a 'Gothic', black-letter typeface to announce an evening of *Olde Tyme Dancing*. Here too, the fact that there are such standard associations between typography and context allows for endless opportunities of language play. To take the above examples, if we wanted to be jocular or ironic, we could set the Brisbane Airport sign with a backwards slant; *Harmony* could appear in a sequence of different typefaces; the undertaker sign could display a riot of bright colours; and the black-letter script could be used on a sign advertising *Modern Alarms*. The black-letter family of typefaces, because of its widely recognized 'olde-worlde' associations, is often used in this way. In a *Punch* cartoon I once saw (but cannot recall when), a monk bangs his thumb with a hammer, and out of his mouth rises elegant, black-letter curses. And in the following example of 'graphic poetry', the whole effect depends on recognizing the conventional meaning of the typographic contrast.[24]

Hagidiscography

Peter and **Paul**.

Simon and *Garfunkel*.

Matthew and **Mark**.

Peters and *Lee*.

Luke and **John**.

Captain and *Tenille*.

Cosmas and **Damian**.

George and *Ringo*.

Cyril and **Methodius**.

Nina and *Frederick*.

Elvis?

It is a short step from here to utilizing the properties of graphic language in order to add visual shape to a poem – as famously illustrated in George Herbert's 'The Altar', where the lines of text build up an altar-shape, Dylan Thomas's 'Vision and Prayer' sequence, in which poems are diamond- and X-shaped, or E. E. Cummings's 'The Grasshopper', which is shaped like a grasshopper. We are near the world of concrete poetry now, where graphic possibilities are exploited to the limit, and poems can be created in virtually any shape, figurative or otherwise. Any technology can be used: for example, the 1960s saw the emergence of the 'typewriter poets' – Bob Cobbing, Peter Finch, Sylvester Houedard, Meic Stephens and others, who created extraordinary effects through typed patterns of overlapping letters and space variation.[25] In an electronic age, animated typography is the vogue: letters can be made to change shape and move about to suit your purpose.

Cartoonists often exploit the graphic potentiality of language play. In one of Edward McLachlan's, a car cheekily drives through the space between the two words painted on a road, *NO ENTRY*; in another, a man is seen balancing precariously on a large capital *E*, which is falling away beneath the other letters in a sign – the rest of the sign says *DANG R*. Some hot-off-the-drawing-board creations in this vein are illustrated on p. 153.

Graphic designers, as their title would lead us to expect, play the most with the letters and words of written language, often in the cause of advertising a product (p. 94). In a 1980s catalogue, the fashion firm Streets of London presented the word *streets* in lower-case letters, with the *r* reversed and below the line, and the final *ets* with each letter reversed. It is a good example, for present purposes, because the reason for the ludic typography is actually given an editorial gloss. A policy statement in the catalogue reads:

Out on its own. A style all its own. Streets veers off the beaten track. Exploring new trends. Going beyond the norm ... Distant. Different. And desirable. Break away and break the monotony.

Going beyond the norm. Precisely what language play is about.

The portfolio of any international graphic designer provides dozens of examples of visual language play. Here are some from Australian designer, Ken Cato:

19 CARTOONOGRAPHS

o A design for an information and technology trade fair, to be held in Australia, used the theme *Intelligent Australia*; in an exhibit advertising the event, the *i* of the first word and the *t* of the second were raised off the line, thus highlighting *i t* and simultaneously suggesting an upbeat approach to the subject.

o The Borneo Pub, a bar at the Citraland Hotel, Jakarta, had its name designed as a native mask, with the *N* of *BORNEO* elongated to form a nose, the two *o*'s enlarged to form the eyes, and the word *PUB* making the mouth.

o A government research company in Singapore, the Applied Research Corporation, was given a corporate identity by playing with its initials: the chief feature of the design was the way the capital *R*, printed in a rounded typeface, lost its left leg and a dot was placed under its right leg. This made the letter appear like a reversed question-mark – an apt symbol for a research corporation.[26]

Lastly, as an indication of the potentialities of graphic language play, there is the ambigram – words designed to be read upside down, back to front or in the mirror – as well as in their usual way (in English, from left to right). We have already seen the role of palindromes in the history of language play (p. 67). Ambigrams take the quest for graphic symmetry much further. *SWIMS* will read the same upside-down. *TOOT* will read the same if a mirror is placed at one end or at the other. And a surprisingly large number of words can, with judicious and artistic manipulation, be read in an inverted way – as demonstrated by such graphic artists as Scott Kim, Douglas Hofstadter and John Langdon. The title of Langdon's book *Wordplay* (1992) illustrates the genre.[27] Turn the book upside-down to see the effect (but remember to re-invert before you try to read on).

That this is an art-form falling centrally within the domain of language play is made clear in Langdon's preface:

Designing an ambigram is not like designing a typeface. In the design of a typeface, each letter must perform well, functionally and aesthetically, on either side of every other letter in the alphabet. I call this an 'open system'. An ambigram is a 'closed system'. The letters that are drawn for one specific ambigram may not even be recognizable outside the context of that ambigram. This allows the artist significant latitude beyond the rules of everyday typography. For instance, it might be necessary to mix capital and lowercase forms. Nevertheless, readability will be best served if we can avoid breaking any more rules than necessary.

Don't break any more rules than necessary: wise words for anyone engaged in language play (p. 11).

THE THEOLOGIANS

Almost as a footnote to this chapter, I add the promised (p. 93) reference to theology. It is here to make a point – that a surprisingly wide range of people have a professional interest in language play. This chapter has not tried to cover them all. Psychiatrists, teachers, speech pathologists, media specialists, broadcasters, management consultants ... Anyone who is professionally concerned with language will at some point have to deal with questions of usage that are hovering at the edge of language, on the boundary between what is acceptable and what is unacceptable, and will thus have to consider the implications of language play. Everyone, not just poets, has to face up to what T. S. Eliot calls 'the continual wrestle with words and meanings'. Theologians and philosophers do this more than most. They are the people who are professionally 'trying to say what cannot be said'.

The phrase 'the edge of language' is in fact used by a US theologian, Paul Van Buren, as the title of a book, *The Edges of Language* (1972), in which he explores the fuzzy boundary which exists between sense and non-sense. The book was part of a flurry of publications which emerged in the 1960s and 1970s in which people expressed themselves dissatisfied with the traditional language for talking about God, and demanded new forms of expression. 'Our image of God must go', argued John Robinson, the then Bishop of Woolwich; and German theologian Paul Tillich in his writing argued for a 'rebirth' of words. The flurry brought results. New prayers and new linguistic rituals are now everywhere in evidence, especially noticeable in baptismal, marriage, funeral and other high-profile ceremonies. There are even new Bible 'translations', using such unexpected varieties of English as broad Yorkshire dialect or the hip language of the New York streets.

o This is the beginning of the Christmas story, as told by Arnold Kellett in *Ee By Gum, Lord!* (1996):

'As-ta ivver thowt abaht why it wor in t' little tahn o' Bethle'em wheeare it all started? Well, it come abaht this rooad . . . Ther' wor a joiner called Joseph, livin' i' Nazareth – that wor in t' north, tha knaws – nut all that far from t' Sea o' Galilee. But Joseph's ancesters wer' off-corned-uns – southerners, really. An' their native tahn wor a little place bi t' name o' Bethle'em, abaht five mile sahth o' Jerewsalem. Nah it so 'appened 'at t' Roman Emperor – a feller 'oo went bi' t' name o' Caesar Augustus – decided 'at 'e'd better reckon up just 'ah much brass 'e could gather i' taxes – from all 'is conquered territories, like. So 'e gives aht an' order 'at all t' fowk mun bi properly registered – an' this meant 'at the' 'ad to go back ter wheeare the'r forefathers belonged, does-ta see? . . .[28]

o And this is the beginning of the Sermon on the Mount, according to Carl Burke in *God is Beautiful, Man* (1969):

You are like the stuff you put on hamburgers. If it gets so it tastes rotten you can't make it taste good again. So it's no good and gets thrown in the junk bucket and the city dump guys haul it away. You are like a good streetlight. You can't hide it, everybody sees it unless it gets busted. If it's put on the pole it lights up the whole street. So if you are real cool, people will get the word and be glad that you know God.

If you think I came to ease out what you already got to know, you just are not with it, man! I just want you to know that they were for real too!

Grab this man! Nothing, but nothing is gonna get pushed aside as long as there's a world, see!

If you mess up what you get told or them things called commandments you just ain't gonna be much in heaven and when you ain't much there, you just ain't much!

But if you do the best you can and helps other kids do the best they can you got nothing to worry about.[29]

The devising of new ways for talking about God is always a controversial activity, given the conservative forces which exist within religions; but it is always there, and sometimes takes surprising linguistic forms, involving elements of language play. You only have to hear a

preacher in one of the black Baptist communities in the USA – and most people have seen such performances on film, if not in the flesh – to appreciate the extent to which unusual, imaginative and figurative language is employed to fire the enthusiasm of a congregation in speech, chant and song. God can be likened to a flower, a bird, a geologist – to almost anything. (A geologist? Remember the 'Rock of Ages'.) This is tapping exactly the same kind of ludic creative process as we have seen elsewhere in this book.

Advertisers and news editors, comedians and collectors, writers of all kinds, theologians ... these are the professionals who play with language for a living. But they are not that different from the rest of us. The kinds of linguistic manipulation which make their reputations, and sometimes their bank balances (whether in this world or the next), are different only in degree from those which the rest of us engage in for free. That of course is why it is possible to become ludic linguistic professionals in the first place: the games they play with language are games which everyone recognizes, because everyone plays them too – albeit more sporadically and amateurishly. So where do the differences between amateur, enthusiast and professional come from? Perhaps those who become linguistic professionals were given a head start when they were young? Did they play more with language themselves? Did they have parents who were always punning or doing crosswords? The questions multiply. Where does the impulse to play with language come from? How does it grow? When do children acquire ability in it? From Scrabble (Chapter 3) and Drabble (above), accordingly, we must turn our attention now to Babble.

5

THE CHILDREN

The question pile continues to grow. Where does our fascination with language play come from? Why do we slip so naturally into it? Why do we find it so enjoyable being part of a playful linguistic interchange? Why is it so satisfying when we complete a language game successfully? To find answers to such questions, we need to examine the way we first encounter language in our early childhood. That is why, at the end of Chapter 4, we moved in the direction of 'babble' – used there as a convenient mnemonic for the domain of child language acquisition. So: when do we first learn to play with language?

THE FIRST YEAR

And the answer is: from the very beginning. Language play is at the core of early parent–child interaction. Virtually as soon as a baby is born, it becomes part of a ludic linguistic world. Many audio and video recordings have now been made of the way in which parents (and other carers) talk to newborns. What is so noticeable is to see the adults displaying such an instinctive readiness to manipulate the rules of the language – producing the range of effects which are loosely described as 'baby talk'. Baby talk is a highly distinctive way of speaking, in which normal sounds, grammar, vocabulary and patterns of discourse are altered, in varying degrees, so as to foster a communicative rapport with the child. We cannot say much more than 'rapport', when we are talking about newborns. The baby cannot yet comprehend what is being said to it, and certainly cannot answer back. The best adults can hope for, by way of a response, is an engaging of attention, a meeting of needs, perhaps a fostering of mutual recognition. Yet despite our awareness that the child is linguistically incompetent, our interactions are not carried on in silence. Even though we know that infants cannot possibly understand a word of what is being said to them, we none the less persist in talking to them as if they do.

But not in normal English. Not using the language of formal, adult discourse. We simplify, and one of the ways in which we can make simplification enjoyable (for both parties) is to engage in language play. In particular, the phonetic properties of speech become dramatically extended – difficult to describe on the printed page, but immediately apparent to anyone who eavesdrops on a mother talking to her baby. There is a noticeable extra rounding of the lips and a lengthening of vowels. The speech is louder, more rhythmical and at a higher pitch level. Glissandos of melodic movement are used throughout a greatly extended pitch range. At the same time there is frequent use of nonsense vocalizations of endearment – tongue clicking, lip smacking and other noises accompanying the kissing, cuddling and nuzzling which is part of normal interaction. There is nothing quite like it anywhere else in human linguistic expression – the nearest exception being the way we talk to animals. I recall from teenage days my mother being highly embarrassed when I played back to her a tape recording I had surreptitiously made of her conversation with her budgerigar. That was language play with a vengeance. (And my tape recorder was banned from the kitchen, too, as a result – an early instance of the trials which beset all who would be empirical linguists.)

Other features of speech also change markedly in baby talk. Sentences become simpler and shorter, and structures are frequently repeated. One recorded dialogue (if that is the right word) went like this – the whole thing said in a rhythmical, bouncy, jocular, mock-theatrical manner:

Mother (looking at her baby's face while jiggling the child in her lap):
You are lovely, aren't you! You are lovely! Oh yes you are! You are! You're gorgeous! You're a gorgeous, gorgeous bit of baba. A gorgeous baby bouncy bit of baba (etc.).

The last phrase was repeated several times, with strong stresses on each of the main words, with the baby bounced up and down in time with the stress pattern. Both parties seemed to be hugely enjoying the experience – notwithstanding its unorthodox grammaticality. Nor are such sequences restricted to positive words. Mock-threat, mock-disgust and mock-horror are just as readily employed. The baby only has to burp, sneeze, be sick or produce a predictable but none the less unwelcome smell to elicit such comments as (I select three maternal reactions to the latter event) 'You're disgusting', 'What a horrid stinky pong!', and 'You're going back where you came from!' The tone of voice and facial expression make it plain (to any baby who might be precocious in lexical learning) that the mother doesn't really mean it. It is language play.

Special words may be invented to reflect the noises of the real world, such as *woof* (for 'dog') or *nee-naa* (for an emergency vehicle). Words may be structurally altered so that their sounds are repeated – perhaps reflecting an instinct on the part of the mother to make the

sounds more salient, and therefore easier to learn, and also reflecting the way children themselves talk, as they grapple with more complex pronunciations. Such reduplications, as they are called, are illustrated by *woof-woof*, *nana* ('banana'), *ta-ta* ('thank you'), and *choo-choo* ('train'). Not all adults like to use words in this way. Indeed, some scrupulously avoid them, believing that they will interfere with the child's learning of normal vocabulary. But this is to underestimate the immense language learning capability of young children, who are able to assimilate without difficulty several language varieties (or, for that matter, languages), including the distinction between playful and serious uses. Indeed, in a very short period of time (the third year) they will actually be heard to make use of these differences themselves, when they in turn play at being 'mummies and daddies' with their dolls and teddies. Parents sitting around a group of children in a nursery often hear their own baby-talk echoed in the play behaviour of their child – sometimes with embarrassing accuracy. Everything has been internally taken down and is ready to be used as evidence. Out of the mouths of babes, indeed.

Language play in the early months of life encompasses far more than baby talk, of course. A very noticeable activity is the way in which parents chant or sing to their children, sometimes using nonsense syllables with no particular tune, sometimes using real words in a traditional tune, such as lullabies and nursery rhymes. By six months of age, most children have heard several such rhymes and have begun to develop 'favourites'. Even more significant are the early play routines parents use, in which everyday activities are turned into a simple but effective game, with visual and tactile contact being used along with language to increase the chances of getting a response. Among the earliest examples are the various nuzzling and tickling routines, especially when the baby is being changed, or having a bath. The sight of a piece of bare tummy is usually enough to stimulate a face-to-tummy nuzzle – but the point is that such activities are not carried on in silence. As the face approaches the tummy and makes physical contact, there is usually a crescendo of nonsense syllables; as the lips caress the tummy, there is often a noisy, blowing lip-vibration, which invariably elicits squeals of delight. The message is plain: vocalization is fun.

And most of the vocalization in the first year of life – over 90 per cent, according to the studies – is fun. The 'serious' side of language acquisition, of the 'That's a car', 'Be careful' type, where the parent is drawing the child's attention to the fact that there is some learning to be done, comes later – building up only as children approach their first birthday. The same applies to 'sensible' dialogues about eating, crawling, sitting and the many other activities which are signs of the developing child. They grow in frequency as the child grows in maturity. But in the first year they are far outnumbered by the instances of play language, which is also growing in complexity as the games become more subtle – finger-walking, peeping sequences, bouncing games, build-and-bash games and much more. A great deal of learning is taking place here too.

Learning through play is a major theme in developmental psychology. And as child psychologists such as Jerome Bruner have pointed out, these playful interactions have a clear-cut structure. They present the child with a set routine, containing a limited number of important elements, and they are played over and over until the child is 'fluent' in them. Then, when the child *is* fluent (or simply bored), the parent moves on to new games, or maybe changes the structure of the game – varying the outcome, demonstrating fresh possibilities. For example, a finger-walking game such as 'round and round the garden' has a loud and highly tactile climax. In one version, it goes like this:

> Round and round the garden,
> Like a teddy bear;
> One step, two steps,
> And tickle *him/her* under there!

There are three stages of tactile contact: the circular stroking of the child's palm during the first two lines; the finger-walk up the arm during the third line; and the dramatic tickling under the arm during the fourth line. Now, after this game has been played several (thousand?) times, parents seem to instinctively know when to top up the enjoyment levels by making the child 'wait for it' – deliberately introducing a pause at the end of the third line. During the pause, the child giggles or wriggles in anticipation. Line four is then brought into play, but with an even greater crescendo, thus eliciting an even better response. A nice 'double whammy'.

This game illustrates the close link between language play and tactile experience. Many other games at this age are totally dependent on a corresponding collaboration between language and visual experience. The best example is the 'peep-bo' (or 'peek-a-boo') game. It is not enough to play this game by using vision alone: to peer out from behind a face-cover and return there in silence. Nor is it possible to play the game using language alone: to stand in front of a child, with face uncovered, saying urbanely *peep-bo*. No, to play the game properly, we need to time our actions so that the words *peep-bo* are heard just at the point when the face appears from behind its covering. Vocal–visual choreography of this kind (or vocal–tactile, as in the previous example) is an essential part of most language play in the first year.

GROWING UP

Given the remarkable emphasis placed upon language play in child-directed speech during the first months of life, we would expect it to be a central element in subsequent language development. And so it proves to be. Playing with very general qualities of sound seems to be the first step. Researchers into language acquisition have made recordings of children, from around age 1, with no one else around, in which there occur long sequences of vocal modulation that seem to be a primitive form of vocal play. These vocalizations become increasingly noticeable while the child is doing things – humming, chanting and simple 'tuneless' singing – a kind of primitive 'whistle while you work'. Symbolic noises increase, and sounds are brought in to represent actions, such as to represent ambulances, police cars, telephones, motor horns and things falling down. Several early utterances use primitive words which reflect this noisy world, such as *ding ling* and *beep beep*.

When children find themselves in pairs or small groups, at this age, they often begin to 'talk funny', for no apparent reason, deviating from their normal level of articulation: everyone in the group might talk in a squeaky or a gruff way, for example, and the sounds themselves seem to be the main focus of the play. They may converse with each other (or with their parents) in mock-conversation, producing a string of nonsense syllables with apparently normal sentence melody (a phenomenon which is sometimes described as 'jargon'): it sounds like a real sentence, but it is saying nothing at all. They also begin to play with tones of voice: in one babbling monologue, from a child aged fifteen months, the babble accompanying play with a (small) toy rabbit was uttered in a high pitch range, almost falsetto in character, while that with a (large) toy panda was spoken much lower, in a deep, chesty voice.

From around age two, a much more sophisticated kind of sound play emerges, in which children start to manipulate their growing inventory of vowels and consonants. Syllables are lengthened, shortened, duplicated; sounds are swapped about; pauses are introduced within words. One influential study, Peter Bryant and Lynette Bradley's *Children's Reading Problems* (1985: 48), drew particular attention to the way in which children of this age have already learned about rhyming:[1]

Not only does the two-and-a-half-year-old child recognize rhyme and produce rhyming sentences with ease: she also changes the very form of words which she knows to suit the rules of rhyme.

And they quote several examples from various researchers to prove their point, recorded from pre-school children:

> I'm a whale
> This is my tail
>
> I'm a flamingo
> Look at my wingo

The red house
Made of strouss

An American child language researcher, Catherine Garvey, reported one three-year-old girl who spent nearly fifteen minutes engaged in taking apart and varying the syllable structure of just one word, *yesterday* – the versions being mostly whispered in a soliloquy as she played with various objects in the room. The word obviously fascinated her – so she played with it.

This kind of play is typically a solitary behaviour, often heard in the kind of drowsy monologues produced by children of this age as they are drifting off to sleep. One of the first language acquisition studies to listen carefully to what children actually say, Ruth Weir's *Language in the Crib* (1962), found many such play sequences at night-time. Here is her Anthony at around two years six months:

bink . . . let Bobo bink . . . bink ben bink . . . blue kink . . .
berries . . . not barries . . . barries . . . barries . . . not barries . . . berries . . .

We should not be surprised at this: when you are alone in the dark, at this age, there is not much else you can do but play with language. Delight in the sound of words is also reported by the British educationist James Britton (1970), who tells the story of a small boy, brought to collect his father from a psychology conference, who went dancing through the hall chanting repeatedly the phrase *maximum capacity*. 'Words are voices' said a two-year-old, Clare, when asked about words. And this same two-year-old's enjoyment with the sound of words comes across clearly in these extracts (she is talking to herself while drawing):

Draw a coat down.
Draw a ling-a-ling-a-ling.
Draw a little thing – little ear squeer – big eye – little eye here – eye!
A little girl called Sinky and she's walking.
And there's Humpty Dumpty – pull him down!
Is that too tight? No it isn't! . . .

I'm writing to my sister – I'm writing to my sister – and my big sister's
  called Hunkron, isn't she?
And Daddy's sister's called Grandma and my sister's called
  Kronkilanma.
My sister's called Mac – aunty Mac – not uncle Mac – aunty Mac – not
  uncle, aunty Mac. And aunty Clare and aunty Mac – aunty Nance –
  aunty . . .

Within a year, these monologues can become very complex – Britton
calls them 'spiels'. They may be spoken alone or to an audience.
Here's an example from Clare, now nearly three:

There was a little girl called May
and she had some dollies –
and the weeds were growing in the ground –
and they made a little nest out of sticks
for another little birdie up in the trees
and they climbed up the tree –
and the weeds were growing in the ground –
I can do it much better if there's some food in my tum –
The weeds were growing in the ground –
the ghee was in the sun and it was a Sunday –
Now we all gather at the seaside
and the ghee was in London having dinner in a dinner-shop
and the weeds were growing in the ground . . .

This is not communicative language: the tone of voice is sing-song,
meditative, and there is no logic to the sequence of ideas. It is asso-
ciative freedom, what Britton calls 'a kind of celebration' of past
experience – a process of recall for its own sake, with the favourite
bits often repeated. *The weeds were growing in the ground* turns up
twice more in the next few utterances. It is a primitive poetry. Such
speech may sound like a dialogue, but the one child performs both
parts. If there are other children in the room, they tend to ignore
these vocalizations, not treating them as communicative. Sharing of
language play seems to follow later. (There is just one exception to

20 CHILD'S PLAY

Spontaneous rhyming and wordplay can be heard in young children's playtime dialogues as soon as they are able to carry on a conversation with other children – certainly by the beginning of the third year. And, as the following extract shows, the same ludic drive is still producing a lot of language play during the early years of school. It is from a recording made by American child-language researcher Catherine Garvey, in which two five-year-olds are playing together, wandering about and handling a variety of objects, not looking at each other very much. The example shows a variety of effects – the use of nonsense words motivated purely by their sound, the repetition of words which must sound nice, the changing of the sounds within a word, and the use of alliteration and rhyme. There is also considerable play with pitch movement, on certain words, but this isn't shown here.

M: And when Melanie and . . . and you will be in here you have to be grand mother grand mother. Right?

F (*distorted voice*): I'll have to be grand momma grand momma grand momma.

M: Grand mother grand mother grand mother.

F: Grand momma grand momma grand momma.

M: Grand mother grand mother grand mother.

F: Grand momma grand mother grand momma.

M: Momma.

F: Momma I . . . my mommy momma. Mother humpf.

M: Hey.

F: Mother mear (*laugh*) mother smear.

M: (*laugh.*)

F: I said mother smear mother near mother tear mother dear (*laugh*).

M: Peer.

F: Fear.

M: Pooper.

F: What?

M: Pooper. Now that's a . . . that's a good name.

this: twins, who do play with each other's vocalizations at this age.)[2]

Between three and four, children start using each other's play language as a trigger for further variations. They may add rhymes: A says *Go up high*, B says *High in the sky*. They may alter the initial sounds of words, sometimes to make real words, sometimes to coin nonsense words, as shown in the dialogue on p. 168. By five, this dialogue play can be very sophisticated. There might also be play with the morphology – the grammatical endings of words. A good game is to add an ending to various nouns: *teddy* leads to *fishy*, *snakey* and others. Here is an example of this kind of play from Catherine Garvey (between two five-year-olds):

A: *Cause it's fishy too. Cause it has fishes.*
B: *And it's snakey too cause it has snakes and it's beary too because it has bears.*
A: *And it's . . . it's hatty cause it has hats.*

This is the first sign of children trying to outdo each other in verbal play, trying to score over the previous speaker, in the manner of ping-pong punning (p. 4), or maybe just trying to keep the game going.

Original sin manifests itself in the young child very early on. Once they learn a way of behaving, or are told how to behave, they seem to experience particular delight in doing the opposite, with consequential problems of discipline for the parent. This is obvious at the non-verbal behavioural level. What is less obvious is that exactly the same process goes on at the linguistic level too. Being naughty with language seems innately attractive. If there *is* a LAD (a 'Language Acquisition Device', as proposed by Chomsky and others),[3] it seems to be a BADLAD. From as early as 3, children can be heard to home in on an inadvertently dropped adult obscenity with unerring instinct. Within hours of arriving at school they learn their own rude words, such as *bum* and *knickers*, which will keep them surreptitiously giggling throughout the infants. They will be rude at adults or other children by altering the sounds of words: *Dad Pad* said one five-year-old to me in a real fury, as he was stopped playing in order to have a bath. His whole demeanour showed that it was the worst insult he could imagine saying, to express his disapproval. And name-changing is done for fun, too. Nonsense names might be *Mrs Poop*, *Mr Ding*, *Mr Moggly Boggly* – these examples all coming from four-year-olds. Nicknames appear soon after, and certainly after arrival in school. These children often deliberately misname for fun, calling a cup a saucer, or mislabelling the objects in a picture. They break the rules of polite behaviour, such as saying *good morning* when it is night time. I think all parents have encountered the 'silly hour' when they seem unable to get their child to talk sense.

Verbal play exists in many forms by six, both serious and humorous, and rapidly increases in sophistication over the next few years. The children play clever-clever concatenation games, in which one rhyme is joined to another in a list.[4] Here is an extract from an American counting-out game, which could go on indefinitely, or could be terminated by an end-of-rhyme formula, such as 'Minnie and a minnie and a ha-ha-ha':

> *I went downtown*
> *To see Mrs Brown.*
> *She gave me a nickel,*
> *To buy me a pickle.*
> *The pickle was sour,*
> *She gave me a flower.*
> *The flower was dead,*
> *She gave me a thread.*
> *The thread was thin,*
> *She gave me a pin.*
> *The pin was sharp,*
> *She gave me a harp* (etc.).

This is no less than primitive rapping (and not so primitive, either, given the simplistic rap lyrics of some pop songs).

Puzzles and formal language games emerge at this age, some of which will become quite intricate – such as Pig Latin or talking backwards. For example, Nelson Cowan (1989) monitored a boy's acquisition of Pig Latin throughout the year preceding first grade; he was five years and three months at the beginning of the study, and six years five months at the end – though informal observations continued until after he was seven.[5] This is a game where the onset of the first syllable is shifted to the end of the word and followed by *ay* – *please* becomes *izplay*, *cat* becomes *atkay*, and so on. At the beginning of the period, following an explanation of the game, the boy seemed unable to transform any words; but his performance rapidly improved. By six years nine months he was really quite fluent, though he still made errors. Cowan and his colleagues also studied backwards speech in some detail, and were able to show that children develop their ability to talk back-to-front by around age eight or nine. Plainly, a great deal is being learned about linguistic manipulation during these early school years.

Verbal games such as 'Knock-knock' and 'Doctor, doctor' also become fashionable at around age seven. Riddle comprehension grows and the type of riddle used increases in subtlety. There is a classic study of children's humour by Martha Wolfenstein showing how joke preferences and performances vary with age (from four to seventeen). She found an important transition at about age six, from the improvised and original joking fantasy to the learning and telling of ready-made jokes (typically the riddle):

With striking punctuality children seem to acquire a store of joking riddles at the age of six. As one six-year-old girl remarked: 'We didn't know any of these jokes last year.'[6]

I can confirm that from personal experience. When two of my children were aged (nearly) seven and (just) five, they were sitting together watching Basil Brush on BBC television. (Basil Brush, for those who do not know, was a puppet fox with a raucous laugh and an insatiable desire to construct puns and riddles, whose brilliance he would personally signal by shouting 'Boom Boom!' after each one – an utterance which actually became a catch-phrase in Britain during the 1970s, and which can still be heard today.) After each riddle, the seven-year-old devoured each riddle, laughing uproariously; but his enjoyment was persistently diminished by his five-year-old sister who kept asking him 'Why is that funny?' and at one point turned to me and asked 'Why can't I laugh too?' I think I said, 'You're not old enough' or some such remark – which, as a response, was about as academically accurate as it was emotionally unsatisfactory.

The riddle preference pattern does not last long. There is a continual quest for something new. Wolfenstein found that at age six or seven about three times as many joking riddles are told as jokes in any other form; but in the following three years the percentage of riddles falls to little over half; and by eleven or twelve it is reduced to a third. Riddles are being discarded in favour of anecdotes and a freer and more elaborate narrative. The delight in rhyming also seems to peak at around age eight, then fall rapidly away. Stories and gossiping become increasingly centre-stage, and the child's behaviour becomes – linguistically, at least – much more adult-like. Awareness of adulthood over the horizon can be seen in the pseudo-intellectual speech by children from about age ten onwards, using tautologies and very long words, often with no real sense of appropriate meaning:[7]

I presume that your presumptions are precisely incorrect. Your sarcastic insinuations are too obnoxious to be tolerated. . . . If you insinuate that I tolerate such biological insolence from an inferior person like you, you are under a misapprehended delusion.

There is also the adolescent use of nonsense as a means of fostering group solidarity – a phenomenon nicely portrayed by British dramatist Jack Rosenthal in a television play – *P'tang yang kipperbang* (1982). One member of a gang of male classmates recites, *sotto voce*, the words in the play's title, and this triggers an obligatory grunt response from the others; they do this often, but he is then discomfited to find that a female classmate (whom he very much admires) thinks this behaviour is puerile. However, it isn't just puerile, in the literal sense of that word. Adult members of 'gangs' trade in-group noises and arcane formulae too: witness the 'old boy' honks of solidarity expressed by people who used to go to the same school or college but who haven't seen each other for years. Old boy? It does seem to be a predominantly male bonding ritual. But, male or female, it is a good example of the continuities which exist between child and adult language play.

THE LANGUAGE OF THE PLAYGROUND

The best hunting ground for language play is not the home, but the street – or the park, or the playground, or wherever children find themselves in groups. These are the settings in which British folk-lorists Iona and Peter Opie worked while collecting the material for their pioneering *The Lore and Language of Schoolchildren* (1959).[8] The book is notable for its wealth of examples, showing how different expressions and games have travelled around the country (or indeed, the world), introducing local variations on the way; but for present purposes what is of interest is the way children use a small set of linguistic stratagems (rhyme, in particular) to express a wide range of functions. Here are some of the commonest uses of language play.

o It can be an essential part of regulating the activities within a game, such as skipping with a rope, bouncing a ball (see p. 52), marching together, or counting out partners in a game:

One, two, three,	*'Left* (pause), *'left* (pause),
Mother caught a flea,	*I 'had a good 'job and I 'left* (pause)
Put it in the tea-pot	(repeated ad nauseam).
And made a cup of tea.	
The flea jumped out,	*I like coffee,*
Mother gave a shout,	*I like tea,*
In came father	*I like radio*
With his shirt hanging out.	*And TV.*

o It can mark out a certain kind of narrative, such as the 'horror story' – in this example, conveyed by repetition, a low, slow, menacing tone of voice and a sudden last-word *Psycho*-like shock.

21 BEGINNING AT THE BEGINNING

Counting-out (or choosing-up) rhymes are used by children, usually between the ages of six and eleven, as a ritual way of choosing who shall be 'it' (given a special role), 'in' (a side), or 'out' (left out) in a game, so that it can begin. The following examples, taken from Roger D. Abrahams and Lois Rankin's *Counting-Out Rhymes: A Dictionary* (1980) show the variable length and complexity of this genre, and also the way it mixes intelligible words and nonsense. Rhyme, wordplay and metrical rhythm are the constant factors.

A. E. I. O. You.

Eggs and ham
Out you scram.

All the monkeys in the zoo
Had their tails painted blue.
One two three – out goes you.

Ickety rickety rah rah rah,
Donna macka shicka shocka
Rom pom push.

In a dark, dark wood, there was a dark, dark house,
And in that dark, dark house, there was a dark, dark room,
And in that dark, dark room, there was a dark, dark cupboard,
And in that dark, dark cupboard, there was a dark, dark shelf,
And in that dark, dark shelf, there was a dark, dark box,
And in that dark, dark box, there was a GHOST!!

o It can provide a way out of a difficult situation, or be a means of telling someone to keep their distance. In each of these examples, A's question is totally innocent and B is being perverse (perhaps seriously, perhaps for fun):

My mother, your mother, lives across the way,
At 514 East Broadway,
And every night they have a fight,
And this is what they say:
Acka, backa, soda cracka,
Acka, backa, boo.
If your father chews tobacco,
Out goes you.

Onery, twoery, tockery, teven,
Alabone, crackabone, ten and eleven.
Pin, pam, musky dam
Tweedledum, twadledum, twenty-one.

Calcium, potassium,
Magnesium beer,
Nitrogen, oxygen,
Hydrogen dear,
Compound unit, atom fat,
You're the fool
Who's not at bat.[G21]

A: Where are you going?
B: There and back to see how far it is.

A: You know what?
B: I know his brother.

A: What's the time?
B: Half past nine.
   Hang your knickers on the line.

o It can be a means of tricking someone into doing something silly, or a commentary on what someone has just done, as in these famous instances:

Adam and Eve and Pinch-me
Went down to the river to bathe.
Adam and Eve were drowned,
Who do you think was saved?

Made you look, made you stare,
Made the barber cut your hair.
Cut it long, cut it short,
Cut it with a knife and fork.

And the whole world of language can be temporarily banned by issuing a rhyming edict:

Silence in the courtyard,
Silence in the street,
The biggest twit in England
Is just about to speak – starting from now!

o A lot of language play is simply 'being clever', for its own sake, as in this parody of a carol:

We three kings of Orient are,
One in a taxi, one in a car,
One in a scooter, blowing his hooter
Following yonder star.

We are close to a catfrontational world here (p. 2).

There are numerous other contexts for childish language play, such as oath-taking ('on your honour', 'cross your heart'), betting, making bargains, getting possession ('bags I that one'), swapping things, or opting out (crossing your fingers while saying 'barley', or one of its many variants). In most of these cases, the ludic language is being used performatively – that is, the simple act of using the language makes things change in the real world. When you cross your fingers and say *barley* (or whatever), you don't just ask for immunity from the game, or want it to happen. It happens. If only life stayed that way.

Nor must it be forgotten that language play is used, not only for 'nice' purposes such as making friends, but for the less pleasant side of child life: jeering at such targets as spoilsports, swots, dunces, copy-cats, nosey parkers, swanks, starers (stare-cats), cowards, cry-babies, sneaks (tell-tale-tits), and other unfortunates. Rhyme is at the heart of most cat-calling:

Copy-cat, copy-cat
Don't know what you're looking at.

Cowardy cowardy custard
Your face is made of mustard.

Finally, as with adult language, many instances of children's language play seem to have no purpose at all, other than to express their own youthful exuberance. It is 'just for fun'. Into this category fall all kinds of jingles, tongue-twisters, nonsense rhymes, parodies of popular songs, ridiculing of events and risqué jokes. Rhyme drives so much of this play along too:

A: Do you want a sweet?
B: Yes.
A: Suck your feet!

A: Do you want treacle?
B: Yes.
A: You're a big fat beetle!

Happy birthday to you!
Squashed tomatoes and stew!

Here comes the bride!
All fat and wide.

And many rules are being broken – of logic as well as of language – in these famous examples of child nonsense:

I went to the pictures next Tuesday
And took a front seat at the back.
I said to the lady behind me,
I cannot see over your hat . . .

One fine day in the middle of the
*   night,*
Two dead men got up to fight,
Back to back they faced each
*   other,*
Drew their swords and shot each
*   other . . .*

These are indeed complex manipulations of logic and of language –

as the Opies point out, all the more remarkable for being produced by individuals who are in many cases less than seven years old.

TOWARDS EDUCATION

It would be nice to be able to give more precise information about the way children play with language, but very few quantitative studies have yet been made. It is one of those topics in the study of child language acquisition which has been surprisingly neglected. But every now and then it is possible to find a study in which a researcher says something precise about what is going on. For example, Richard Ely and Alyssa McCabe (1994) looked at several categories of language play in children between five years five months and six years eight months, and found instances of it in 23 per cent of the utterances – almost one in four.[9] They studied natural discourse, where it is evidently much more common than in experimentally controlled settings or those where a teacher or other adult is present. Language play here was defined broadly: it included distinctive sound play, word play, role play (adopting another voice) and all kinds of 'jokey' verbal humour. Sound play represented nearly a third of all language play, showing the persistence of this modality from the first years of life.

Plainly, there is a lot of ludic linguistic behaviour about; and it is difficult to escape the conclusion that language play is a continuing feature of development, as children progress through school. Dylan Thomas was one who spotted it, commenting on the 'tumbling and rhyming' of children as they spill out of their classrooms. It is so obviously there, indeed, when we take the trouble to look, that it is surprising so little mention is made of it and that so little research has been done on it. Indeed, it has been so neglected that the phenomenon is not mentioned at all in the standard child language anthology of the 1980s, nor is it mentioned in the corresponding major anthology of the 1990s.[10] But occasional voices have been raised, and none louder than that of Russian educationist Kornei Chukovsky, who in his book *From Two to Five* (1963) talks about language play as something quite fundamental:

. . . the inexhaustible need of every healthy child of every era and of every nation to introduce nonsense into his small but ordered world, with which he has only recently become acquainted. Hardly has the child comprehended with certainty which objects go together and which do not, when he begins to listen happily to verses of absurdity. For some mysterious reason the child is attracted to that topsy-turvy world where legless men run, water burns, horses gallop astride their riders and cows nibble on peas on top of birch trees.[11]

The various collections of children's play make this point empirically – as we have already seen in the vast amount of rhyming material collected by the Opies, in such domains as counting out, jumping rope, or bouncing ball, much of which is so nonsensical that the only possible explanation has to be delight in the sound as such. As these authors say, at the very beginning of their book, 'Rhyme seems to appeal to a child as something funny and remarkable in itself, there need be neither wit nor reason to support it'. And if one asks why they do it, there is no better account of the various factors than that provided by the Opies who, commenting on the jingle 'Oh my finger, oh my thumb, oh my belly, oh my bum', remark:

[this] is repeated for no more reason than that they heard someone else say it, that they like the sound of the rhyme thumb *and* bum, *that it is a bit naughty, and that for the time being, in the playground or in the gang, it is considered the latest and smartest thing to say – for they are not to know that the couplet was already old when their parents were youngsters.*[12]

What is the value of language play to the developing child? The child psychologists, Jean Piaget and Lev Vygotsky, among others, have drawn attention to the notion of 'play as practice'. Children, they argue, are most likely to play with the skills which they are in the process of acquiring. And Jerome Bruner has commented that language is 'most daring and most advanced when it is used in a playful setting'.[13] So this is the chief message: that language play actually helps you learn your language. And if this is so, then the opposite is likely to be true: the persisting absence of language play in a child is going to be an important diagnostic indication that something is wrong. Kornei Chukovsky suggests as much, with reference to rhyme:

Rhyme-making during the second year of life is an inescapable stage of our linguistic development. Children who do not perform such linguistic exercises are abnormal or ill.

And indeed, children with language delay or disorder are known to have very poor ability even to imitate simple patterns of language play (copying rhythmic beats, for instance) and tend not to use it spontaneously.

All aspects of spoken language in children can be implicated. Language play, the arguments suggest, will help the development of pronunciation ability through its focus on the properties of sounds and sound contrasts, such as rhyming. Playing with word endings and decoding the syntax of riddles will help the acquisition of grammar. Readiness to play with words and names, to exchange puns and to engage in nonsense talk, promote links with semantic development. The kinds of dialogue interaction illustrated above are likely to have consequences for the development of conversational skills. And language play, by its nature, also contributes greatly to what in recent years has been called *metalinguistic awareness*, which is turning out to be of critical importance in the development of language skills in general and of literacy skills in particular.

Our metalinguistic awareness is our ability to use words and phrases in order to talk about the properties of language. It extends from the most primitive awareness – simple terms for describing voices as 'high' or 'loud', and suchlike – to the most complex, as when we muster some impressive terminology in order to describe the syntactic structure of a subordinate clause. All the technical terms you need for describing a language – the names of the parts of speech, the phonetic labels for describing sounds, the names of letters of the alphabet and so on – are part of this metalanguage. Putting it in a nutshell, a metalanguage is 'a language for talking about language'.

To be able to talk *about* language in this way involves a distancing, a 'stepping back', from the normal use of language. It is as if we are looking down on language from a special vantage point. Language is 'down there'; our ability to talk about it is 'up here'. And it turns out that this ability to step back from language is itself an important feature of language development. The argument goes something like this: if we are good at stepping back, at thinking in a more abstract way about what we hear and what we say, then we are more likely to be good at acquiring those skills which depend on just such a stepping back in order to be successful – and this means, chiefly, reading and writing, which are both one remove away from the natural state of speech. When we learn to read, we need to understand how letters, punctuation marks and the other features of graphic expression relate to speech sounds – and this involves some pretty complex thinking.

Here, the argument continues, is where language play fits in. Just as metalinguistic skills in general require a stepping back, so too does language play. To play with language requires that, at some level of consciousness, a person has sensed what is normal and is prepared to deviate from it – what I have referred to as the 'bending and breaking' of rules (p. 11). Language players are in effect operating within two linguistic worlds at once, the normal and the abnormal, and trading them off against each other. It therefore seems very likely that, the greater our ability to play with language, the more we will reinforce our general development of metalinguistic skills, and – ultimately – the more advanced will be our command of language as a whole, in listening, speaking, reading, writing and spelling.

Several educational studies have now reached this conclusion. An important finding – demonstrated by Bryant, Bradley and others – was that the ability of young children to use and respond to alliteration and rhyme is associated with later success in learning to read. The language play evidently helps them analyse words into their constituent sounds, and this kind of analysis is a prerequisite for successful reading and spelling. A child's early progress in nursery rhymes would thus predict early progress in literacy skills. Similarly, the ability to understand riddles can also be shown to have a relationship with reading ability.[14] Mary Sanches and Barbara Kirshenblatt-Gimblett go even further: they conclude that 'speech play is instrumental to the acquisition of adult verbal art' – all of it, including poetry, rhetoric and other forms of eloquence.

THE LOGICAL CONCLUSION

Given the high profile of language play within adult society, its prominence during the years when children are learning to speak, and its relevance to literacy and verbal art, you would naturally expect that it would have a privileged place in those materials and settings where children are being taught to read and write, or to develop their abilities in the use of spoken language. You would expect reading schemes to soak themselves thoroughly in it. You would expect authors writing for very young children to make copious use of it. You would expect curriculum documents to draw special attention to it.

Well, if you do have these expectations, you will be severely disappointed. For when we look for ludic language in the books and materials which children have traditionally encountered in school, while learning to develop their abilities in listening, speaking, reading and writing – as we shall do in the next chapter – we shall find next to nothing there.

6

THE READERS

The evidence of Chapter 5 makes a simple but much-neglected point: that at the stage when children arrive in school, their linguistic life has been one willingly given over to language play. Not only have they learned a significant proportion of the structural rules of the language – most of the pronunciation system and a great deal of the grammar, as well as a considerable vocabulary (approaching 10,000 words) – they have learned how to bend and break these rules in the service of play. They take evident pleasure in language; they enjoy playing with language; they have interacted with adults who enjoy it too. From a child's point of view, language play must surely be what language is chiefly for.

Then they arrive in school.

Where language play has traditionally been frowned upon. For, if a child dared to play with language in the classroom – adopt a funny voice or say some of the silly things illustrated in earlier chapters – what would most teachers do? Would they welcome it, reinforce it, praise it? Or would they perhaps say (and I am now quoting from classroom observations) that such language is 'better off in the play-ground', that this is 'where we are sensible, not silly', that we 'don't use words like that in here'? George, don't do that!¹ Or, just as much to the point, will the children be likely to encounter in their class-rooms language-teaching materials filled with the spirit of language play? Will they find wordplay and riddles in their reading schemes? Will they find rhymes and bouncy rhythms, alliteration and non-sense, cheeky metaphors and all the other effects we have described in this book?

THE LUDIC GAP

They will not. Or – to be more precise – until very recently they would not. Language play has been conspicuous by its absence. There has been an extraordinary gap between the real linguistic world which children inhabit and the linguistic world which they encounter when they start learning to read; yet hardly anyone has remarked upon it. The debate in recent years between the relative merits of 'reading schemes' and 'real books' in the teaching of reading has focused on many things – but not language play. Yet, from the perspective of child language acquisition, it is a critical point. For the axiom which should underlie all work on language intervention, whether in classroom or clinic, is the same as that which underlies all good educational practice: that one will make most progress when teaching can be related to what the student already knows. Putting this in linguistic terms, the more we know about the language skills of children, both in terms of comprehension and production, as they begin the task of learning to read, the better we shall be able to present them with literacy tasks which build systematically on what they know and do, and which do not conflict with it. If the language of reading materials is essentially familiar, if the child can identify what reading is about, then a barrier to learning is going to be removed. But no such language can be familiar if it ignores language play.

I see this argument as no more than an extension of what teachers have been doing in their language work in the past – but it is an extension which involves a more radical altering of perspective. In the 1970s a great deal of attention was devoted to evaluating the words and sentence patterns found in reading materials in relation to the stages of spoken language acquisition which children would normally have achieved. The words in the first stages of a scheme were carefully matched with those which would fall within the child's own experience. Grammatical constructions which a normal five-year-old would not yet have learned to use in speech (such as the passive – *The mouse was chased by a cat*, etc.) were replaced. Unreal constructions (ones which would never be used in natural spoken language, such as *A tall red jug stood next*) were avoided. Then, during the 1980s, more attention was paid to making materials sociolinguistically familiar, especially in relation to such areas as gender and race – what Carolyn Baker and Peter Freebody, in their *Children's First School Books* (1989), have called 'the culture of literacy'.[2] It is perhaps only a small parody of the linguistic climate of readers of the period to say that 'Fetch your grandmother a Martini' was being replaced by 'Get your nan a Four X'. And in the 1990s we have seen continuing progress in the movement to make materials more contemporary and intrinsically appealing, both in book form and electronically. All of these developments remain important: if materials are too difficult, structurally, or too alien or stereotypical, socially, or are simply unappealing, aesthetically, unnecessary barriers have been put in place.

But I am at this point struck by a simple fact. If all this excellent research and debate had provided us with satisfactory answers to our questions about literacy, we would not still be reading in the press about national concern over standards. We would not find publishers producing major new reading programmes. We would not have so many soul-searching conferences about language and

literacy. But editorials, schemes and conferences there are, plenty of them, and there seem to be just as many questions calling out for answers as there were thirty years ago. They are rather different questions now, admittedly; things have moved on. But no one would say that the problem of how to teach reading has gone away. It seems as large as ever. Which suggests to me that perhaps people have been looking in the wrong directions for their solutions to the literacy challenge. And perhaps the right direction – or one of the right directions – is language play.

The reason I find language play such a plausible candidate is because it provides a bridge between the two domains of language structure and language use, both of which have long been considered essential aspects of a child's linguistic development. This point needs a brief historical excursus, by way of explanation.[3] Once upon a time, in the learning of language, children were given training in structures only: they would be taught to parse sentences, analyse clauses, name parts of speech, list rhetorical figures and identify metrical patterns, but with very little sense of how these features of language could be put to use in real-life situations. Then this formal approach to language, which lasted from the mid eighteenth century until the 1960s, was largely replaced by a 'language in use' movement, in which children explored the linguistic world which surrounded them – advertisements, newspapers, church services, broadcasts . . . – but were given no training in the techniques of linguistic description. They had no 'language for talking about language' (p. 180). In many countries, two generations of teachers were distinguished by these emphases: those who had been brought up on a diet of parsing and who could tell a preposition from a conjunction, but who weren't always quite sure why they needed to; and those who didn't know what a preposition was – unless, as one listener to BBC's Radio 4 remarked, it was something to do with a strategy for mounting a horse.

In the late 1980s, fresh efforts were made to find ways of bringing these two domains together. The principle was evident: one should not teach structures without showing children how these structures are used in real-life situations; and conversely, one should not introduce children to the language of real-life situations without giving them some means of talking about it precisely. Structure and use should be seen as two sides of the same coin – a view which is present in the guidelines which led to the new British National Curriculum course on English. But the question remained: how exactly can these domains be brought together? How do you give structure a perspective of use, or use a perspective of structure? Teachers began to grapple with these issues in the 1990s. But progress has been limited – and perhaps this is because the debate has largely ignored the central role of language play.

The argument, in essence, has four steps.

(1) Children are used to playing with language, and encounter language play all around them.

(2) Language play chiefly involves manipulating language structures.

(3) A major aim is to improve children's ability with language structures. Therefore:

(4) We should make use of their abilities in language play – before going on to teach them other uses of language with which they are less familiar.

Language play, on this account, becomes a bridge between the familiar and the unfamiliar linguistic world. Manipulating structure brings, as we have seen in Chapter 5, an increased awareness of the way language works – the rather vague verb 'works' here referring to the way language varies according to different purposes, contexts and uses, which will become increasingly divergent and demanding as the child moves up through the school. Moreover, language play is a permanent bridge, not just one which applies at age 5. As we have seen, growing children manipulate language in increasingly sophisticated ways, and the strategies of language play are thus always available to the teacher as a point of connection with the rest of the curriculum. But the impact of any ludic linguistic perspective will be greatest at the very beginning of literacy education; so that is where the detailed illustration of this perspective must begin.

THE MISSING PLAY

For decades, there was little or no language play at all in the various reading schemes. Here are just a few extracts from early readers to illustrate the staid linguistic flavour of an approach which can be traced back to Victorian times.[4]

Scot will dig in the sand. He will like to play there. But he must not go in the pond. He is too small.

Jane and Peter play in the water. They like to play on the boat. Come on, says Peter.

Or, from a more advanced reading level:

The horses seemed very big, standing there in their stalls. But they were very quiet. When they saw the children, they stretched out their heads and blew softly through their nostrils. That was their way of saying, 'Good morning.'

I read through some 200 early British readers from before the 1970s, in researching this chapter, and could not find a single example of language play. Likewise, Carolyn Baker and Peter Freebody, using an Australian corpus, made no reference to it at all in their thorough account of early school books, and their copious examples showed no sign of it. I was pleased to find riddles being given some prominence at one point in the 'Janet and John' series, but had to discount it, as they were plainly being included only as an interest topic – there is a separate chapter called 'Riddles' in *Days in the Sun*, in which the adults and children swap some riddles. The subject has curiosity value, and that is all. Once that particular story is over, language play disappears again.

It is not that Janet, John and the other children live in a world which lacks language play. On the contrary, they must know it well, as two passages in the story indicate:

When it rained and the cold mist rolled down the mountain, Granny and Dan would pass the time playing 'I Spy' and asking riddles . . . Dan asked Granny all the riddles he had learnt from the other children at school.

They seem to be normal children, all right; but you would never guess from the language they are given to use elsewhere.

Even if we look for the most established category of language play, the use of imaginative figures of speech – metaphors and similes, in particular – there is little to report. Taking some books at random: in the whole of Ladybird 6a, there is only one such figure in 333 sentences (*'The time does fly,' says Jane*), and that is so cliched that it hardly counts as play. Three stages later, there is only one – of a rather better quality – in 403 sentences (9b: *This cupboard is like a treasure house*). There is nothing at all in the early books of 'Janet and John'; and even well into the series, in *High on a Hill*, we find only eleven instances in 256 sentences. Here are four of them:

> *a sleepy little river*
> *the white gate was wide and friendly*
> *lily leaves spread themselves like green plates*
> *frogs made a chorus*

These are promising, but the average is still only one instance in twenty-three sentences. The only category of figurative language which occurs with any frequency is personification, such as when a bird is given the attributes of a human being, and the story talks about his/her family, friends, furniture, etc. The contrast with the earlier speech norms of children is striking.

Of course, there were a few exceptions in the traditional reading world, especially in the more adventurous phonic readers. Dr Seuss is probably the classic case; indeed, his *Fox in Socks* (1965) is sub-titled 'A Tongue-twister for Super Children', and the first page advises: 'Take it slowly. This book is dangerous', as is plain when we find such sentences as:

Now we come to
Ticks and tocks, sir.
Try to say this
Mr. Knox, sir . . .
Clocks on fox tick.
Clocks on Knox tock.
Six sick bricks tick.
Six sick chicks tock.

Poor Knox, who complains:

Please, sir. I don't
like this trick, sir.
My tongue isn't
quick or slick, sir.[5]

This is genuine language play – though some have argued (and I shall agree, below) that Dr Seuss may be overdoing it. But apart from this kind of inventiveness, you have to go back to Victorian times, in the comic alphabet books of that period, before you find a genre which is willing to routinely incorporate language play. Although the contrasts between the relatively unreal linguistic world of traditional (i.e. mid twentieth-century) readers and the greater reality of modern materials have often been commented on, I have never seen the lack of language play in the former stressed – and it may be the most dramatic difference of all.

Is it too much to suggest that the lack of a perspective derived from language play is the biggest single factor hindering children from seeing what the task of reading is all about? (Indeed, the conventional wisdom of describing reading as a 'task' illustrates the mind-set which is endemic. None of the examples in the first two chapters of this book could sensibly be described as a 'task': it is not a 'task' to tell a joke, or make a silly rhyme, or see a figurative resemblance.) If language play is the normal perspective for pre-school children, how far will the lack of this perspective become a barrier, as they try to acquire another linguistic skill? If it is not present in the reading materials they see or, perhaps more importantly, in the attitudes of those who work with those materials, what follows? If absence of language play is a sign of pathology, as we saw towards the end of Chapter 5, then how are we to interpret the textual dimension of early readers? Is it not then a pathological world? How much, indeed, have readers improved in this respect in recent years?

Until the mid 1990s, I would have had to say: not a lot. You would have to search a long time in a children's library before you found a book which gave prominence to language play. I did search. After two days of doing little else than read through books aimed at young schoolchildren, and published before 1990 – an exercise, I should warn, which can seriously impair your perception of reality – I found very few cases. Here are four of them:

o The nonsense names in Lonzo Anderson's *The Haganinny* (Level 9.2 of *Reading 360*) are a cross between Lewis Carroll and *Star Wars*:

The worst day of my life, I guess, was the time I made that trip into the zangles of Arroom. I had been hired by the Blazon of Ammerwok to hunt down the hateful haganinny that was threatening the Blazon's people who lived in the zangles.

o *Fuzzbuzz* Level 2 contains a story in which a jester tries to cheer up a grumpy king by actually telling him a riddle (and it takes the king a while to get it).

o *Gay Way* (Pink Level Core Reader) presents a Lewis Carroll *doublet* game, as the reader crawls down a caterpillar from *cup* to *wet*, with each word changing just one letter at a time.

o *Mount Gravatt* Level 1:24 has a booklet called 'Monster Things' which has a triple rhyming sequence:

> *I'm making monster things on the wall.*
> *This one's got paws,*
> *and claws,*
> *and two big jaws.*[6]

It is the extension to three rhymes which makes this interesting –
going beyond the expectations of the traditional rhyming couplet.

Those reading schemes which involve the child in truly imaginative
play are much more prepared to be linguistically daring. A clear
example of this at the very outset is in Level 1 of the Mount Gravatt
scheme, where we inhabit a universe of pretend (playing buses, making shapes) and negative facts (as in *Who Am I? – I'm not a bird, or a
dog or a fish . . .*), which is a short step away from metaphor. Choosing
ten booklets at random, I found six items in 100 sentences, such as the
metaphors in *I'm the wind* (*I'm making a song in the leaves*) and *Rain*
(*The raindrops make a river in the gutter*). This is one in seventeen.
Although still very low, better ratios are hard to find.

Until recently, scheme readers did not seem to favour this kind of
innovation. Rather, the world of formal readers was one where language play was conspicuous by its absence. To the child, surely,
Wordsworth's words (from *Intimations of Immortality*) must therefore seem particularly apt:

> *Heaven lies around us in our infancy!*
> *Shades of the prison-house begin to close*
> *Upon the growing boy.*

The prison-house metaphor suggests that children come to reading
prepared by their previous experience of language play to have fun,
then find that there is no fun there. They encounter a world which (in
language terms) is serious and conventional. Beautiful pictures;
lovely story; linguistically unimaginative text. And before very long,
by copying older children, the teachers and the textbooks, they
become linguistically conventional themselves and models for the
next generation.

Some developmental studies have actually observed this process
taking place. In 1975 a study by Howard Gardner and colleagues
looked at the development of what they called 'metaphoric skill' in
children between four and nineteen years, using a simile completion
task. The children were presented with a simile which lacked an end-

ing – such as *as big as* . . . – and they had to finish it off. How did the children perform?

o The pre-schoolers used some empty and conventional allusions (*as tall as you, as cold as snow*), and demonstrated some possible confusions (*as warm as snow*), but produced several creative endings (*as sad as a pimple, as soft as a rainbow*).
o The seven-year-olds were more literal, concrete and conservative (as *soft as a pillow, as bright as the sky*).
o The eleven-year-olds were also quite concrete and conventional, but their imaginative elaborations began to increase.
o And some interestingly vivid comparisons emerged at ages fourteen and nineteen (*as warm as a summer's night in Montana, colours as light as an old folk tune*).

The most surprising finding, though, was that the pre-schoolers produced a higher number of metaphors than any other age group. This impressed Gardner and his colleagues; they called it 'surprising precocity'. To some extent this might simply reflect incomplete knowledge of the meaning of a word (as in the 'warm as snow' muddle – if it is a muddle), but the researchers conclude that it more likely suggests an ability to be creative:

The young subjects may have produced appropriate metaphors because conventional responses are less likely to vault to mind; they are more willing to follow their sensory imagination and to throw caution to the winds.[7]

Older subjects, in other words, increasingly learn conventional means of metaphorical expression, become less willing to be creative, to break the rules. In short, they conform.

Now there is nothing in this book in support of a social psychological revolution. Conformity is not my *bête noire*. I accept that linguistic conformity is integral to society, and reading must introduce children to it. But conformity has to take its place alongside creativity, and my argument is therefore threefold.

o First, given the amount of language play in pre-school child society, there should be a principled transition in early readers enabling children to move from a world in which language play is so important to a world in which language play has been so marginalized.

o Second, given the amount of language play in adult society, it should be possible to encounter it more regularly in a child's reading world than is currently the case – to make it less marginal.

o Third, because there is so little, linguistically, in early readers which children can use as a model to refine their creative language interests and skills, the books give children no basis for approaching the more imaginative domains of language use, such as poetry and satire, and may actually impede the implementation of a child's creative urge. Something ought to be done about that, too.

This last point is crucial. In talking to children over the years, I am left in no doubt that they have a view that certain kinds of linguistic inventiveness are definitely 'out of bounds', as far as using them in writing is concerned, and this must partly be the result of lack of play models in reading or teaching. All three arguments amount to the view that there is an enormous cultural gap between the world of child reading and the world of real language. Whatever else reading schemes are, they are certainly not perceived as fun. This is not to deny that children find readers from many schemes these days highly enjoyable, with interesting stories; but enjoyment is not fun. So-called 'real books' are, by contrast, regularly perceived to be fun. And the distinction between these two categories, from a linguistic point of view, is chiefly a matter of their willingness or otherwise to engage in language play.

Language play has not yet been incorporated into general educational thinking about literacy. I stress here that we are talking about language play – not situational play. There are of course plenty of examples of playful or absurd situations in modern literacy materials. Reading books these days, whether structured or 'real', do typically display much greater thematic relevance to the child's world than used to be the case, with imaginative and ingenious story lines taken from what we know to be motivating in children's everyday experience and fantasy. The dialogues, indeed, can be colloquial and vivid. But from a ludic point of view, the text is invariably sanitized. The illustrations can be wacky, but the captions are not. An alien spacecraft crashes into the sea, full of weird and wonderful creatures, but the text describes the event using the conventional word *Splash!* – not *Splaaaash!*, *Splooosh!*, *Kerashhh!*, or any of the other crazy spellings which are a routine part of the child's comic world. Any comic, in fact, will show vastly more sound symbolic creativity: in one *Desperate Dan* annual, we see him use a range of emotional vocalizations which include (just taking letter Y) *yah*, *yahoo*, *yeeha*, *yeow*, *yeuch*, *yeurgh*, *yikes*, *yip-yip*, *yipes*, *yowch* and *yup*.[8] We tend not to see this kind of thing in reading books. The amazing creativity which has characterized children's readers in recent years has been channelled very largely into character and plot, rather than language.

FROM CREATIVITY TO INTERVENTION

Is it possible to bridge this gap and thus move from one form of creativity, through intervention, to another? Is the way forward to increase the language play perspective in conventional reading materials and promote a readiness to play with language texts on the part of teachers and others? There is certainly evidence to show that it is *possible*, as can be seen by the following set of examples relating to different aspects of language structure and use. How far people are willing to think about the other factors is an educational issue that has so far been little addressed.

PRONUNCIATION

Some poems, anthologies and stories are based entirely on language play (as illustrated in John Foster's *What a Lot of Nonsense!*), and much of the humour is phonological. Nonsense names, for example, are found throughout (p. 30), and there is delight in words as sound.

The different verses of Dennis Lee's 'On Tuesdays I polish my uncle'
build up by degrees: verse 5 reads:

> I started the ark in the dark.
> My father was parking the shark.
> And when we got home we had ants in our pants,
> Dirt in our shirt, glue in our shoe,
> Beans in our jeans, a bee on our knee,
> Beer in our ear and a bear in our hair,
> A stinger in our finger, a stain in our brain,
> And our belly-buttons shone in the dark.[9]

Poems of this kind reflect, in a highly crafted way, what children do
naturally all over the world, as the Opies, among others, have illustrated.

Similarly, it is possible to introduce a bridge between structure and
use in written work. A good example of a more structured approach
to writing, again grounded in the principles of language play, can be
found in Ronald James and R. G. Gregory's splendid (though much
undervalued) book, *Imaginative speech and writing* (1966), which so
strongly supported linguistic innovation in written work. This project
showed that, with appropriate support, children are very ready to
continue using language play in writing. For example, in a section
devoted to the way sounds move into words, James and Gregory illustrate a story by a seven-year-old using made-up words, called 'Putting
up the fair':

Glunk glunk glunk glunk
Lock lock lock lock
Buzzz Buzzz Buzzz Buzzz
rolla clatter rolla clatter
patter patter
tip tip tip
wing wang wing wang
bang bang
clatter clatter

squeek squeek
clug clug clug
bang.

Other sections deal with playing with intonation and stress, nonsense verse and various kinds of sound symbolism.[10]

ORTHOGRAPHY

At this level, the chief examples are all letter-orientated, as part of the task of improving letter recognition. Comic alphabet books have been doing this since Victorian times and there have been many stories in which individual letters are personified, given families, get lost and get into various (spelling) scrapes, as we have seen in Chapter 4. Typical of the enlivening alphabet book are Eric Carle's *All about Arthur (An Absolutely Absurd Ape)* (1974) and John Burningham's *ABC* (1964); the story genre can be illustrated by Richard Scarry's *Find Your ABC's* (1973).[11] For example, Eric Carle's book relies on copious alliteration – even to the extent of using words which are well beyond the vocabulary levels of a typical four-year-old (a common failing of alphabet books which use the 'A is for —' principle):

In Atlanta one autumn day an absolutely absurd accordion-playing ape named Arthur felt all alone.

In Baltimore Arthur befriended a bashful banjo-playing bear named Ben. Ben was bored beyond belief.

And so the story continues, with the usual problems of finding words beginning with Q and X. Lyn Wendon's *Letterland* makes letters the basis of a whole teaching approach: each letter is associated with a human or animal personality, and a fictional world is created in which all kinds of linguistically relevant activities take place:

The Hairy Hat Man (h) hates noise, so he never speaks above a whisper. Sammy Snake (s) loves making a hissing sound – there aren't many hisses he misses!

So . . . whenever Sammy Snake is next to the Hairy Hat Man, what do we hear? 'sh . . .!', as the Hairy Hat Man turns around and tells Sammy to be quiet.[12]

There is more going on here than simply letter recognition and spelling practice. Look at the words being used – *noise, whisper, hissing, sound* . . . The children are taking some early steps in learning metalanguage (p. 180)

GRAMMAR

A fine example at this level is the *Find a Story* technique used in the 1970s in the supplementary course published by Penguin Education called 'Reading and Language Development', by Maureen Vidler.[13] Each book contained a number of sentences with a similar syntactic structure. By carefully laying out a sentence down the page, and horizontally cutting each page between different parts of the sentence, 150,000 different stories could be created by combining the strips in different ways. In Book 5, for example, the first page reads:

Did you know
that huge hairless
hippos
keep cool by
wallowing in mud?

By turning the middle strip over, the child can replace 'hippos' by 'little boys / slugs / poodles / young girls / baby elephants / headmasters / goldfish / grandmothers / policemen / teachers'. By turning the bottom strip over, 'wallowing in mud' can be replaced by 'wearing ribbons on their tails / standing on their heads / squirting water down their noses' and others. Children invariably want to make their own books along these lines – though they need help, for it is harder to do than they think – and given that it is possible to tightly control and grade the sentence structures involved, a neater bridge between language structure and language use is difficult to imagine. It is an exercise in the identity of phrase and clause elements, totally motivated by the forces of language play.

SEMANTICS

There are, of course, many word books which present vocabulary in an entertaining manner: Richard Scarry's *Best Word Book Ever* (1964) must represent this genre – but this is again situational play, not language play. Rather fewer books play with the meanings of individual words. Here are three examples.[14]

o Joan Hanson has written a series on antonyms, homonyms, homographs and synonyms (1972). In *Homonyms*, for example, we see funny drawings on opposite pages representing word pairs which sound the same but have different meanings, such as *hare* and *hair*.
o Sometimes a scheme devotes a whole book to language play: *Jokes, Jests and Jollies* is a collection of jokes, puns, riddles and tongue-twisters as part of *Reading 360* (Level 9, Book 3). But this is to take language play as a topic, rather than as a guiding ethos.
o *Fortunately* (by Remy Charlip, 1964) is entirely based on a spread-by-spread contrast between a happy situation and an unhappy one. In this respect, it resembles the format of a children's game, such as Consequences. A delightful story in its own right, from a structural linguistic point of view it can also be seen as an exercise in developing the child's awareness of sentence-connecting adverbs.

Fortunately one day, Ned got a letter that said, 'Please Come to a Surprise Party.'
But unfortunately the party was in Florida and he was in New York.
Fortunately a friend loaned him an airplane.
Unfortunately the motor exploded.
Fortunately there was a parachute in the airplane.
Unfortunately there was a hole in the parachute (etc.).

The publication of a single book is of course by no means the same as trying to introduce a spirit of language play throughout a series, and it is unusual to see this effort being made. The *Skylarks* language development programme (1975) was one such attempt. This was a series of eight-page booklets aimed at children in the early stages of learning to read, devised primarily by British teacher Jeff Bevington, with the graded structural input provided by myself. Several of the early booklets, which aimed to provide a transition from single-sentence texts to sentence pairs, used unexpected sequences of ideas, typical of the world of language play. For example, on clause sequence (A2) we had:

Ducks quack, but they can't sing.
Frogs croak, but they can't play the flute.

On sentence sequence (A7):

Fish don't wear pyjamas. What about whales?
Birds can't read books. Not even bird books?

By the end of the series, two booklets are devoted to figurative language (F7–8):

Tom went as white as a sheet.
The robber in the mask is going to be caught red-handed.

Waves of shadow went over the wheat.
The snow wrapped the land in a cloak of white.[15]

PRAGMATIC ISSUES

Introducing language play is one way of effectively reducing the chief pragmatic problem facing authors and teachers: how to make the language real. We need to find topics which interest children, motivate teacher–child interaction and avoid the problem of what I have called 'postillion sentences'.[16] These sentences take their name from the legendary sentence in foreign language learners' phrase books, *The postillion has been struck by lightning*, cited as an example of a useless sentence, because no learner would ever have occasion to use it (notwithstanding the occasion when there really was a thunderstorm during the Lord Mayor's procession in London). Traditionally, pragmatic issues of this kind were disregarded in reading books. A picture of a cow might have a caption sentence: *This is a cow*. The point here is to note the remove from daily reality. When would the sentence *This is a cow* ever be used in everyday speech? One does not usually talk about what is obvious (from the picture, in this case). To have such sentences permeate a reading scheme is to distance that scheme from the foundation of usable spoken language that the child has already acquired.

It doesn't take much to turn such language into usable, reinforcing language. Partly hiding the cow behind a barn in the picture, and asking *Is that a cow?* makes it a real sentence – and even more would be a context where a worried adult asks the same question, unsure whether the animal approaching is a bull! Or, to take an example from the *Mount Gravatt* booklet referred to above, *Who am I?* (Book 13, Level 1): here the opening page shows only an eye looking through a hole in a fence. *That's my eye*, says the text. The parts of an animal gradually unfold, and the reader is presented with a guessing game:

I'm not a girl.
I'm not a boy.
I've got two ears.
I'm not a dog.
I'm not a cow.
That's not my milk . . .

The last page reveals the mystery to those who haven't guessed it – a horse. Some simple crossword-puzzle clues (p. 68) are not far removed from this.

Of course, it is a risky business, entering the real cultural world of children's talk. You have to be prepared to include some surprising vocabulary. Faced with a picture of a meal on a plate, children do not describe what is on the plate, but talk about their likes and dislikes, directly or indirectly. *Where's the tomato sauce?* was one such reaction, evidently, when Rod Hunt was investigating caption material for the *Oxford Reading Tree*.[17] A great deal of surprising vocabulary arises from the world of language play. *Gallop*, for example, turns up as a verb of similar frequency to *hear* and *hold* in Bridie Raban's 1988 report on the spoken vocabulary of five-year-old children.[18] Why? Because this is a word the five-year-olds used frequently as they played at 'being horses' in their school playgrounds. Moreover, you have to decide what to do about the vocabulary which is not so pleasant. Raban's report includes such items as *kill*, *gun*, *bombs* and *bullets* – presumably (I hope) also reflecting a world of play – as well as *bum*, *bugger*, *titties* and *fart* (this last as frequent as *bath* and *clock* and, interestingly, as *God* and *Guinness*). There is something fascinating about any survey in which *Henny Penny* turns up in the same frequency range as *machine-gun*. It seems there can be murder even in fairyland.

METALANGUAGE

By the beginning of the 1990s, there was a significant shift, as books became increasingly daring, in the extent to which they not only made use of language play, but devised plots which were totally dependent on the children's capabilities in this respect. This can be seen in two very different publications.

o In the 'Dr Xargle' series, Jeanne Willis has 'translated into human' books written by the alien, Dr Xargle, who is attempting to teach his pupils how we live on earth. For example, in *Dr Xargle's Book of Earth Tiggers* (1990) – cats, to us – we are presented with the babytalk of adults, as well as a great deal of play with patterns of word structure: *beddybyes*, *walkies*, *leggies*, *tigger* (cat) and *tiggerlet* (kitten), *houndlet* (puppy), *earthlets* (people). New words are used, such as *stinkpod*, *meatblob*, *cowjuice* (milk), *muckworm*, *gibble* (found in dustbins), *pigrolls* (sausages), and *fishstick* (goldfish). There is even play with spellings: *feelers* are *pheelers*. Here is a short extract:

A healthy Earth Tigger also needs cowjuice, tandoori cluck bird, muck-worm and old green gibble in dustbin gravy . . . When Earth Tiggers are born, the Earthlet gives them a bed made from knitted twigs and a bag of birdfluff. This the Tiggerlets hate . . .[19]

o In *The True Story of the Three Little Pigs* (by A. Wolf, aka Jon Scieszka), we see the language of a traditional story pulled and pushed in several directions – in effect, a play about a play:

Everybody knows the story of the Three Little Pigs. Or at least they think they do. But I'll let you in on a little secret. Nobody knows the real story, because nobody has ever heard my side of the story . . .

   Way back in Once upon a Time time, I was making a birthday cake for my dear old granny. I had a terrible sneezing cold. I ran out of sugar.

   So I went next door to ask if I could borrow a cup of sugar. Now the guy next door was a pig. And he wasn't too bright, either. He had built his whole house out of straw. Can you believe it? I mean who in his right mind would build a house of straw?

And so the story continues: the cold makes his nose itch, he huffs and puffs, sneezes and the house falls down; the pig dies in the accident, and, as Al the Wolf says:

It seemed like a shame to leave a perfectly good ham dinner lying there in the straw. So I ate it up. Think of it as a big cheeseburger just lying there.

The success or otherwise of this book depends on the child's ability to recognize the language (not just the story line) of the original. We are in the same position when we watch Tom Stoppard's *Rosencrantz and Guildenstern are Dead*.

OTHER DOMAINS?

Language play continues to be relevant as children develop their linguistic skills. One of the goals of mother-tongue language teaching with somewhat older children is to help them become aware of the conventions which distinguish different language varieties, such as spoken vs written, formal vs informal, standard vs nonstandard, and the range of occupational 'dialects' which exist, such as the English we associate with legal, religious, journalistic, advertising, broadcasting and other contexts. Here too it is possible to play, as a means of increasing awareness. Here is one example, taken from a radio script I wrote on the relationship between spoken and written English – a fifteen-minute programme called *Put it in Writing* for the BBC series *Patterns of Language* (1986). It begins with the familiar (to British ears) sound of six pips introducing the evening news. The script then runs as follows, read by Brian Perkins, one of the impeccably authoritative 'voices' of Radio 4:

This is the six o'clock news. Now, let me see, oh yeah ... there's been a fantastic traffic jam in London this afternoon, you know – really amazing – went on for, oh I dunno, about three hours, more or less, before the coppers came in and sorted it all out. Oh, and another thing, the poor old Prime Minister got stuck in it too ...

The presenter (Brian Redhead) sternly intervenes:

Hold on a moment. That's not the right sort of language for a news broadcast! You sound as if you're chatting on the street corner. This is a schools programme, you know. You should get it right.

The presenter apologizes – he just felt like a change, that's all – and then he does it again properly:

This is the six o'clock news. One of the largest traffic jams which London has seen for some time took place in the city this afternoon ...[20]

And the programme continues with a discussion of the reasons for the differences between speech and writing. Some of the teachers who have used this material have told me that children's intuitions about what comprises a formal newsreading style are much sharpened by hearing what happens when the wrong language is used. It is evidently not a difficult matter for a teacher to take some of the 'wrong' features, explore why they are inappropriate and put the children to work finding better versions. This is exactly how a bridge from structure to use can be built via language play.

Even the forbidding world of grammar can be brightened in this way. There is nothing particularly novel in this observation – though those who remember their grammar lessons from school as being particularly dreary will be surprised to be told so. In the mid nineteenth century there were several books published which promised to brighten up your grammatical day. In 1840 Percival Leigh wrote *The Comic English Grammar*, in the hope that through humour (in the spirit, as he puts it, of 'Merry England') he would be able to eradicate the 'violations of grammar' which greatly annoyed him. The book is well worth reading, despite its prescriptivism, for its jocular style and comic examples. As an illustration, here is the way Leigh begins his chapter on syntax:

'Now then, reader, if you are quite ready, we are – All right! ****'
The asterisks are intended to stand for a word used in speaking to horses. Don't blush, young ladies; there's not a shadow of harm in it: but as to spelling it, we are as unable to do so as the ostler's boy was, who was thrashed for his ignorance by his father.
'Where are we now, coachman?'
SYNTAX
'The third part of Grammar, Sir, wot treats of the agreement and construction of words in a sentence.'
'Does a coachman say wot for which because he has a licence?'
'Can't say, Ma'am?'
'Drive on, coachman.'
And we must drive on, or boil on, or whatever it is the fashion to call getting on in these times.[21]

205

22 GRAMMATICAL PLAYTIME

Writers have been trying to inject some enjoyment into the learning of grammar for at least a century. Here is the opening chapter of *The Play Grammar*, a popular book in mid Victorian England.

'Oh Mamma,' said little Fanny, one morning, after breakfast, 'will you tell Herbert and me how to play the game you spoke of last night, and which you called the Play Grammar?'

'Do, mamma!' exclaimed Herbert. 'I should like to know more about it.'

'And so should I,' repeated Fanny; 'for my birth-day will soon be here, and our cousins are coming to spend the day, you know; so we could amuse them with it, and puzzle them, as you puzzled us, last night. Julia is fond of puzzles and riddles.'

'Well, my dears,' said their mamma, 'I have not the least objection; so, if you like, we will begin, now.'

The Play Grammar was brought, and the two children sat down at the table with their mamma, who asked Fanny how many days would elapse before her birth-day.

The little girl counted the days with her fingers, and found there would be twelve.

'Then you will just have time to get through our Play Grammar,' said her mamma, 'for it is in ten divisions, and we will take one of them each day.'

Less well known is W. Newman's *Round Games and Amusing Exercises Upon Grammar*. This includes such gems as 'A Rhyme of Forty Adverbs', which runs as follows:

> *Tit-tat-toe,*
> Proudly *they go,*
> *Twenty stout ADVERBS*
> *All of a row.*

'Will this game teach us grammar?' asked Herbert.

'Yes, my dear, it will teach you something of grammar; in the same way that your puzzle-maps teach you something of geography.'

'Oh! that will be capital,' said Herbert; 'because we shall learn, and be amused too. I am impatient to begin.'

And they do begin, working their way day by day systematically through the different parts of speech.

As a reward, for children who reach the end of the book, there are twenty adverb conundrums (*Which adverb wears a shoe? Answer, A-foot*), a game of linguistic consequences, and a further set of conundrums on the different parts of speech, some examples of which are given below. (You will have heard at least the first one before.)

When is a door an adverb?

Which preposition of two syllables might be spelt with one letter and one numeral?

What conjunction holds liquids?

Out of which pronoun are coals brought?

Why are verbs like teeth?

You'll never get the last one: 'Because they are regular, irregular, and sometimes defective.' Boom, boom! (The answers to the others are on p. 237.)

> Ably *and* stably; clearly *and* dearly,
> Calmly *and* warmly; closely, jocosely,
> Fleetly *and* neatly; meetly, completely,
> Duly *and* truly; fully *and* newly,
> Brightly *and* lightly; rightly *and* tightly.
> *Twenty stout ADVERBS pleasant to see,*
> *Papa with his compliments asks them to tea.*

> *Tit-tat-toe,*
> *How very slow,*
> *Twenty poor ADVERBS*
> *Creepingly go.*
>
> Badly *and* sadly; gruffly *and* roughly,
> Poorly *and* sorely; grimly *and* dimly,
> Barely *and* sparely; *skeletons* merely,
> Grumblingly ever, *but* pleasingly never;
> Ill always horribly, well never. *Deary me!*
>
> *Twenty poor ADVERBS sad to behold,*
> *I wish them good evening, my tea's growing cold.*

Lists of this kind are no longer in fashion, but the use of rhyme and rhythm is certainly in tune with the ludic mentality illustrated earlier in this book. Write a poem consisting only of adverbs?

Today, there is slow, almost reluctant recognition of the relevance of a ludic approach to the teaching of grammar. I say reluctant because I am well aware that to many people, grammar is not a laughing matter. For those who had parsing drilled into them as one of the signs of an educated gentleperson, or who were flogged each time they split an infinitive, the possibility that grammar might be fun would seem a ridiculous prospect. But it is certainly possible, and several books on language for schools written in the 1990s have incorporated elements of language play, along with cartoons and other appealing devices. For example, in the *Longman Book Project* (1994), there are several grammatical exercises (aimed at children aged around nine or ten) of a playful kind. Noun phrases are introduced by devising a game for a child to play with a partner: 'Grow your own noun phrases.' You start with a noun, then add words in turn to make the phrase grow. The example the authors give illustrates the playful tone:

pudding
a pudding

a pink pudding
a sweet pink pudding
a sweet pink pudding with custard
a sweet pink pudding with custard on top
a sweet pink splodgy pudding with custard on top (etc.).

And they focus attention on punctuation by borrowing from Victor Borge (p. 37): each punctuation mark is given its own sound (a comma is *boing*, a period is *splat*, three dots is *zzzzzz* and so on), and the children are invited to read some text aloud.[22]

Any aspect of language can be given the ludic treatment. In my *Language A to Z*, aimed at teenage pupils, I approach the task of helping children to become more aware of what a *sentence* is by means of a detective story:

The police burst into the room. Murphy lay on the settee, his chest covered with blood. Branson went over to him. There was very little time. 'Who did it, Murphy?' Branson put his ear next to the dying man's lips. 'Who did it?' Murphy's eyes flickered. 'It was . . . It was . . .' His head fell back. Branson cursed. Their last lead had gone.

And the text continues:

Branson's problem was that Murphy didn't finish his sentence – though poor old Murphy didn't really have much choice in the matter! . . .

Interrogative sentences are introduced by an interrogation scene using mock-foreign accents: 'You haf slept well?', 'You are goink to be cooperative?'. The beginning of the entry on *intensifiers* illustrates them by overusing them (much in the manner of the Victorian adverbs example):

This is going to be a splendidly well-written entry. I'm absolutely certain of it. I'm going to be extremely careful to put an intensifying word or phrase into every sentence. It's awfully tricky, though. When you write sentences like this, they can sound totally artificial, after a while. Incredibly artificial. In fact, I'm hardly able to keep it up (etc.).

To take an example from semantics: the entry on *archaisms* begins by playfully putting modern vocabulary into an old style:

Lo! Get thee gone. The milkman hath been, and thou art late for school.

And to take an example from phonetics: the entry on *plosives* begins by quoting some 'explosive' sounds from a comic strip, then drawing a contrast with inappropriate sounds:

Pow! Kabam! Crack! Bop!
  This is a learned quotation from a Superman comic. Superman, you gather, has caught up with a bunch of baddies, and is letting them have it. As his fists make explosive contact with several chins, these words appear on the page. They're good words. The sounds make you think of the noises you imagine them to be in real life. You wouldn't get Soo!, Mame! or Loash!, for instance . . .[23]

The use of a ludic perspective for 'serious' language work is beginning to be given some recognition, but it is grudging. I looked for signs of it in an account of the English Programme of Study of the British National Curriculum being circulated in the mid 1990s. There is regular reference to the use of poetry and other genres of creative writing, but specific features of language play receive only sporadic mention. 'Word games' are mentioned in relation to 'Speaking and Listening' at the earliest two stages in the curriculum (Key Stages 1 and 2), as one of the activities which can help to develop vocabulary; and alliteration, sound patterns, rhyme and figurative language are mentioned in relation to 'Reading' (but not to 'Writing'). And that's it. Language play isn't mentioned for the older children (Key Stages 3 and 4). The message seems to be that play is just for little kids. Little kids? Wrong. Kids? Fine. As long as that includes all of us. For are we not all children at heart?

A NEW CLIMATE?

These children's books are each excellent, in their own way, but they are isolated instances: they do not form a climate of opinion. Maybe they have individually played their part in helping to form such a climate, for certainly in the mid 1990s there are signs of significant development, with language-play titles increasing in frequency. For example, from the USA in 1996 came Cynthia Rylant's *The Old Woman Who Named Things*, a story about someone who gives a name to everyday objects:

Once there was an old woman who loved to name things.
She named the old car she drove 'Betsy.'
She named the old chair she sat in 'Fred.'
She named the old bed she slept on 'Roxanne.'
And she named her old house 'Franklin.'

This then allows the author to take off:

Every morning she would get out of Roxanne, have a cup of cocoa in Fred, lock up Franklin, and drive to the post office in Betsy . . .

From Australia in 1997 came a new series called 'Exaggerations', with such titles as *There's a Most Massive Spider In My Bedroom* and *The Worst Pizza In The World*.[24] Exaggerating, with its dramatic tones of voice and often invented vocabulary, falls well within the domain of language play. And in 1993, from Britain, came the 'Jets' series, aimed at children, the publishers' blurb says, 'who are just beginning to enjoy reading'.[25] Enjoy is the operative word. And it was good to see so much language play in the different books – suggested by the alliteration, rhyme and word-play of several titles: *Changing Charlie, Grubble Trubble, Clever Trevor, Hiccup Harry, Rhyming Russell, The Fizziness Business, Cowardy Cowardy Cutlass*. Especially important are examples where it isn't necessary at all, for the story line, to bring in language play, but the author does so none the less – as in *Sharon and Darren* (1993), where the opening lines make a metalinguistic point:

I've got a boyfriend.
His name is Darren.
Sharon and Darren –
we make a poem.

This is exactly how language play works in real life – the surprise factor. Hey, I've been a poet, and I didn't know it!

A number of books in the 'Jets' series play with several linguistic levels at once. In *Ernest the Heroic Lion-Tamer*, the main text is supplemented by accompanying cartoons, in which can be found all sorts of language play:

o characters make comic-like noises ('Aaah!', 'Cor!'), as do objects ('Ker-blam');
o they make smart remarks about what they see: 'She's hot', says someone at the sight of the fire-eater;
o they use pseudo-intellectual language – 'Jollity! Jollity!' says someone, at the sight of the clowns;
o they use 'clever' wordplay – 'Splats entertainment, folks', says another;

o they make rhyming lists – the ringmaster says to Ernest: 'It's time to act on the fact of what your act lacked. With tact; it's time for your act to face facts'.

At several points in the book, cartoons play with the meaning of an idiom. The text says '. . . the drums rolled', and this is followed by a picture of a drummer chasing his drum and calling 'Stop rolling!' As the lion-tamer is about to put his head inside the lion's mouth, the text says 'Not a soul stirred'; this is followed by a cartoon showing several members of the audience, one of whom is seen to be stirring a cup of something – 'Except me!' he says, and around the spoon can be seen the words 'Stir! Stir!', using the standard comic technique of verbalizing object noises. There is pragmatic fun, also, with the voice of the *reader* seen in a speech bubble making an observation about the way the story is being told. 'Brian Lion opened his jaws WIDE' says the text, printed inside the lion's open mouth. 'Scary, isn't he?' adds the author. And a bubble identified as *Reader's voice* says 'Phew! Scarier than a mutant man-eating spider, I reckon!' Of course, readers aren't to be allowed to intrude without comment, and the author immediately responds to the intervention: 'In that case, before we go any further, there's something you should know', and goes on to explain the truth about Brian Lion.

Language play is thus an integral part of the text. Indeed, in the case of Ernest, there is an additional dimension given to the play, for the reader's metalinguistic awareness is being invoked as well. The conversational interaction between the author of the story and the imaginary reader returns with a vengeance on p. 32. The reader's interruptions begin to really irritate Ernest:

READER'S VOICE: *Oh boy, he's got a nerve, talking to Brian Lion that way!*

ERNEST: *A nerve? Actually I've got* millions *of nerves, you silly little reader!*

And on p. 35 (see p. 214), Ernest gets support from the *author*, who also asks the reader not to interrupt so much. And Ernest agrees, star-

23 DEAR READER

Page 35 of Damon Burnard's *Ernest the Heroic Lion-Tamer*, where the interfering reader gets thoroughly ticked off.

And so Brian put up with the moods and did as he was told, because he hoped it would make Ernest cheerful again.

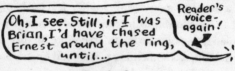

Oh, I see. Still, if I was Brian, I'd have chased Ernest around the ring, until...

Reader's voice-again!

Reader?

Yes?

Please try not to interrupt so much!

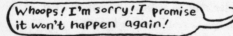

Whoops! I'm sorry! I promise it won't happen again!

Thank you.

Yeah! Put a sock in it, Motor-mouth!

ing out at the reader and telling him/her to 'put a sock in it, motormouth'. The (real) author ganging up with his (fictitious) characters against the (fictitious yet real) reader. We are truly being daring with linguistic realities now – stepping back and stepping back (p. 181). French semioticians would have a field day with this. Then, on the last page, Brian the lion, who has saved the day, asks Ernest, wistfully:

if anyone ever writes a book about us ... promise me it'll be called 'Ernest and Brian', and not just 'Ernest the Heroic Lion-Tamer'.

I promise, Bri, I promise ...

replies Ernest, ironically – leaving it to the reader to recall what the title of the book really is.

Of especial importance in fostering a new ludic climate was the appearance of two new reading schemes in 1996, produced by major British publishing houses, both of which pay special attention to language play – the first ones to do so. Rhyme, rhythm and alliteration are the focus of the 'Rhyme and Analogy' programme in the *Oxford Reading Tree*. Roderick Hunt's *Bad Day, Good Day*, for example, has this kind of thing:

> *Thursday was a late day.*
> *The sort of day I hate – day.*
> *Had to run – day.*
> *Dropped my bun – day.*
> *Thursday was a late day.*[26]

The same emphases are to be found in *Cambridge Reading*, where there are books like *Rhyming Riddles*, nursery rhyme books and books of number rhymes. In *A Very Hot Day*, for example, rhyme is used to add some zip to a selection of everyday vocabulary.

> *Shoes by the door.*
> *Jeans on the floor.*
> *Socks on the stair.*
> *T-shirt on the chair.*

Vest on the mat.
Pants on the cat.
I'm in the pool![27]

Children are encouraged to adapt a published story to write a new story of their own – another way of showing how it is possible to deviate from established norms. Both series are accompanied by extensive teachers' materials which draw attention to the relevant theoretical background. We are no longer talking 'exceptions' here: these are serious, systematic and courageous attempts to introduce a fresh perspective.

There are risks, of course. With missionary zeal, it is always possible to go too far – as some people have argued about Dr Seuss's tongue-twisters. Whole books are written in rhyme, in the new schemes. And this, of course, is a possible problem. If everything rhymes, rhyme ceases to have its point. It loses its effect. Moreover, rhyme is not the whole story. It has been shown to be important for phonological awareness, and thus for early reading – but there is far more to language development than phonological awareness, and far more to language play than rhyme. And if rhyme is focused upon to the exclusion of everything else, it is in danger of creating a world which is just as artificial as the rhymeless world of before.

I do none the less applaud these efforts to introduce aspects of ludic language on such a large scale, and they may well play an important role in developing a new climate of opinion; but we are still far removed from any kind of pedagogical orthodoxy. There is as yet no general expectation that materials should include elements of language play, nor much discussion of what happens when such elements are included, nor how teachers should incorporate a ludic perspective within their teaching. The earlier debate about 'play as practice', referred to in Chapter 5, is not entirely relevant, for Piaget, Bruner and the others were talking about play in general, not about language play; and the real nature of the link between language play and later linguistic ability has still to be explored.

There is still a major cultural gap between the linguistic world of early childhood and the linguistic world children encounter when they begin to learn to read. These gaps can evidently be bridged, and the thrust of this chapter is to suggest that a promising means of bridging this gap is to introduce a perspective from language play. I doubt whether there could be any greater motivating force for children (or, for that matter, for adults). Reading and writing do not have to be a prison-house. Release is possible. And maybe language play can provide the key.

7

THE FUTURE

The mood has changed, since the beginning of this book. Chapter 1 presented the topic of language play in rare good humour, eavesdropping on a moment of ping-pong punning during a mildly winey evening conversation; and the jocularity continued in the following chapter. This is probably what most readers would have expected, in picking up a book called 'language play': a bit of a laugh. But Chapter 3 will have made it plain that there is much more to language play than being funny: it is really to do with a broader notion – that of enjoyment, or entertainment. The array of linguistic puzzles and games presented there takes us well beyond humour, into surprise and discovery, challenge and satisfaction. The professionalisms introduced in Chapter 4 open up the topic still further, allowing us to enter several different worlds of creativity and originality, and – especially through the medium of literature – bringing us into mimetic contact with the whole of human experience. Chapters 5 and 6 indicate ways in which a focus on language play can bring to light important social and educational consequences – a kind of applied ludic linguistics.

Language play is evidently a much bigger topic than it appears to be at first sight. That is why it deserves a whole book to itself – and, moreover, a treatment of a rather different kind from what it has traditionally received. It is usually presented as an end in itself, as a shop-window of fascinating linguistic frolics. This has been the pattern since Victorian times, seen in the compendiums of jokes, games and puzzles compiled by such masters of the ludic arts as C. C. Bombaugh, Dmitri Borgmann and Willard Espy. But I did not want to produce yet another 1000 games for (grown-up) kids. There is far more to language play than this.

WHY PLAY?

Language play is important socially. It brings people into rapport with each other, as we saw with the very first example in Chapter 1 (the 'catfrontation' episode); and repeatedly, with the examples in Chapter 2 that showed how groups of people bond by sharing each other's language play. Word games may be the means of bringing people into organized relationships, such as a club or a competition, as we saw in Chapter 3; or they may simply help people break the ice, as when a comment on the day's crossword puzzle may be the only vocal exchange allowed to break the silence in a commuting railway compartment. Permitting others to play with your name (a pet name or nickname) is an important signal of intimacy; rejecting someone's use of that name is just as important an intimation of distance. Enjoying others' language play is a sure sign of a healthy social relationship; and disaffection with someone's language play is just as sure a sign that a relationship is on the way to breaking down. When you

get annoyed by someone's silly voices, find their mock regional accents extremely irritating, or their favourite word game pointless and boring, then all is definitely not well.

We have also seen that language play is important personally. It adds to our quality of life, providing opportunities for personal enjoyment that are both free and unlimited. If we perceive it as a challenge, in relation to the games reviewed in Chapter 3, then it is one to which few sports can compare, except perhaps a game like golf, where there is You, The Ball and That Hole – nothing else counts. With language play, there is You and The Language – that's all. You can set your own targets for achievement. And if you choose to engage in competitive language play, then if the course of language acquisition has run smoothly, everyone starts on a level playing field – as I argued at the end of Chapter 3. Language play is a fundamentally egalitarian pastime.

We have seen that language play is important educationally. Children value it too. That was the point of Chapter 5. They grow up within a world of language play. It permeates their lives. It is their main means of achieving rapport with their parents and peers. And they quickly become competent in it themselves. By the time they get to school they know that language play is one of the more enjoyable reasons why anyone should want to engage in the task of language learning. That is why a school world without language play is so alien, and perhaps one of the reasons why the progress of so many children towards literacy and advanced language skills has been slow. Arguing that cause was the purpose of Chapter 6.

And we have seen that language play is important creatively. Chapter 4 is the longest chapter in the book, simply because it tries to pay a respectable amount of attention to the many domains in which people express themselves creatively through language. I cannot prove it, but I do believe that the more children are given opportunities to play with language and respond to language play, as they move up through the school, the more sophisticated will be their eventual prowess in the verbal arts. Poetry has to be the critical factor here; it ought to be presented to all children as a natural expressive medium, as soon as they walk into school. But it is not the only one; and

Chapter 4 shows that there are many other ludic linguistic worlds also waiting to be creatively explored.

These are some of the reasons why language play is so important, as a topic of enquiry.[1] And also why it is surprising to see that it has been so much ignored in our definitions and descriptions of language. As I pointed out in Chapter 1, the ludic function of language is generally not mentioned in dictionaries or introductory texts – or is at best marginalized. Yet it is one of the most important dimensions of language. How can it have been so neglected? Perhaps because our academically enquiring minds, over the centuries, have been taught to look steadfastly only in one direction – that of 'language as information'. Or perhaps scholars have unconsciously dismissed language play as being too trivial a topic for serious study. I do not know. But I do know that the situation shouldn't stay that way.

Perhaps we should not intellectualize too much about all this. I very much sympathize with the feelings of Walter Redfern who, at the end of a fine analysis of the nature of puns, throws the whole pack of cards up into the air:

Why defend wordplay? Play is indefensible. It simply is. Perhaps nothing else simply is quite so exquisitely and wholeheartedly as play.

And he goes on:

In studying the ludic element in culture, literary and everyday, I should logically also posit a similar element in those who receive and respond to wordplay: that is, all of us. Punning is a free-for-all available to everyone, common property; it is a democratic trope. It is the stock-in-trade of the low comedian and the most sophisticated wordsmith: James Joyce and Max Miller (and who comes first?). It is and always has been. God was the first logonaut.[2]

And we, according to one view, were created in God's image. In the beginning was the pun? The *word* and the *Word*; *man* and *wo-man*. Maybe.

THE FINAL STEP

But I have to take one further intellectualizing step, before throwing my cards up in the air; and that is because I am left with the nagging 'why?' questions I have been asking throughout this book. Why is there so much ludic behaviour? Why do we enjoy it so? Why is it so prominent in early child language acquisition? I could just stop with the previous answer: because God made us so – and for many that would be answer enough. However, it is more fashionable, though not always more illuminating, to discuss the question in evolutionary terms. Might it be that language play is actually what makes us human? Chapter 5 argued that language play is important for the development of metalinguistic skills in children, and thus for the development of their language as a whole. If we can think this way ontogenetically, for the individual, might we not also think it phylo-genetically, for the race? May we take a truly dramatic step, and claim for language – and thus for language play – some evolutionary privileges? Is it sensible to talk about the survival of the linguistic fittest? Is skill with language an evolutionary plus? If it is, there is good reason for the human race to have developed a facility in language play.

As a linguist I cannot see so far back by myself; but it is possible to get a better view by hoisting myself up on to a couple of pairs of broad evolutionist shoulders. One pair belongs to Richard Dawkins. In *River Out of Eden* (1995), he argues that language is one of the major thresholds which any 'planetary replication bomb' can be expected to pass through. From his point of view, language 'is the networking system by which brains ... exchange information with sufficient intimacy to allow the development of a cooperative technology.'[3] That sounds like a pretty important evolutionary step to me. And an even stronger statement about the significance of language comes from Terrence Deacon, in *The Symbolic Species* (1997) – a book which he subtitles 'the co-evolution of language and the human brain'. I shall not attempt to paraphrase the argument of this powerful book, but content myself with a series of quotations which seem to make my case – first, regarding the centrality of language and other symbolic behaviour in evolution (*homo symbolicus*):

o 'The remarkable expansion of the brain that took place in human evolution ... was not the cause of symbolic language but the consequence of it.'

o 'What aspects of human social organization and adaptation wouldn't benefit from the evolution of language? From this vantage point, symbolic communication appears "overdetermined". It is as though everything points to it. A plausible story could be woven from almost any of the myriad of advantages that better communication could offer: organizing hunts, sharing food, communicating about distributed food sources, planning warfare and defense, passing on toolmaking skills, sharing important past experiences, establishing social bonds between individuals, manipulating potential sexual competitors or mates, caring for and training young and on and on.'

o 'Symbolic analysis is the basis for a remarkable new level of self-determination that human beings alone have stumbled upon ... [giving us] unprecedented capacity to generate independent adaptive behaviours.'

And then, more specifically in relation to language play, there are these words:

o 'laughter played an important role in the maintenance of group cohesion and identity during a major phase of hominid evolution ... The role of laughter as a play signal, especially in mock aggression (as in response to tickling), may also offer some hint as to an older evolutionary role ...'

o [in relation to 'getting' a joke] 'This ability simultaneously to entertain inconsistent alternative perspectives extrapolated from the same initial context is something that only we humans have.'

o 'Consider the intensity with which contemporary humans pursue mysteries, scientific discoveries, puzzles and humor, and the elation that a solution provides. The apocryphal story of Archimedes running naked through the streets yelling "Eureka!" captures this experience well. The positive emotions associated with such insights implicate more than just a cognitive act. The reinforcement that is intrinsic to achieving such a recoding of the familiar may be an important part of the adaptation that biases our thinking to pursue this result. A call that may primarily have been selected for its role as a symptom of "recoding" potentially aggressive actions as friendly social play seems to have been "captured" by the similar recoding process implicit in humor and discovery. In both conditions, insight, surprise and removal of uncertainty are critical components.'[4]

This linking of humour and discovery is something which is at the heart of language play. It is what unites my Chapter 2 and my Chapter 3. And it is no coincidence, according to Deacon, that we find ourselves laughing after the puns, jokes and riddles of the former, as well as after the ingenious puzzles and solutions of the latter. We encounter a particularly difficult crossword clue – and we laugh. We solve it – and we laugh. We pick out of a Scrabble bag seven vowels – and we laugh. We find ourselves getting rid of all seven letter tiles in one brilliant move – and we laugh. 'Laughter', says Deacon, ' is not just an expression of emotion. It is a public symptom of engaging in a kind of mental conflict resolution.' It has a pre-symbolic function, antedating language. And maybe language itself arose out of the playful manipulations of the vocal tract, once it began to dawn on early hominids that ludic sound could be used for a more serious purpose. *Homo symbolicus*, yes; but *homo ludens* first. And although language play shares many features with play in general – the attempt to outdo each other in pun-capping, for example, has clear similarities with the way people compete in manipulative computer games – the remarkable complexity of language provides an array of ludic possibilities which cannot be matched elsewhere in human behaviour. As we saw in Chapter 2, there is an extraordinary amount of linguistic structure to be played with. And the fact that people have, by and large, the same linguistic competence enables them all to play in the same league. That is why language play is unlike all other forms of play. X may be interested in playing computer games and hate sports. Y may be interested in football and can't stand computer games. But both use language and are qualified to engage in language play.

'Recoding potentially aggressive actions as friendly social play'? Certainly, it is a common experience that language play can help us survive. There is plenty of anecdotal evidence. Take the famous case of Emperor Claudius, as recounted by Robert Graves, who survived through his ability to play the fool.[5] Two millennia on, and Gene Wilder and Richard Pryor repeatedly get themselves out of trouble in the film *Stir Crazy* through their linguistic play. I expect thousands of schoolchildren have managed to avoid being bullied or achieved a prestige standing within their class by using their abilities in language play. And several of these former children, after becoming famous comedians – Billy Connolly is one who comes to mind – have testified to the survival value attached to language play. Peter Ustinov, indeed, in his autobiography talks openly of survival during his days in preparatory school: 'I learned at Mr Gibbs' how to survive by emphasizing the clumsy and comic aspects of my character . . .'[6]

There we have it. One of life's linguistic fittest, surviving through language. No wonder we should celebrate language play.

NOTES

The notes for the Games People Play are included at the end and are numbered according to the game.

1 THE LUDIC VIEW

1 For further examples of ping-pong punning, see Delia Chiaro, *The Language of Jokes: Analysing Verbal Play* (London: Routledge, 1992), pp. 113–117. This also contains a further example of the kind of *'armless* sequence I refer to on p. 5.
2 The reference is to Steven Pinker, *The Language Instinct* (Harmondsworth: Penguin, 1994). His first chapter is headed 'An instinct to acquire an art', and this accords very well with my general argument. Pinker's book is not about language play, however, though he uses it elegantly to make a number of points.

2 THE AMATEURS

1 A. A. Milne, *Winnie-the-Pooh* (London: Methuen, 1926). Quotations from Ogden Nash are taken from L. Smith and I. Eberstadt, *Candy is Dandy: The Best of Ogden Nash* (London: Deutsch, 1983).
2 Michael Kilgarriff, *1000 Jokes for Kids of All Ages* (London: Wolfe Publishing, 1974); *Oh No! Not Another 1000 Jokes for Kids* (London: Ward Lock, 1983); Mary Danby, *The Most Awful Joke Book Ever* (London: Fontana, 1984) – earlier books in the series having been called *The Awful Joke Book* and *The Even More Awful Joke Book*; Nigel Blundell, *Sick as a Parrot* (London: Pan, 1982).
3 Howard Jacobson, *Seriously Funny: From the Ridiculous to the Sublime* (Harmondsworth: Penguin, 1997).
4 M. Mahood, *Shakespeare's Wordplay* (London: Methuen, 1979), p. 30.

5 Michael Johnstone, *1000 What's What Jokes for Kids* (London: Ward Lock, 1986).

6 Dialect humour books: Rawbone Malong, *Ah big yaws?* (Cape Town: David Philip, 1972); Afferbeck Lauder, *Let Stalk Strine* (Sydney: Ure Smith, 1965), *Nose Tone Unturned* (Sydney: Ure Smith, 1966), *Fraffly Well Spoken* (Sydney: Ure Smith; London: Wolfe Publishing, 1968); Frank Shaw, Stan Kelly and Fritz Spiegl, *Lern Yerself Scouse* (Liverpool: Scouse Press, 1966), Linacre Lane, *Lern Yerself Scouse 2 or The ABZ of Scouse* (Liverpool, Scouse Press, 1966), Brian Minard, *Lern Yerself Scouse 3* (Liverpool: Scouse Press, 1972); Jim Everhart, *The Illustrated Texas Dictionary of the English Language* (Lincoln, Nebraska: Cliff's Notes, 1968); Sam Llewellyn, *Yacky dar moy bewty!* (London: Elm Tree Books, 1985). Other books include: Colin Bowles, *G'Day! Teach Yourself Australian* (London: Angus and Robertson, 1987) and Jackie Mason, *How to Talk Jewish* (New York: St Martin's Press, 1990).

7 Kel Richards, *Father Koala's Nursery Rhymes* (Gosford: Ashton Scholastic, 1992).

8 John Foster, *What a Lot of Nonsense!* (London: Robert Royce, 1985).

9 Examples of split books: James Riddell, *Animal Lore and Disorder* and *Hit or Myth* (London: Atrium Press) – no date, but bought for a child in the 1950s. *Move Over Mrs Markham* (1972) is available through Warner Chappell Plays Ltd, London; the quotation is from Act 2 (p. 104).

10 *The Meaning of Liff* (London: Pan Books, 1983). The idea that words should 'earn their keep' is an old one. It turns up, for example, in Alice's conversation with Humpty Dumpty (Lewis Carroll, *Through the Looking Glass*, 1872, Chapter 6). He comments:

'I meant by "impenetrability" that we've had enough of that subject, and it would be just as well if you'd mention what you mean to do next, as I suppose you don't mean to stop here all the rest of your life.'

'That's a great deal to make one word mean,' Alice said in a thoughtful tone.

'When I make a word do a lot of work like that,' said Humpty Dumpty, 'I always pay it extra.'

'Oh!' said Alice. She was too much puzzled to make any other remark.

'Ah, you should see 'em come round me of a Saturday night,' Humpty Dumpty went on, wagging his head gravely from side to side, 'for to get their wages, you know.'

11 Charles Connell's poem is reprinted in John Foster, *What a Lot of Nonsense!* (London: Robert Royce, 1985), p. 32.

12 Belviso's nursery rhymes and other play of this kind are illustrated in

Willard R. Espy, *An Almanac of Words at Play* (New York: Potter, 1975), pp. 38–9, 72–3.

13 Eric Partridge, *Comic Alphabets: Their Origin, Development, Nature* (London: Routledge and Kegan Paul, 1961). The quotation from Swift on p. 22 appears towards the end of the first conversation: see Partridge's annotated edition, *Swift's Polite Conversation* (London: Deutsch, 1963, p. 117). For other alphabets, see Ruth M. Baldwin, *100 Nineteenth-Century Rhyming Alphabets in English* (Carbondale: Southern Illinois University Press, 1972).

14 Gloss: for those unable to decode the sources of the author's distortions: 486, B format, Windows CE, default, ethernet, Fortran.

15 For a fine early collection of limericks, see Langford Reed, *The Complete Limerick Book* (London: Jarrolds, 1924).

16 See the entry on Little Richard: Donald Clarke, *The Penguin Encyclopedia of Popular Music* (New York: Penguin, 1989) p. 711.

17 Iona and Peter Opie, *The Lore and Language of Schoolchildren* (Oxford: Oxford University Press, 1959), p. 113.

3 THE ENTHUSIASTS

1 Mark Cohen, *The Puffin Book of Tongue-Twisters* (Harmondsworth: Penguin, 1984), p. 56. Another collection is Ken Parkin, *Anthology of British Tongue-twisters* (London: Samuel French, 1969), which classifies them phonetically.

2 James Thurber, *The Wonderful O* (New York: Simon and Schuster, 1957).

3 Howard Bergerson, *Palindromes and Anagrams* (Dover, 1973).

4 A good example of an anagram book which pulls no punches is William Tunstall-Pedoe and Donald L. Holmes, *Anagram Genius* (London: Coronet Books, 1995), and this book contains details of how to buy the software which helped to generate the examples. Another source of computer-generated anagrams can be found at: www.wordsmith.org.

5 The search for ciphers in the works of Shakespeare is best illustrated by Ignatius Donnelly's remarkable two-volume work, *The Great Cryptogram* (London: Sampson Low, Marston, Searle and Rivington, 1888).

6 Words which begin and end with the same letter? Here is Gyles Brandreth's list (from *The Joy of Lex*, London: Guild Publishing, 1987), p. 19: aloha, blob, cynic, dad, ewe, fluff, grinning, health, iambi, Jernej, kick, lull, mum, neon, octavo, pop, Qaraqalpaq, razor, syllables, tot, unau, valv, wow, Xerox, yolky, zizz.

7 There are hundreds of other word games for the enthusiast recorded in

Gyles Brandreth's *The Joy of Lex* (cf. above) or Tony Augarde's *The Oxford Guide to Word Games* (Oxford: Oxford University Press, 1984). Classic publications in the genre include Charles C. Bombaugh's *Gleanings for the Curious from the Harvest Fields of Literature* (1874), reissued as *Oddities and Curiosities of Words and Literature* (New York: Dover Publications, 1961), Dmitri Borgmann's *Language on Vacation* and *Beyond Language*, the many books by Willard R. Espy, such as *The Game of Words* (Newton Abbot: Readers Union Edition, 1971) and *An Almanac of Words at Play* (New York: Potter, 1975), and those by Ross Eckler, such as *Word Recreations*, *Names and Games* and *Making the Alphabet Dance* (New York: St Martin's Press, 1996). Typical word puzzle books are: Veronica Millington, *Word Teaser* (London: Longman, 1985); Janet Whitcut and Brian O'Kill, *Word Quiz* (London: Longman, 1984).

8 The thirty-six-page booklet, *God Proved by Words and Figures*, was compiled by John Hughes and published by ABC Publishers of London. It has no date, but it cost 2 shillings, and postage was 2½d, so I imagine it was in the 1950s.

9 The Latin square has two translations: 'The sower Arepo holds the wheels at work' or 'Arepo the sower holds the wheels with force'. Many explanations about its origin and meaning have been suggested, but without agreement. There is a good discussion by Roger Millington in Chapter 4 of *The Strange World of the Crossword* (London: Hobbs, 1974).

10 A STITCH IN TIME SAVES NINE – starting with the A in column 1 line 3, and ending with the E in column 10 row 5.

11 The London Zoo story is recounted, among many others, in Roger Millington's *The Strange World of the Crossword* (London, 1974), p. 25.

4 THE PROFESSIONALS

1 For a discussion of traditional advertising goals, see J. V. Lund, *Newspaper Advertising* (New York: Prentice-Hall, 1947); and for a linguistic perspective, Torben Vestergaard and Kim Schrøder, *The Language of Advertising* (Oxford: Blackwell, 1985), especially Chapter 3; Michael L. Geis, *The Language of Television Advertising* (New York: Academic Press, 1982); the Crazy Cow ad is discussed on p. 167. The examples in Games People Play 13 are taken from a range of magazines from different countries between the 1960s and today, and include some examples from G. N. Leech, *English in Advertising* (London: Longman, 1966) and G. E. Wood, *The Wordsmiths* (Wellington, New Zealand: Consumer Council, 1964).

2 The fencing story is in the *Vancouver Sun*, 6 July 1993, p. D12.

3 Stanley Unwin, *Deep Joy* (Whitby: Caedmon of Whitby, 1984).

4 The extracts from *The Two Ronnies* dialogue: 'Hello.' 'Hello.' 'Are you busy?' 'Yes we are busy.' 'Have you any eggs?' 'Yes we have eggs.' 'Have you any ham?' 'Nein.'

5 *The Goon Show* extracts in the main text are all from Spike Milligan, *The Goon Show Scripts* (London: Woburn Press, 1972). The extract in Games People Play 15 is from Spike Milligan, *The Lost Goon Shows* (Harmondsworth: Penguin, 1988), 'The Silent Bugler', first recorded in 1958 but not transmitted until 1986.

6 Nigel Rees, *Graffiti Lives, OK* (London: Unwin, 1979); *Graffiti 2* (1980); *Graffiti 3* (1981); etc.

7 Wolfgang Mieder and Stewart A. Kingsbury (eds), *A Dictionary of Wellerisms* (Oxford: Oxford University Press, 1994); John Train, *Remarkabilia* (London: Allen and Unwin, 1984); Russell Ash and Brian Lake, *Bizarre Books* (London: Macmillan, 1985; Sphere Books, 1987).

8 The error books include: Fritz Spiegel, *What the Papers Didn't Mean to Say* (Liverpool: Scouse Press, 1965), Earle Tempel, *Press Boners* and *More Press Boners* (New York: Pocket Books, 1968), and Kermit Schafer, *Typo-bloopers* (New York: Avenel Books, 1977).

9 A word of explanation regarding the parenthesis, for non-British readers. 'It's good to talk' became a mid-1990s catch-phrase in the UK. It was originally a slogan used on television to advertise British Telecom (BT).

10 The extracts are from *Josh Billings: His Sayings* (New York: Carleton, 1866), sections 1, 28, 53; *The Complete Works of Artemus Ward* (London: Chatto and Windus, 1899), p. 118.

11 For clerihews, see: *The Complete Clerihews of E. Clerihew Bentley*, with an introduction by Gavin Ewart (Oxford: Oxford University Press, 1981).

12 Miles Kington's piece is in *The Franglais Lieutenant's Woman* (London: Robson Books, 1986), p. 63.

13 Pedro Carolino, *English As She Is Spoke* (New York: Dover Publications, 1969); this edition also reprints an enthusiastic introduction by Mark Twain. The extracts are from pp. 38–39 and 107ff.

14 The extract is from Leo Rosten, *The Return of H*Y*M*A*N K*A*P*L*A*N* (London: Gollancz, 1959; first published in 1938), p. 41. Several of the Kaplan stories originally appeared in the *New Yorker* and *Harper's Magazine*.

15 Malcolm Bradbury, *Rates of Exchange* (London: Secker and Warburg, 1983; Harmondsworth: Penguin, 1985). The quotations (from the latter edition) are on pp. 83–4, 279.

16 Umberto Eco, *The Name of the Rose* (London: Secker and Warburg, 1983; London: Pan, 1984). The quotation is on p. 46 of the Pan edition.

17 Anthony Burgess, *Joysprick: An Introduction to the Language of James Joyce* (London: Deutsch, 1973), p. 152.

18 Paul Ferris, *Dylan Thomas: The Collected Letters* (New York: Macmillan, 1985). The quotations are from a letter to John Davenport (29 May 1947), p. 632, and one to Margaret Taylor (3 August 1947), p. 656.

19 Samuel Beckett, *Waiting for Godot* in *The Complete Dramatic Works* (London: Faber and Faber, 1986), p. 42.

20 Harold Pinter, *The Birthday Party* (London: Methuen, 1960), pp. 50–52.

21 Margaret Drabble, *The Radiant Way* (London: Weidenfeld and Nicolson, 1987; Harmondsworth: Penguin, 1988, p. 396).

22 Most of the works discussed can be found in Tilman Osterworld, *Pop Art* (Cologne: Taschen, 1991); see also Edward Lucie-Smith, *Art Today* (Oxford: Phaidon, 1989, 3rd edn).

23 A good selection of modern and experimental typefaces can be found at LettError, a design studio in The Hague, run by Just van Rossum and Erik van Blokland (www.letterror.com).

24 Graphic poetry is illustrated as part of a discussion of the semantic effects which can be conveyed by typography in my 'Towards a linguistic typography', *A TypI Annual Conference*, University of Reading, 1997.

25 For typewriter poets, see: Peter Finch (ed), *Typewriter Poems* (Cardiff: Second Aeon Publications, 1972).

26 The Cato examples are taken from Ken Cato, *Cato Design* (London: Thames and Hudson, 1995; Rockport, MA: Rockport Publishers, 1995).

27 John Langdon, *Wordplay* (New York: Harcourt Brace Jovanovich, 1992).

28 From 'T' Babby Born in a Mistal', in Arnold Kellett, *Ee By Gum, Lord! The Gospels in Broad Yorkshire* (Otley: Smith Settle, 1996), p. 2. There is an accompanying tape recording.

29 From 'Preaching on a Hill', in Carl Burke, *God is Beautiful, Man* (National Board of Young Men's Christian Associations, USA, 1969; London: Fontana, 1970, p. 51); earlier books by Carl Burke were *God Is For Real, Man* and *Treat Me Cool, Lord*.

5 THE CHILDREN

1 Peter Bryant and Lynette Bradley, *Children's Reading Problems* (Oxford: Blackwell, 1985), p. 48; Catherine Garvey, 'Play with language and speech', in Susan Ervin-Tripp and Claudia Mitchell-Kernan (eds), *Child Discourse* (New York: Academic Press, 1977), pp. 27–47; Ruth Weir, *Language in the Crib* (The Hague: Mouton, 1962); James Britton, *Language and Learning* (London: Allen

Lane, The Penguin Press, 1970), pp. 77, 84.

2 For examples of twin conversation, see Eleanor Keenan, 'Conversational competence in children', *Journal of Child Language* 1, 1974, pp. 163–83.

3 For more on LAD, see Steven Pinker, *The language instinct* (Harmondsworth: Penguin, 1994).

4 Several examples of concatenated rhyme-play are given in Mary Sanches and Barbara Kirshenblatt-Gimblett, 'Children's Traditional Speech Play and Child Language', in Barbara Kirshenblatt-Gimblett (ed.), *Speech Play: Research and Resources for Studying Linguistic Creativity* (Philadelphia: University of Pennsylvania Press, 1976), pp. 65–110.

5 For Pig Latin and other games, see Nelson Cowan, 'Acquisition of Pig Latin: a case study', *Journal of Child Language* 16, 1989, pp. 365–86; Nelson Cowan and Lewis A. Leavitt, 'Talking backward: exceptional speech play in late childhood', *Journal of Child Language* 9, 1982, pp. 481–95; 'The developmental course of two children who could talk backward five years ago', *Journal of Child Language* 14, 1987, pp. 393–5.

6 Martha Wolfenstein, *Children's Humor: A Psychological Analysis* (Glencoe: Free Press, 1954). The quotation is from p. 94.

7 Examples of pseudo-intellectual language are discussed in Sanches and Kirshenblatt-Gimblett, 1976, p.101.

8 Iona and Peter Opie, *The Lore and Language of Schoolchildren* (Oxford: Clarendon Press, 1959).

9 Richard Ely and Alyssa McCabe, 'The language play of kindergarten children', *First Language* 14, 1994, pp. 19–35.

10 The two child language anthologies are Paul Fletcher and Michael Garman (eds.) 1986. *Language acquisition*, 2nd edn (Cambridge: Cambridge University Press, 2nd edn, 1986) and Paul Fletcher and Brian MacWhinney (eds.) *The Handbook of Child Language* (Oxford: Blackwell, 1995).

11 Kornei Chukovsky, *From Two to Five* (Berkeley: University of California Press, 1963). The quotation is on p. 96.

12 The Opies' quotations are from p. 17 (see above).

13 Jerome Bruner, 'Language, Mind, and Reading', in H. Goelman, A. Oberg and F. Smith (eds.), *Awakening to Literacy* (Exeter, NH: Heinemann, 1984), p. 196.

14 For riddles, see Ely and McCabe (above); also Kathy Hirsh-Pasek, Leila Gleitman, and Henry Gleitman, 'What Did the Brain Say to the Mind? A Study of the Detection and Report of Ambiguity by Young Children', in R. J. Jarvella and W. J. M. Levelt (eds), *The Child's Concept of Language* (New York: Springer, 1978).

6 THE READERS

1 The reference is to Joyce Grenfell's nursery sketches: *George – Don't Do That* (London: Futura, 1978).

2 The notion of the 'culture of literacy' is presented in Carolyn D. Baker and Peter Freebody, *Children's First School Books* (Oxford: Blackwell, 1989). On general issues of taking into account what the child already knows, see Marie Clay, *Reading: The Patterning of Complex Behaviour* (London: Heinemann, 2nd edn 1979) and Emilia Ferreiro and Ana Teberosky, *Literacy Before Schooling* (London: Heinemann, 1983).

3 The recent history of ideas in educational language thinking is reviewed in my *Cambridge Encyclopedia of Language* (Cambridge: Cambridge University Press, 1997), Chapter 44; for a fuller account, *Child Language, Learning and Linguistics* (London: Edward Arnold, 1987, 2nd edn).

4 The extracts from traditional schemes are from *I Went Walking*, an early text in the 'Janet and John' series (London: Nisbet, 1949); *Things We Like*, Book 3a in the Ladybird Reading Scheme (Loughborough: Wills and Hepworth, 1964); and *Days In The Sun*, a later book in the 'Janet and John' series.

5 Dr Seuss, *Fox in Socks* (New York: Random House, 1965).

6 Lonzo Anderson, *The Haganinny* (Reading 360.) (Lexington: Ginn, 1974); *Fuzzbuzz* (Oxford: Oxford University Press); *Gay Way* (Basingstoke: Macmillan Education, 1985); *Mount Gravatt Reading Series* (Sydney: Addison-Wesley, 1977). The booklets used in the Mount Gravatt example were 2, 5, 9, 13, 17, 19, 20, 22, 23, 30.

7 Howard Gardner, Mary Kircher, Ellen Winner, and David Perkins, 'Children's metaphoric productions and preferences', *Journal of Child Language* 2, 1975, pp. 125–41.

8 The Desperate Dan example is illustrated further in my *Cambridge Encyclopedia of the English Language* (Cambridge: Cambridge University Press, 1995), p. 250.

9 John Foster, *What a Lot of Nonsense!* (London: Robert Royce, 1985), p. 8.

10 Ronald James and R. G. Gregory, *Imaginative Speech and Writing* (London: Nelson, 1966).

11 Eric Carle, *All about Arthur (An Absolutely Absurd Ape)* (New York: Franklin Watts, 1974); John Burningham, *ABC* (London: Cape, 1964); Richard Scarry, *Find Your ABC's* (London: Collins, 1973).

12 Lyn Wendon, *Letterland* (Cambridge: Letterland Ltd, 1968).

13 Maureen Vidler, *Find a Story* (Harmondsworth: Penguin Education, 1974).

14 Richard Scarry, *Best Word Book Ever* (London: Hamlyn, 1964); Joan

Hanson, *Homonyms* (Minneapolis: Lerner, 1972); H. Hoke, *Jokes, Jests and Jollies* (Reading 360.) (Lexington: Ginn, 1974); Remy Charlip, *Fortunately* (New York: Parents' Magazine Press, 1964).

15 Jeff Bevington and David Crystal, *Skylarks* (London: Nelson, 1975).

16 Postillion sentences are discussed in David Crystal, 'Postillion sentences', *Child Language Teaching and Therapy* 11 (1), 1995, 79–90.

17 *Oxford Reading Tree* (Oxford: Oxford University Press, 1986).

18 Bridie Raban, *The Spoken Vocabulary of Five-year-old Children* (University of Reading: Reading and Language Information Centre, 1988).

19 Jeanne Willis and Tony Ross, *Dr Xargle's Book of Earth Tiggers* (London: Andersen Press, 1990); Jan Scieszka, *The True Story of the Three Little Pigs* (London: Viking Kestrel, 1989).

20 *Patterns of Language* (London: BBC, 1986).

21 Percival Leigh: *The Comic English Grammar: an Introduction to the English Tongue* (London: Richard Bentley, 1840; London: Bracken Books, 1989). *The Play Grammar* was one of the educational books compiled by 'Miss Corner' for the London publishing house of Dean and Co, probably in the 1850s. There is no date on the book, but the copy I have says that it is the 25th edition, so it was evidently popular.

22 The examples are from Sue Palmer, *Language Book 1* (level: Language 3) (London: Longman, 1994), pp. 24, 39.

23 The examples are from D. Crystal, *Language A to Z*, Books 1 and 2 (London: Longman, 1991).

24 Cynthia Rylant, *The Old Woman Who Named Things* (New York: Harcourt Brace, 1996); Quentin Flynn and Sarah Farman, *There's a Most Massive Spider in my Bedroom* (Melbourne: John Parsons, 1997), and other stories.

25 The *Jets* series is published in London by A. and C. Black; the quotations are from Nigel Gray, *Sharron and Darren* (1993) and Damon Burnard, *Ernest the Heroic Lion-Tamer* (1993).

26 Roderick Hunt, *Bad Day, Good Day* (Oxford: Oxford University Press, 1996).

27 Juliet Partridge, *A Very Hot Day* (Cambridge: Cambridge University Press, 1996).

7 THE FUTURE

1 I could add that language play is important for linguists too. In the 1990s, phonologists have been exploring the properties of play languages (they call them *ludlings*) to learn about the nature of phonological systems in general:

there are several references in John A. Goldsmith (ed.), *The Handbook of Phonological Theory* (Oxford: Blackwell, 1995).

2 Walter Redfern, *Puns* (Oxford: Blackwell, 1984), p. 175.

3 Richard Dawkins, *River Out Of Eden* (London: Weidenfeld and Nicolson, 1995), pp. 157–8.

4 Terrence Deacon, *The Symbolic Species: The Co-Evolution of Language and the Human Brain* (New York and London: W.W. Norton, 1997). The quotations are from pp. 340, 377, 419–21.

5 Robert Graves, *I, Claudius* (London: Arthur Barker, 1934).

6 Peter Ustinov, *Dear Me* (Harmondsworth: Penguin, 1978), p. 64

GAMES PEOPLE PLAY

G2 Richard Lederer, *Get Thee to a Punnery* (New York: Bantam Doubleday Dell, 1988), pp. 20 and 112. For more examples, see Bennett Cerf's *Treasury of Atrocious Puns* (New York: Harper and Row, 1968) – or any of the writings of US humorist, S. J. Perelman.

G4 *Mouthsounds* (New York: Workman Publishing, 1980). Its dedication reads: 'This book is dedicated to the little guys – the class clowns and the office cutups. Those unsung heroes who, in addition to shooting paper clips and photocopying their faces, rescue us from what would otherwise be lackluster afternoons.'

G9 Tom Stoppard, *Rosencrantz and Guildenstern are Dead* (London: Faber and Faber, 1967), pp. 30–32.

G11 2–3. SALES 4–5. RECEIPT 6–7. MERE 10–11. DOVE 14–15. MORE 18–19. HARD 22–23. LION 26–27. EVENING 28–29. EVADE 30–31. ARE 8–9. FARM 12–13. RAIL 16–17. DRAW 20–21. TIED 24–25. SAND 10–18. DOH 6–22. MORAL 4–26. REVERIE 2–11. SERE 19–28. DOVE F–7. FACE 23–30. NEVA 1–32. RULE 33–34. NARD N–8. NEIF 24–31. SIDE 3–12. SPAR 20–29. TANE 5–27. TRADING 9–25. MIRED 13–21. LAD

You would be forgiven for not getting *neif* – an obsolete form of *nieve*, a fist, known in northern dialects of Middle English. But it *is* in the unabridged *Oxford English Dictionary*. So is *tane*, another obsolete northern dialect form, from 'that ane' (= that one).

Horizontals

1. BOB 4. ASH 7. ERA 8. VIA 9. TELLERS 11. DEN 12. SEWAGES 16. TRI 17. EEL 18. YEN 19. DRY

Verticals

1. BET   2. ORE   3. BALDWIN   4. AVENGED   5. SIR   6. HAS   10.
LEA   12. STY   13. ERE   14. EER   15. SLY
Eer is a variant of *ever*, like *e'er*.

G14 The correlations are: 1D; 2L; 3H; 4F; 5C; 6J; 7I; 8G; 9B; 10K; 11A; 12E. The
chief allusions are as follows: 1 A pun on *common sense*. 2 The elocution scene
in *Pygmalion/My Fair Lady*: 'the rain in Spain lies mainly in the plain'. 3 The
proverb 'A bird in the hand is worth two in the bush'. 4 The catch-phrase,
'That's the way the cookie crumbles', with a pun on *cookie/kooky* (= 'zany').
5 *Ab*, the article makes clear, is an (unusual) abbreviation of *abdomen*; the
allusion is to the title of the popular British television series, *Ab Fab*
('Absolutely Fabulous'). 6 Another proverb: 'Where there's a will, there's a
way'. 7 The song 'Fings (= 'things') ain't what they used to be', from the
musical. 8 An everyday idiom. 9 A specifically British allusion, to the income
tax system, 'Pay as you Earn'. 10 A melodramatic metaphor, 'web of intrigue'.
11 The chanted catch-phrase heard in such US comedy shows as *Rowan and
Martin's Laugh-In*, 'Here come de (= 'the') judge'. 12 A colloquial idiom, 'the
best thing since sliced bread'.

G21 Roger D Abrahams and Lois Rankin (eds), *Counting-Out Rhymes: A
Dictionary* (Austin and London: University of Texas Press, 1980).

G22 The answers to the conundrums: *When it's a-jar*; B4 (*before*); *but* ('t');
mine.

INDEX

abbreviations 47–8, 66

ABC Arithmetic 80

Abrahams, Roger D. 174, 237

absurdist poetry 29–30

accents 11, 19–22, 24–30, 126, 210, 219

acrostics 58–61

Adair, Gilbert 64

Adams, Douglas 36

Addison, Joseph 60

adverbs 206–8

advertising 46, 94–100, 152, 154

Ah Big Yaws? 22, 228

Alice 58, 228

alliteration 30, 40–41, 58, 98, 138, 181, 197, 212, 215

Almanac of Words at Play, An 72

alphabet books 197

alphabetic words in a sentence 76–7

alphabets 36, 40–45, 66–7, 73, 79–80

amateurs 9–53

ambigrams 154–5

anagrams 68–72, 110–11

Anderson, Lorenzo 191, 234

anecdotes 172

animal noises 26–7

animals, talking to 50–51

animation 152

antigrams 69

antonyms 199

Appleton, Victor 90

Applied Research Corporation 154

appreciation, expressing 26

appropriateness 205

archaisms 210

Archimedes 223

'argument clinic' sketch 108

Armstrong, Louis 51

art, verbal 182

artists 148–55

Ash, Russell 121, 231

As I Opened Fire 149

assumptions 14

Atkinson, Rowan 105

Augarde, Tony 230

Australian dialect 22–3

Australian nursery rhymes 24

authors 134–7, 137–48

baby talk 50–51, 159–64, 202

backwards talk 170–1

Bacon, Francis 71

Bad Day, Good Day 215

Baker, Carolyn 185, 188, 234

Baldwin, Ruth M. 229

Ball, Lucille 105

Baloo 51

'banter' sketch 109

Bard, Wilkie 56

Barker, Ronnie 105–6

BBC 204

Bean 105
Beckett, Samuel 7, 145, 232
Belviso, Bob 39, 228
Bentley, Edmund Clerihew 129, 231
Bergerson, Howard 67, 229
Bestie 104
Bevington, Jeff 200, 235
Bible 71
Billings, Josh 127–9, 231
Birthday Party, The 145–6
Bizarre Books 121
black-letter typography 151
Blankety Blank 92
Bloodnok, Major 112
bloopers 121–2
Bluebottle 28, 112–13
Blundell, Nigel 227
Bombaugh, Charles C. 62, 218, 230
bonding 28, 52, 219
bon motorists 6–7
Book of Nonsense 45
Borge, Victor 37, 209
Borgmann, Dmitri 78, 218, 230
Borneo Pub 154
Boswell, James 5
Bowles, Colin 228
Bowman, Isa 59
Bradbury, Malcolm 135–6, 231
Bradley, Lynette 165, 181, 232
Brando, Marlon 25
Brandreth, Gyles 229, 230
British Telecom 231
Britton, James 166–7, 232
broadcasting 89–92
Bronx cheer 26
Browne, Charles Farrar 127–9
Bruner, Jerome 163, 179, 216, 233
Brush, Basil 171
Bryant, Peter 165, 181, 232
Bugs Bunny 25

Burgess, Anthony 143, 232
Burgess, Gelett 88
Burke, Carl 156, 232
Burnard, Damon 214, 235
Burningham, John 193, 234

Cambridge Encyclopedia, The 81, 122–7
Cambridge Encyclopedia of Language, The 234
Cambridge Encyclopedia of the English Language, The 234
Cambridge Reading 215–16
Call My Bluff 92
captions 104
Carle, Eric 197, 234
car licence plates 6–7
Carlson, Wayne 78
Carolino, Pedro 132, 231
Carroll, Lewis 58–60, 70, 191, 228
cartoon 152–3, 212–13
  captions 104
  speech 38, 113
  voices 29
Catch Phrase 92
catch phrases 94, 98, 111, 112, 231
catfrontation episode 2–5
Cato, Ken 152, 232
Cendrar, Blaise 148
Cerf, Bennett 236
Chain Letters 92
Chambers Dictionary 2, 89
Chaplin, Charlie 105
Chapman, John 32
Charlip, Remy 199, 235
Chairo, Delia 227
chicken behaviour 27
child language 52–3, 159–82
  and reading 183–217
Chomsky, Noam 169

choosing-up games 174–5
Chukovsky, Kornei 178–80, 233
Clapham and Dwyer 43
Clarke, Donald 229
class dialects 18–19
classroom language 183–7
Claudius, Emperor 225
Clay, Marie 234
clerihews 129–30, 231
clowns 52
Cobbing, Bob 152
Cockney 21, 42, 49–50
code-switching 131–2
Cohen, Mark 57, 229
coining words 2–5, 30–36, 95–6, 117
collectors 117–27
comedy 12, 105–16
comic
    alphabets 40–45, 190
    strips 38–9, 149, 210, 212
    writers 127–36
Comic Alphabets 40–5
Comic English Grammar, The 205
communication view of language 1
competition 220, 224
concatenation games 170
concrete poetry 140, 148, 152
conformity 193
connectivity 199
Connell, Charles 38, 228
Connolly, Billy 225
consequences 199
consonants 10, 13, 165
'contradiction' sketch 109
conversation 2–3, 9, 11, 24, 30, 53, 73,
    147, 168, 180
Cook, Peter 105
Cooney, Ray 32
copyright in jokes 17
Corbett, Ronnie 106

Coren, Alan 130–31
Corner, Miss 235
counting-out games 170, 174–5
Cowan, Nelson 170–71, 233
Crazy Cow 98
creativity 8, 193–4, 220
Critchley, John 150
crossword
    clues 33, 68, 69, 224
    puzzles 83, 85–8
Cubists 148
culture of literacy 185
Cummings, E. E. 140, 152

Danby, Mary 227
Davenport, John 232
David Copperfield 30
Dawkins, Richard 222, 236
Deacon, Terrence 222–4, 236
'dead parrot' sketch 109–10
Dee, Jack 28
definitions, playful 33
Desperate Dan 38, 195, 234
deviation 10
dialect humour 18–24
dialogue play 168–9, 180
Dickens, Charles 23, 30, 120–21
dictionaries, use of 89
Diddymen 116
Dingbats 73
di Sciullo, Pierre 150
discovery 224
Disney, Walt 52
'doctor-doctor' games 171
Dodd, Ken 116
Donald Duck 24
Donaldson, Tim 150
Donnelly, Ignatius 229
doublets 191
Drabble, Margaret 147, 232

drama 144–6
Dr Awkward and Olson in Oslo 68
Dr Xargle 202–3
Dryden, John 18

Eberstadt, Isabel 227
Eccles 112
Eckler, Ross 60, 64, 230
Eco, Umberto 136, 231
edges of language 155–6
education and language play 178–82, 220
Ee By Gum, Lord! 156
Eliot, T. S. 155
Eller, Jim 150
eloquence 182
Ely, Richard 178, 233
emotional nonsense 49
English as She is Spoke 132
English Now 34
enthusiasts 54–92
Ernest the Heroic Lion-Tamer 212–15
Ervin-Tripp, Susan 232
Espy, Willard R. 72, 218, 229, 230
Everhart, Jim 228
evolution 222–5
Ewart, Gavin 231
exaggerations 212
examination howlers 33

Farman, Sarah 235
Fazah, Ziad 55
Ferreiro, Emilia 234
Ferris, Paul 232
figures of speech 147, 189, 200
Finch, Peter 152, 232
Find a Story 198
Finnegans Wake 139, 143
Fitzgerald, Ella 51
Fitzgerald, F. Scott 63

Fletcher, Paul 233
fluddle 33
Flynn, Quentin 235
Fonseca, José da 132
fonts 150–55
foreign language learning 18, 132
formulaic jokes 17–18
Fortunately 199
Foster, John 30, 195, 228, 234
Fox in Socks 189–90
fractured English 132–7
Fraffly Well Spoken 22, 228
Franglais 131–2
Freberg, Stan 29, 105
Freebody, Peter 185, 188, 234
French 18, 76, 131, 132
friends 28
Fuzzbuzz 191, 234

Gadsby 63
Gaillard, Slim 51
Games magazine 60
gangster slang 50
Gardner, Howard 192, 234
Garis, Howard 90
Garman, Michael 233
Garvey, Catherine 166, 168, 232
Gay Way 191, 234
Geis, Michael L. 230
gematria 80–83
Georgetown University 83
German accent, mock 25
Gilbert, W. S. 47, 56
Gladiators 92
Gleitman, Henry 233
Gleitman, Leila 233
Godfather, The 25
God is Beautiful, Man 156–7
God Proved in Words and Figures 80, 230

Goelman, H. 233
Goldsmith, John A. 236
golf 220
Goon Show, The 28, 29, 52, 112–16
graffiti 117
Graham, Elizabeth 60
grammar 13, 180, 184–5
    in reading 198–9
    non-standard 95–7, 127–9, 132–7
    play 205–10
graphic design 148, 150–55
graphic poetry 151
Graves, Robert 11, 137–8, 225, 236
Gray, Nigel 235
Grease 51
Greek, Classical 63
Gregory, R. G. 196, 234
Grenfell, Joyce 234
grid games 83–9
Grosset and Dunlap 90
Guardian 101
guide-book language 137–8
guide songs 52
Guinness Book of Records, The 55
Gulliver's Travels 71

Hagidiscography 151
Hall, Rich 33
Hanson, Joan 199, 235
'hate anagrams' sketch 110–11
Hay Literary Festival 61
headlines 101–5
Hebrew 80
Heineken 99–100
Henry V 134
Herbert, George 151
hesitation 26
heteroliteral texts 77
hey 42
Hirsh-Pasek, Kathy 233

Hofstadter, Douglas 154
Hoke, H. 235
Holland, Lord 62
Holmes, Donald L. 229
homographs 199
homoliteral texts 77
homonyms 199
homo symbolicus 223
horror-story play 173–4
Houedard, Sylvester 152
Howerd, Frankie 105
howlers 33
Hughes, John 230
humour 12, 14, 93, 105–16, 218, 224
Humpty Dumpty 228
Hungarian, mock 136–7
Hunt, Roderick 202, 215, 235
Hyman, Kaplan 134–5, 231

identity 28, 150–55
Idle, Eric 109, 111
*Illustrated Texas Dictionary of the
    English Language, The* 22, 228
Imaginative Speech and Writing
    196
improvisation 73
I'm Sorry, I Haven't a Clue 45
Indiana, Robert 149
-inge 29
Inge, Charles 46
Intelligent Australia 154
intensifiers 210
Internet 44–5
interrogatives 210
intimacy, expression of 27, 51, 219
Irish 19, 21, 25, 45
-ish 32
Italian 149
    mock 39
It'll Be All Right on the Night 123

Jacobson, Howard 14
James I 71
James, Ronald 196, 234
Janet and John 188–9, 234
jargon 165
Jarreau, Al 51
Jarvella, R. J. 233
jazz 51
'Jets' series 212
Johnson, Samuel 59
Johnstone, Michael 228
jokes 12–22, 105, 171–2, 199, 223
Jones, Terry 109
Joyce, James 11, 139–40, 143, 147
Jungle Book, The 51
Just a Minute 92

Keenan, Elinor 233
Kellett, Arnold 156, 232
Kelly, Stan 228
Kilgariff, Michael 227
Kim, Scott 154
Kingsbury, Stewart 120, 231
Kington, Miles 131–2, 231
Kircher, Mary 234
Kirshenblatt-Gimblett, Barbara 181, 233
Kit-Kat 98
'knock-knock' games 171
Knox, Ronald 46

LAD 169
Ladybird Reading Scheme 188–9, 234
Laggard Bros 132
Lake, Brian 121, 231
Lamb, Charles 15
Lane, Linacre 228
Langdon, John 154, 232
language
    disability 180, 191

    game 148
    instinct 7
    in use 186–7
    teaching 183–7, 204
Language Acquisition Device 169
Language and Lore of Schoolchildren, The 173
Language A to Z 209–10
Latin 83–4, 230
Lauder, Afferbeck 22, 228
laughter 14, 223
Lear, Edward 30, 45
learning through play 163
Leavitt, Lewis A. 233
Lederer, Richard 6–7, 236
Lee, Dennis 196
Leech, G. N. 230
Léger, Fernand 148
Leigh, Percival 205, 235
Leonardi, Alessio 150
Lern Yerself Scouse 22, 228
Let Stalk Strine 22, 228
letter
    recognition 197
    transposition 71
LettError 232
Levelt, W. J. M. 233
Levine, Lawrence 68
Lichtenstein, Roy 149
Liddell, Alice Pleasant 58
limericks 30, 45–9
Lindon, J. A. 67
linguistics 55, 235
lipogram 63–6
literacy 180–82, 183–217, 220
literature 134, 137–48
Lions 25
Little Richard 229
Liverpool dialect 22–3
Llewellyn, Sam 20, 228

Lloyd, John 36
London dialect 22–3
London Zoo 88
Long, Chris 84
Long John Silver 25
Longman Book Project 208, 235
Longman Dictionary of the English Language 2
Loren, Sophia 52
Los Angeles Times 101
Louis XIII 71
Lovelock, Terry 99
Love Rising 149
Love's Labour's Lost 15
Lucie-Smith, Edward 232
ludic view of language 1–8, 218–25
ludlings 235
lullabies 162
Lund, J. V. 230

McCabe, Alyssa 178, 233
McLachlan, Edward 152
McNicholas, Neil 34
MacNicholl, Tony 81
MacWhinney, Brian 233
Mahood, Molly 15
major-general's song 56
Malong, Rawbone 228
Mason, Jackie 228
Mastermind 92
Matthews, Harry 79
Meaning of Liff, The 36, 228
media 89, 92
metalanguage, playing with 116, 202–3
metalinguistic awareness 180–81, 198, 212–15, 222
metaphor 143, 147, 189, 192–3
Midsummer Night's Dream, A 60
Mieder, Wolfgang 120, 231

milk ad 95
Milligan, Spike 30, 231
Millington, Roger 230
Millington, Veronica 230
Milne, A. A. 29, 227
Minard, Brian 228
misprints 121–7
missing words 33
Mitchell-Kernan, Claudia 232
mock foreign languages 113, 210
monologue play 166–7
monosyllables 76
Monty Python 28, 107–11, 114–16, 136–7
Moore, Dudley 105
Morecambe, Eric 105
Morley, Christopher 6
morphology 169
Morse Code 40
Mount Gravatt Reading Series 191–2, 201, 234
mouthplay 26
Mouthsounds 27, 236
Move Over Mrs Markham 32, 228
Muppets, The 28
music halls 56
My Fair Lady 237
My Word 92

names
  anagrams in 71
  play with 36, 113, 170, 195, 219
narrative 172–3
Nash, Ogden 10–11, 37–8, 227
National Curriculum 187, 211
negative prefixes 32
neo- 31–2
neologism 30–36, 143
neo-pop art 149
-ness 31

Newman, Frederick R. 27
Newman, W. 206
newspapers 89, 101–5
news reading 204
Newton, Robert 25
nicknames 170
Nilsen, Don L. F. 7
noises, copying 26–7
nonce words 30–36, 143
Norden, Denis 123
nonsense 49–53, 112, 156, 162, 165,
        168, 170, 172, 177, 179–80, 195–7
Not Necessarily the News 33
novel 146–7
number rhymes 215
nursery rhymes 39, 52, 162, 181, 215

Oberg, A. 233
obscenity 169
occupational dialects 204
OK games 118–19
O'Kill, Brian 230
*Old Woman Who Named Things,
        The* 211–12
onomatopoeia 29, 52, 149
Opie, Iona and Peter 52, 173, 179,
        196, 199, 233
orthography 151, 197–8
Osterworld, Tilman 232
O'Toole, Peter 51
out-takes 123
Oxford English Dictionary 2, 52, 66,
        84, 236
Oxford Reading Tree 202, 215

Pace, Alleen 7
Palin, Michael 111
palindromes 67–8, 84, 154
Palmer, Sue 235
P & O Cruises 95

pangrams 66–7
parent talk 159–64
Parkin, Ken 229
parodies 176–7
parsing 186–7, 208
Partridge, Eric 40–43, 50, 229
Partridge, Juliet 235
Patterns of Language 204
peep-bo game 164
Perec, Georges 64
Perelman, S. J. 236
performatives 176
Perkins, Brian 204
Perkins, David 234
personal function 220
personality 5
personification 189
philosophers 155
phonetic language 37
phonetics 22, 160, 210
phonic readers 189–90
phonology 140, 143, 165, 181–2, 195–7,
        216, 235
phrase-book language 132–3, 136–7,
        201
Piaget, Jean 179, 216
Picasso 148
Pickwick Papers, The 10, 30, 120–21
Pig Latin 170–71, 233
ping-pong punning 4, 139, 169
Pinker, Steven 227, 233
Pinter, Harold 145–6, 232
Pirates of Penzance, The 56
place names 36
play as practice 179, 216
Play Grammar, The 206–7, 235
playground language 173–8
play routines 162–3
plays 144–6
plosives 210

poetry 137–9, 140–2, 152–3, 182, 220
  absurdist 29–30
  acrostic 58–60
  transpositional 78–9
  univoalic 62–3
Polite Conversation 42
Pop Art 148, 150
pop songs 51–2
Portuguese 132–3
postillion sentences 201, 235
pragmatics 200–202, 213
preaching 158
prefix play 31–2
professional language players 93–158
pronunciation 10, 36–7, 47, 94, 98,
    160–61, 178, 180, 195–7
prose, literary 146–7
proverbs 69, 98, 120, 127–9, 132–3
Pryor, Richard 225
pseudo-intellectual speech 172, 212,
    233
P'tang Yang Kipperbang 29, 172
Puffin Book of Tongue Twisters 57,
    229
Pujom, André 71
pun-capping 4–5, 25, 224
Punch 104, 130, 132, 152
punctuation 13, 37, 235
puns 5–7, 14–15, 43, 90–91, 98–9,
    101–5, 116, 120–21, 139, 171, 180,
    199, 221
Pygmalion 237
Pyrex 96–8

Raban, Bridie 202, 235
radio shows 89, 92, 112–16
Rankin, Lois 174, 237
rapping 170
rapport 28, 159–60, 219
raspberry 26

Rawle, Graham 10
read, learning to 181, 183–217
reading 360 199
reading schemes 183–92, 215
real books 184
rebuses 72
received pronunciation 23
Redfern, Walter 221, 236
Redhead, Brian 204
reduplications 162
Reed, Langford 229
Rees, Nigel 117–18, 231
regional dialects 18–24
relationships, human 53
Remarkabilia 121
repetition 107–8
respelling 22
rhetoric 182
rhopalic 77–8
rhyme 37–9, 46–8, 98, 129–30, 138,
    165–6, 168–70, 172–81, 192, 208,
    212–16
rhyming pairs (in jokes) 18
Rhyming Riddles 215
rhyming slang 49–50
rhythm 22, 94, 98, 138, 160, 174, 208,
    215
Richards, Kel 23–4, 228
Riddell, James 228
riddles 171–2, 181, 188–9, 199, 233
Robinson, John 156
Rosencrantz and Guildenstern Are
    Dead 74–5, 203, 236
Rosenthal, Jack 29, 172
Ross, Tony 235
Rossetti, Dante Gabriel 45
Rosten, Leo 134, 231
Round Games and Amusing Exercises
    Upon Grammar 206–8
Round Table in Linguistics 83

rudeness, expressing 26, 169
rule-breaking 10–11, 138–9, 146–8, 155, 181
rules in language play 4–5, 148
'rules O K' 118–19
Rylant, Cynthia 211

Sainsbury's 99
Sanches, Mary 181, 233
Scarry, Richard 197, 199, 234
scat singing 51
Schafer, Kermit 121, 231
Scharf, Kenny 149
Schrøder, Kim 230
Scieszka, Jan 203, 235
Scots 19
scout songs 52
Scrabble 88–9, 224
Scrabble Board 150
Sellers, Peter 28, 29, 52, 105
semantic development 180
semantics 110, 199–200
semaphore 40
semiotics 215
sentence 13, 209–10
Seuss, Dr 189–90, 216, 234
Shakespeare 15, 69, 71–2, 134, 229
Sharon and Darren 213
Shaw, Frank 228
Shaw, George Bernard 45
Shaw, Henry Wheeler 127–9
Sheridan, Richard 30
short story 146
silly hour 170
similes 189, 192–3
simplification 160
singing 162, 164
situational play 194–5, 199
Skylarks 200
Slaka 135–6

slogans 94–100, 231
Smith, Frank 233
Smith, Linell 227
Smith, R. Montague 42
sniglets 33
social function 219–20
sociolinguistics 185
songs 51–2
sonic alphabet 79–80
sound symbolism 13, 24–30, 161, 164, 195, 197
South African dialect 22–3
South China Morning Post 101
Southey, Robert 49
spamming 108
'spam' sketch 107–8, 111–12
Spanglish 131–2
Spanish 131
    mock 113
Spanish Inquisition 89, 111
Speak 149
speech
    bubble 113, 213
    disguise 50
    rapid 23
    vs writing 205
spell, learning to 181
spelling 10, 13, 20–22, 36–45, 47–8, 50, 98, 198
    comic 127–9, 195, 203
Spice Girls 52
Spiegl, Fritz 121, 228, 231
spiels 167
split infinitives 54–5
Star Wars 28, 191
Stephens, Meic 152
stereotypes 19
Stir Crazy 225
Stoppard, Tom 74, 145, 203, 236
Stratemeyer, Edward 90

Streets of London 152
structure vs use 186–7, 196, 199, 205
stylistics 147–8
substitution-games 72
suffix play 31–2
Sun 101
survival 225
swearing 49–50, 112
Swift, Jonathan 5, 42, 71, 229
Sydney Morning Herald 101
syllable play 165–6
Symbolic Species, The 222–4
synonyms 199

taboo words 49–50
tactile play 163–4
Takka Takka 149
Tati, Jacques 105
Taylor, Margaret 232
Teberosky, Ana 234
telephone conversation 43
television shows 89, 92, 105–12
Tempel, Earle 121, 131
Tempest, The 71–2
terminology 180
Texas dialect 22
Tex-Mex 231
theologians 155–8
Thomas, Dylan 143–4, 152, 178, 232
Thurber, James 30, 64–5, 229
Tillich, Paul 156
Tilson, Joe 149
Tom Jones, A History of 10
Tom Swifties 90–91
tongue-twisters 56–8, 177, 189–90,
    199, 216
  visual 48
Torquemada 89
Tower of Babel 61–80
Train, John 121, 231

translation
  between dialects 22–4, 156–7
  between languages 39
transpositional poetry 78–9
True Story of the Three Little Pigs,
    The 203
Tunstall-Pedoe, William 229
Twain, Mark 231
twins 167, 233
Two Ronnies, The 106–7, 231
typewriter poets 152
typographical errors 121–7
typography 140, 148, 150–55
  animated 152

Under Milk Wood 143
univocalics 61–3
Unwin, Stanley 106, 231
usage 155
use vs structure 186–7, 196, 199,
    205
Ustinov, Peter 225, 236

van Blokland, Erik 232
Van Buren, Paul 155–6
Vancouver Sun 101, 230
van Rossum, Just 232
varieties of language 204
verbal duelling 14–15
Verne, Jules 131
Very Hot Day, A 215–16
Vestergaard, Torben 230
Vidler, Maureen 198, 234
visual play 164
vocalizations 160–62, 164–5
Voices 140–42
voices, funny 24–30, 107, 112, 165
Vout 51
vowels 13, 165
Vox Box 149

Vygotsky, Lev 179
Waiting for Godot 145
Ward, Artemus 127–9, 231
Warhol, Andy 149
Warren, Peter 150
Waterhouse, Keith 132
Watson, Leo 51
Weir, Ruth 166, 232
Wellerisms 120–21
Welsh 19
  mock 113
Wendon, Lyn 197–8, 234
West Country 22–3, 25
Whaam 149
Which? 95
Whitcut, Janet 230
Whose Line Is It Anyway? 73
Wilder, Gene 95, 225
Williams, Clarence 51
Williams, Harold 55
Williams, Kenneth 29
Williams, Robin 28
Willis, Jeanne 202–3, 235
Winner, Ellen 234
Winnie-the-Pooh 10, 29
wireless telegraphy 40
Wisdom, Norman 105
Wise, Ernie 105
witzelsucht 7
Wolf, A. 203
Wolfenstein, Martha 171, 233
Wonderful O, The 65–6

Wood, G. E. 230
word
  boundaries 13, 47, 95
  chain 77
  creation 2–5, 30–36, 95–6, 117, 168,
    202–3
  endings 29, 113, 169, 180
  meaning 13
  missing 33
  search 84–5, 230
  squares 83–4
word-cross 85
word-game enthusiasts 54–92
Wordplay 154
words
  alphabetized 76–7
  monosyllabic 76
  not repeated 76
  repeated 107–8
Wordsworth, William 78–9, 192
Word Ways 60, 64
World 85
Wright, Ernest Vincent 63
write, learning to 181, 194
writing, conventions 113, 127–36, 205
Wynne, Arthur 85–7

Ximenes 89

Yacky Dar Moy Bewty 20–21, 23,
  228
'Ying-tong-Song' 52

READ MORE IN PENGUIN

In every corner of the world, on every subject under the sun, Penguin represents quality and variety – the very best in publishing today.

For complete information about books available from Penguin – including Puffins, Penguin Classics and Arkana – and how to order them, write to us at the appropriate address below. Please note that for copyright reasons the selection of books varies from country to country.

In the United Kingdom: Please write to *Dept. EP, Penguin Books Ltd, Bath Road, Harmondsworth, West Drayton, Middlesex UB7 0DA*

In the United States: Please write to *Consumer Sales, Penguin Putnam Inc., P.O. Box 12289 Dept. B, Newark, New Jersey 07101-5289*. VISA and MasterCard holders call 1-800-788-6262 to order Penguin titles

In Canada: Please write to *Penguin Books Canada Ltd, 10 Alcorn Avenue, Suite 300, Toronto, Ontario M4V 3B2*

In Australia: Please write to *Penguin Books Australia Ltd, P.O. Box 257, Ringwood, Victoria 3134*

In New Zealand: Please write to *Penguin Books (NZ) Ltd, Private Bag 102902, North Shore Mail Centre, Auckland 10*

In India: Please write to *Penguin Books India Pvt Ltd, 11 Community Centre, Panchsheel Park, New Delhi 110017*

In the Netherlands: Please write to *Penguin Books Netherlands bv, Postbus 3507, NL-1001 AH Amsterdam*

In Germany: Please write to *Penguin Books Deutschland GmbH, Metzlerstrasse 26, 60594 Frankfurt am Main*

In Spain: Please write to *Penguin Books S. A., Bravo Murillo 19, 1° B, 28015 Madrid*

In Italy: Please write to *Penguin Italia s.r.l., Via Benedetto Croce 2, 20094 Corsico, Milano*

In France: Please write to *Penguin France, Le Carré Wilson, 62 rue Benjamin Baillaud, 31500 Toulouse*

In Japan: Please write to *Penguin Books Japan Ltd, Kaneko Building, 2-3-25 Koraku, Bunkyo-Ku, Tokyo 112*

In South Africa: Please write to *Penguin Books South Africa (Pty) Ltd, Private Bag X14, Parkview, 2122 Johannesburg*

READ MORE IN PENGUIN

A CHOICE OF NON-FICTION

Jane Austen: A Life Claire Tomalin

'I cannot think that a better life of Jane Austen than Claire Tomalin's will be written for many years . . . a truly marvellous book' *Mail on Sunday*. 'As near perfect a Life of Austen as we are likely to get . . . Tomalin presents Austen as remarkably clever; sensitive, but unsentimental' *Daily Telegraph*

A Wavering Grace Gavin Young

'By far . . . the most moving account of Vietnam to be written in recent years' Norman Lewis. 'This delicate, terrible and enchanting book . . . brings the atmosphere of Vietnam so near that you can almost taste and smell it' *The Times*

Clone Gina Kolata

On July 5 1996 Dolly, the most famous lamb in history, was born. It was an event of enormous significance, for Dolly was a clone, produced from the genetic material of a six-year-old ewe. Suddenly, the idea that human beings could be replicated had become a reality. 'Superb' J. G. Ballard, *Sunday Times*

Huxley Adrian Desmond

T. H. Huxley (1825–95), often referred to as 'Darwin's Bulldog', became the major champion of the theory of evolution and was crucial to the making of our modern Darwinian world. 'Nobody writes scientific biography like Adrian Desmond, and this account of Huxley's progress . . . is his best so far' *The Times Literary Supplement*

Cleared for Take-Off Dirk Bogarde

'It begins with his experiences in the Second World War as an interpreter of reconnaissance photographs . . . his awareness of the horrors as well as the dottiness of war is essential to the tone of this affecting and strangely beautiful book' *Daily Telegraph*

READ MORE IN PENGUIN

A CHOICE OF NON-FICTION

Time Out Film Guide   Edited by John Pym

The definitive, up-to-the-minute directory of every aspect of world cinema from classics and silent epics to reissues and the latest releases.

Four-Iron in the Soul   Lawrence Donegan

'A joy to read. Not since Bill Bryson plotted a random route through small-town America has such a breezy idea for a book had a happier (or funnier) result' *The Times*. 'Funny, beautifully observed and it tells you things about sport in general and golf in particular that nobody else thought to pass on' *Mail on Sunday*

Nelson Mandela: A Biography   Martin Meredith

Nelson Mandela's role in delivering South Africa from racial division stands as one of the great triumphs of the twentieth century. In this brilliant account, Martin Meredith gives a vivid portrayal of the life and times of this towering figure. 'The best biography so far of Nelson Mandela' Raymond Whitaker, *Independent on Sunday*

In Search of Nature   Edward O. Wilson

'*In Search of Nature* makes such stimulating reading that Edward O. Wilson might be regarded as a one-man recruitment bureau for tomorrow's biologists . . . His essays on ants tend to leave one gasping for breath, literally speaking . . . Yet he is equally enchanting in his accounts of sharks and snakes and New Guinea's birds of paradise' *The Times Higher Education Supplement*

Reflections on a Quiet Rebel   Cal McCrystal

This extraordinary book is both a vivid memoir of Cal McCrystal's Irish Catholic childhood and a loving portrait of his father Charles, a 'quiet rebel' and unique man. 'A haunting book, lovely and loving. It explains more about one blighted corner of Ireland than a dozen dogged histories' *Scotsman*

READ MORE IN PENGUIN

LITERARY CRITICISM

The Practice of Writing David Lodge

This lively collection examines the work of authors ranging from the two Amises to Nabokov and Pinter; the links between private lives and published works; and the different techniques required in novels, stage plays and screenplays. 'These essays, so easy in manner, so well-built and informative, offer a fine blend of creative writing and criticism' *Sunday Times*

A Lover's Discourse Roland Barthes

'May be the most detailed, painstaking anatomy of desire we are ever likely to see or need again ... The book is an ecstatic celebration of love and language ... readers interested in either or both ... will enjoy savouring its rich and dark delights' *Washington Post*

The New Pelican Guide to English Literature Edited by Boris Ford

The indispensable critical guide to English and American literature in nine volumes, erudite yet accessible. From the ages of Chaucer and Shakespeare, via Georgian satirists and Victorian social critics, to the leading writers of the twentieth century, all literary life is here.

The Structure of Complex Words William Empson

'Twentieth-century England's greatest critic after T. S. Eliot, but whereas Eliot was the high priest, Empson was the *enfant terrible* ... *The Structure of Complex Words* is one of the linguistic masterpieces of the epoch, finding in the feel and tone of our speech whole sedimented social histories' *Guardian*

Vamps and Tramps Camille Paglia

'Paglia is a genuinely unconventional thinker ... Taken as a whole, the book gives an exceptionally interesting perspective on the last thirty years of intellectual life in America, and is, in its wacky way, a celebration of passion and the pursuit of truth' *Sunday Telegraph*

READ MORE IN PENGUIN

LITERARY CRITICISM

The Penguin History of Literature

Published in ten volumes, *The Penguin History of Literature* is a superb critical survey of the English and American literature covering fourteen centuries, from the Anglo-Saxons to the present, and written by some of the most distinguished academics in their fields.

New Bearings in English Poetry F. R. Leavis

'*New Bearings in English Poetry* was the first intelligent account of the work of Eliot, Pound and Gerard Manley Hopkins to appear in English and it significantly altered critical awareness . . . Leavis gave to literary criticism a thoroughness and respectability that has never since been equalled' Peter Ackroyd, *Spectator*. 'The most influential literary critic of modern times' *Financial Times*

The Uses of Literacy Richard Hoggart

Mass literacy has opened new worlds to new readers. How far has it also been exploited to debase standards and behaviour? 'A vivid inside view of working-class culture and one of the most influential books of the post-war era' *Observer*

Epistemology of the Closet Eve Kosofsky Sedgwick

Through her brilliant interpretation of the readings of Henry James, Melville, Nietzsche, Proust and Oscar Wilde, Eve Kosofsky Sedgwick shows how questions of sexual definition are at the heart of every form of representation in this century. 'A signal event in the history of late-twentieth-century gay studies' Wayne Koestenbaum

Dangerous Pilgrimages Malcolm Bradbury

'This capacious book tracks Henry James from New England to Rye; Evelyn Waugh to a Hollywood as grotesque as he expected; Gertrude Stein to Spain to be mistaken for a bishop; Oscar Wilde to a rickety stage in Leadsville, Colorado . . . The textbook on the the transatlantic theme' *Guardian*

READ MORE IN PENGUIN

PSYCHOLOGY

How the Mind Works Steven Pinker

This brilliant and controversial book explains what the mind is, how it evolved, and how it allows us to see, think, feel, interact, enjoy the arts and ponder the mysteries of life. 'To have read [the book] is to have consulted a first draft of the structural plan of the human psyche . . . a glittering *tour de force*' *Spectator*

The Uses of Enchantment Bruno Bettelheim

'Bruno Bettelheim's tour of fairy stories, with all their psychoanalytic connotations brought out into the open, is a feast of understanding' *New Statesman & Society*. 'Everything that Bettelheim writes about children, particularly about children's involvement in fiction, seems profound and illuminating' *Sunday Times*

Evolution in Mind Henry Plotkin
An Introduction to Evolutionary Psychology

Evolutionary theory holds a vital key to understanding ourselves. In proposing a more revolutionary approach to psychology, Professor Plotkin vividly demonstrates how an evolutionary perspective brings us closer to understanding what it is to be human.

The Man Who Loved a Polar Bear Robert U. Akeret

'Six fascinating case histories related with wit and humanity by the veteran psychotherapist Robert Akeret . . . a remarkable tour to the wilder shores of the human mind' *Daily Mail*

Private Myths: Dreams and Dreaming Anthony Stevens

'Its case for dreaming as something more universally significant than a tour across our personal playgrounds of guilt and misery is eloquently persuasive . . . [a] hugely absorbing study – its surface criss-crossed with innumerable avenues into science, anthropology and religion' *Spectator*

READ MORE IN PENGUIN

PSYCHOLOGY

Closing the Asylum   Peter Barham

'A dispassionate, objective analysis of the changes in the way we care for the mentally ill. It offers no simple solutions but makes clear that "care in the community" is not so easy to implement as some seem to believe' *The Times Educational Supplement*

Child Behaviour   Dorothy Einon

Covering the psychology of childcare, this book traces every key theme of child behaviour from birth to adolescence. Dorothy Einon discusses what, at any age, it is reasonable to expect of a child, how to keep things in perspective, and the most interesting and rewarding aspect of parenthood – bringing up a happy, well-adjusted child.

Bereavement   Colin Murray Parkes

This classic text enables us to understand grief and grieving. How is bereavement affected by age, gender, personal psychology and culture? What are the signs of pathological grieving which can lead to mental illness? And how can carers provide genuine help without interfering with the painful but necessary 'work' of mourning?

Edward de Bono's Textbook of Wisdom

Edward de Bono shows how traditional thinking methods designed by the 'Gang of Three' (Socrates, Plato and Aristotle) are too rigid to cope with a complex and changing world. He recognizes that our brains deserve that we do better with them, and uses his gift for simplicity to get readers' thoughts to flow along fresh lines.

The Care of the Self   Michel Foucault
The History of Sexuality Volume 3

Foucault examines the transformation of sexual discourse from the Hellenistic to the Roman world in an enquiry which 'bristles with provocative insights into the tangled liaison of sex and self' *The Times Higher Education Supplement*

BY THE SAME AUTHOR

Who Cares About English Usage?

To boldly split or not to split? Why is life so stressful? Is this something up with which we must put?

Aspects of these and many other questions come under entertaining scrutiny in this book on some of the common questions about English usage. Clearly and wittily presented with short quizzes to stimulate the mind and some pertinent cartoons, this book proves that it's fun as well as worthwhile thinking about our language, how it reflects ourselves and how best to feel at home with it.

Listen to Your Child
A Parent's Guide to Children's Language

Learning to talk is probably the greatest milestone in a child's development – a deeply moving, and often hilarious, experience for all parents. It is also a process which has been intensively studied by psychologists and linguists in recent years – this informative and entertaining study shows us what they have discovered.

In dealing with the whole period from (and before) birth to the early school years, David Crystal provides invaluable advice for parents as well as a painless introduction to a central topic of modern language study.

BY THE SAME AUTHOR

Linguistics

In this excellent and lively guide to what is involved in a linguistic approach to language study, David Crystal shows what the benefits, as well as the problems, are in studying language in a scientific way. His book makes a novel introduction to a significant subject which today concerns not only psychologists, sociologists and philosophers, but teachers, interpreters and even telephone companies.

The English Language

In this marvellously informative guided tour of the English language, David Crystal describes the common structures that unify the language and outlines the major variations that separate the English of Britain, America, Ireland, Australia, the Caribbean and other parts of the English-speaking world.

'[An] illuminating guided tour of our common treasure by one of its most lucid and sensible professionals' *The Times*

An Encyclopedic Dictionary of Language and Languages

With entries for every country and several hundred languages, for literary terms, grammar and word games, for phonetics, typography and speech disorders, this essential guide provides clear and fully cross-referenced definitions of key linguistic terms.

'Clear, objective definitions make this dictionary an essential guide to the terminology of twentieth-century linguistics and phonetics' *Linguistics and Literature*